·TROT ON·

·TROT ON·
SIXTY YEARS OF HORSES

Sallie Walrond and Anne Grimshaw

*This book was produced in a limited edition
of 1000 copies, of which this is number*

160

KENILWORTH PRESS

First published in Great Britain in 2004 by
Kenilworth Press Ltd
Addington
Buckingham MK18 2JR

British Library Cataloguing in Publication Data
A catalogue record for this book is available from the British Library

ISBN 1-872119-77-8

Designed by Paul Saunders
Layout by Kenilworth Press
Printed and bound in China by Midas Printing International Ltd on behalf of Compass Press Ltd

Contents

	Acknowledgements	7
	Parts of the Harness	8
1	The Working Horses of London	9
2	The Knightsbridge Riding School	18
3	A Surrey Riding School	31
4	Stocklands	36
5	Dressage	47
6	Driving and Family Ponies	52
7	Zapateado	70
8	Dolly	86
9	Early Tandems	88
10	A Gypsy Wagon	94
11	Ali	98
12	The 1966 BDS Show	117
13	Judging	120
14	New York	123
15	Books	125
16	An American Rodeo	132
17	Breaking	137
18	Colorado and Wisconsin	145
19	Pupils	152
20	Lowther 1975	165

21 Talking to Gypsies   171

22 Tandem Club   174

23 Channel Islands   178

24 Western Australia   184

25 The Team and Other Ponies   195

26 Belgium   206

27 Judging in Connecticut   211

28 Ireland   217

29 France   221

30 Driving Trials with Raz   226

31 New Zealand   232

32 California I   244

33 California II   252

34 Guitars, Tandems and Gliders   259

35 Disabled Drivers   264

36 New England, USA   270

37 Drive and Hunt   277

38 1991   280

39 Judges   294

40 Dun Ponies   299

41 2003   310

About the Co-Author: Anne Grimshaw   317

Books by Sallie Walrond   326

Acknowledgements

SALLIE WALROND would like to thank Carolyn Henderson for her suggestion that this book should be written and for inspiring her to embark upon the work.

Sallie is indebted to Anne Grimshaw for her transformation of the original manuscript into entertaining text.

She is also grateful to her husband, Bill, for his unflagging support, and to David and Canny Jones for their help in acquiring a computer and learning how to use it.

Both the authors thank the editors of newspapers and magazines and the photographers who have given permission for their work to be reproduced in this book, as well as the many people who have kindly provided photographs and helped with the monumental task of endeavouring to trace the whereabouts of photographers all over the world. Permission to use the illustrations has been obtained where possible and we apologise for instances where we have not been able to contact the copyright holder.

SUFFOLK, 2004

Parts of the Harness

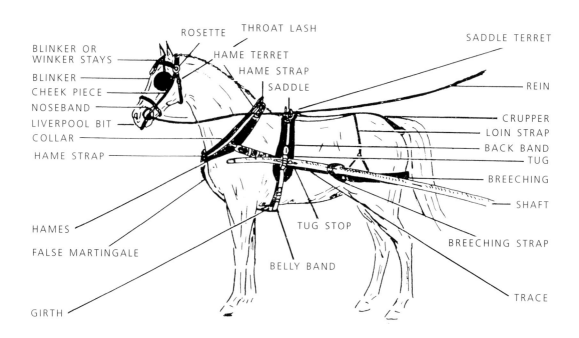

BLINKER OR
WINKER STAYS

BLINKER

CHEEK PIECE

NOSEBAND

LIVERPOOL BIT

COLLAR

HAME STRAP

ROSETTE

THROAT LASH

HAME TERRET

HAME STRAP

SADDLE

SADDLE TERRET

REIN

CRUPPER

LOIN STRAP

BACK BAND

TUG

BREECHING

SHAFT

BREECHING STRAP

TRACE

HAMES

FALSE MARTINGALE

TUG STOP

BELLY BAND

GIRTH

CHAPTER 1

The Working Horses of London

I SAT ON A CHAIR in the bay window of our house in Chiswick, London, waiting for the milkman's horse to arrive. It was during the Second World War and I was eight years old. I had drawn a picture of the horse in his harness. The bridle, collar, driving saddle and reins were to my satisfaction but I could not remember where the rest of the straps, which went over the hindquarters, should be placed. Eventually, the horse arrived. He was a dark-coloured van horse with a hogged mane. He was trace clipped and his tail was cut off just below the dock. He pulled a four-wheeled, pneumatic-tyred, orange-and-white milk cart from United Dairies. I looked closely at the harness and, picking up my pencil, painstakingly drew in the missing straps to complete my picture.

Seeing the working horses that passed our house on a daily basis always thrilled me. The sound of iron-shod hooves on the road had me rushing to the window. One day I plucked up courage to go out and stroke the soft nose of the milk horse whose name I discovered was Blackie. On another day I gave him an apple core, holding it between my fingers as I offered it to him. Blackie nipped the tip of one of my fingers as well as the apple core between his front teeth but let go when I yelped. Tom, the milkman, was watching. He shook his

Sallie with her fairy cycle and toy donkey on a leading rein.

head and smiled kindly,

'Hold your hand out flat. See, like this,' and he demonstrated offering Blackie half of the core that had dropped onto the road, 'that way he can't bite your fingers. Try again.'

I did and Blackie took the prize from my hand leaving my finger-tips intact. I did not make that mistake again. I had learnt my first lesson in handling horses.

One day when we were delivering milk to a block of flats in Chiswick called Watchfield Court, Tom said to me,

'How about a bit of an exchange – between you and me?'

'What do you mean?' I asked.

'How about you taking some of them milk bottles and putting them in the service hatches beside the front doors? Your legs are younger than mine.' I looked at him, puzzled. He continued, 'If you do that you can drive Blackie back to the depot.' I stared at him hardly able to believe my good fortune,

'You mean it? I can drive Blackie all the way back?' I asked incredulously. Tom nodded,

'All the way!' he grinned.

'Yes, please!' The ten-minute drive was a fair exchange for two hours' delivering milk.

Blackie would stand for this period without moving, his head was half-buried in a hessian nosebag that was reinforced at the corners and bound along the top with leather. The bag contained his feed of chaff and a few oats. There was a strap from each side of the nose-bag that passed over the top of Blackie's bridle to keep the nosebag in place even when he tossed it upwards over his head to release any stray food that had got caught in the corners. His Wilson snaffle bit remained on the bridle, which must have made eating quite difficult. The reins were hooked up to the front of the cart on a specially designed rein hook. During cold weather, a quarter sheet with a rubberised outside and a woollen lining was strapped behind the wide serge-lined, driving saddle over Blackie's loins to keep him warm.

One kind lady used to put out some water for us to give to the horse. The container was a washing-up bowl made of metal, enamelled in white with a dark blue rim round the top. Carrying the bowl I would go down in the flats' service lift that we used to take the crates of milk to the upper storeys. I tried very hard not to spill any of this precious water. I would take off Blackie's nosebag so that he could drink, replace it after he had finished the water and return the bowl to the service hatch. Once all the milk had been delivered we prepared to return to the dairy. Empty crates were made safe, Blackie's nosebag was removed and we climbed high up onto the cart for the journey. I was thrilled when I was allowed to drive.

Sallie, with Lulu, a vanner, in the bomb-damaged stable yard of United Dairies.

Sallie, aged about nine, with Peggy.

When we approached the dairy, Tom would take the reins and drive through the entrance. He would draw up alongside the loading bay where we got down and unfastened the bellyband, breeching straps and chain-ended traces. A friendly slap on the quarters and a shout of 'Ger on' were the signals for Blackie to walk forward out of the wooden shafts which then clattered to the ground as they were freed from the tugs. The shafts did not appear to be damaged by this casual treatment. Tom would then unload all the empty crates while Blackie went, on his own, to the water trough by the stable wall. He drank for a long time submerging the lower parts of his bridle and reins into the water. Sometimes he blew bubbles and tossed water up over his face. When he had satisfied his thirst, he turned and walked through the stable door without catching his harness or his hips on the door pillars. He then went along the row of stalls until he came to his own. He would turn into it and wait to be unharnessed and tied up.

Each horse was tied by a headcollar with a rope that passed through a ring fixed to the wall at a height of about three feet (one metre) from the ground. At the end of the rope was a wooden ball called a log. The rope passed through a hole bored into the log and was secured by a large knot. The weight of the log kept the rope between the headcollar and the ring taut enough to prevent an animal's leg getting caught. If the horse chewed the rope then a chain was used.

Each stall was wide enough to enable the horse to lie down to sleep at night and was separated from the next stall by swinging bales. These were planks of wood, like scaffolding boards, which were hung by chains from the ceiling. There were usually two boards hung one above the other, to separate the horses but if one was a kicker there was a third, lower, board to protect his neighbours' hind legs.

When a horse came in, it stood patiently waiting for a groom to come and remove the harness. I loved it when several horses came in within a few minutes of each other because I was allowed to take off the harness. I undid the reins and removed the bridle. Then I pulled the reins out of the terrets and undid the girth. I hauled the harness backwards over the horse's tail and it all slid off. I had to leave the collar and hames on the horse because I was neither tall enough nor strong enough to take them off. I stacked all the harness in a heap on the floor behind the horse then someone collected it and hung it in the warm harness room to dry out ready for the next day. A man came especially once a week to clean and oil the harness.

Each horse was officially known by a number that was branded on a front hoof when the animal was shod at the dairy's own farrier's shop. The same number was stamped onto the collar to avoid a horse

The head horseman at the United Dairies, with a new vanner which had just arrived.

wearing the wrong collar, which could result in sore shoulders. The number was also printed on a rectangular plate that hung on the wall above the horse's head in its stall. Each milkman named his horse and always drove the same one. It soon learned the route and all the waiting places. The horse would walk along the road, keeping near to the kerb and the man would deliver bottles of milk from a bottle carrier to the houses, shouting as he went to the horse to stop or go. A new horse made life very troublesome for the milkman as it did not know the stopping places and it would take time for it to learn them all.

I spent most of the school holidays at the United Dairies' depot close to our home. Occasionally, a call for help would come from a milkman whose cart had a puncture. A horse would be harnessed to a cart loaded with a spare wheel and driven to where the problem was. If I was lucky enough to be around, I was taken and sometimes allowed to drive.

One of the grooms, a man called Bob, must have liked children because he was extremely generous. I learnt a tremendous amount by watching what Bob did and if I asked a question he always took the time to give me an answer. I was, however, terrified of the head horseman. One of his favourite and often-repeated sayings to Bob was, 'Don't give them 'osses too much 'ay'. It was wartime and horse food, as well as human food, was in short supply; he had to make each delivery of hay last for an allotted period and so feed had to be strictly rationed. He was responsible for the wellbeing of a great number of horses.

I don't think that he approved of my 'helping' and was probably, quite rightly, worried in case I got hurt. On one occasion a new horse arrived and had to be isolated because he was said to be vicious. I was told to keep away from him, which I did. Ironically, when a bomb fell on the United Dairies stable the only horse to be killed was this one which had been standing on his own in the part of the stables that had been hit. The next day, my grandmother returned from a walk to the shops and announced that there was flesh all over the road. My mother later discovered that it was, in fact, that poor horse.

Householders were encouraged to put their kitchen waste – potato peelings, apple cores, cabbage stalks and any left-over food of which there was very little due to severe food rationing – into containers known as pig bins which were placed at intervals along the pavement. They were emptied a couple of times a week and the contents used to make swill for feeding pigs. These dustbin-like containers had lids but some horses, such as Blackie, became very adept at creeping forward unnoticed until they could reach the bin. They would expertly nuzzle off the lid then thrust their noses into the stinking contents in search of a goody – but they appeared none the worse for these forays.

There was also a greengrocer who used to come round with an iron-tyred, flat trolley drawn first by a sedate roan cob and later by a high-stepping, hard-pulling, hackney pony. This pony trotted with his head turned inwards as the driver held the reins tightly to steady his furious pace. He could, though, be left with his head buried in his nosebag feed for long periods while his master stopped for his lunch at a house near to ours.

The laundry was collected once a week. Sheets, towels and all kinds of items were labelled and listed in the laundry book. They were all put into a large, wicker laundry-basket with the lid secured by a leather strap. This was collected at the same time as the previous week's laundry was returned by a four-wheeled, covered van pulled by a beautiful chestnut that was more of a riding horse than a harness animal. His harness always gleamed and he was proudly adorned with merit badges presented by the RSPCA that had been awarded to the driver at numerous van horse parades. These were held in Regent's Park, London, to encourage owners and drivers of working horses to maintain high standards of care of their animals. A medallion and a 'first class' award would be given to all of those who, in the opinion of the judges, achieved the required standard.

Large, flat-topped coal carts were hauled by strong, heavy horses like Shires. The smell of sweating horses and coal was, to my young nose, one of the best in London! Similar heavy horses with, I remember, whiskery moustaches on their noses, pulled dustcarts. These carts were large four-wheelers with built-up sides and a curved top comprised several lids. Their smell was foul.

Lamertons, the furnishing company, had a van which was drawn by a team of four skewbald ponies that was primarily used for advertising purposes. The hatters, Scotts of London, had a very smart deliv-

Lamerton's team.

ery van that was drawn by an immaculate bay horse with highly polished, eye-catching harness. A familiar sight were costermongers'
London trolleys pulled by cobs of all shapes and sizes. Their harness
was often quite ornate: coloured edging embellished the saddle, collar and bridle and the white-metal buckles were frequently horseshoe
shaped. The costers took great pride in their animals. Frequently, a
bucket and a nosebag were hung under the vehicle at the back ready
for the lunch break. White rope halters were often worn under the bridle, enabling an animal to be tied up if necessary.

During the war the dairy horses wore such halters so that, in the
event of an air raid, the horse could be tethered while the milkman ran
to the nearest air raid shelter. A loud wailing siren, that seemed to
occur mostly at night, gave the warning of an air raid. If the siren
sounded my mother, grandmother and I would shelter in the cupboard under the stairs as it was said that stairs gave most protection
from falling rubble if the house was damaged by one of Hitler's
bombs. I was more frightened of the thought of a large spider in the
cupboard than any bomb! My father, however, used to go to bed as
usual, refusing to miss his night's sleep. He was totally philosophical
about these occasions. It was a great relief to hear the long, single
drone of the 'all clear' siren. (Even now, sixty years later, if I hear that
siren on the radio, it still sends shivers down my spine.)

I remember hearing the aircraft engines and the whine of falling
bombs. Sometimes I gazed out of the window and saw the bright

beams of searchlights looking for enemy aircraft in the sky. Sometimes I saw a red glow in the sky and we would wonder who the poor victims were of the latest German bombing. We were bombed out twice – windows and doors blasted inwards because of nearby explosions – and we had to move out until repairs were completed.

After the war ended in 1945 motorised traffic increased and the horse-drawn vehicles decreased. By the mid 1950s the art of driving horses was in danger of becoming lost forever.

CHAPTER 2

The Knightsbridge Riding School

WHEN I WAS ABOUT NINE YEARS OLD, a school friend told me that she was having riding lessons in Hyde Park. She suggested that I should go too. The idea appealed to me and I managed to persuade my parents to part with twelve shillings and sixpence (62.5p). This was a lot of money in the 1940s for an hour's ride.

Before I could go for my riding lesson the right clothes had to be bought. Jeans were not generally worn as they are now. I was always dressed in a skirt or frock, as dresses were called then. I did not even possess a pair of trousers. Charity shops did not exist and so there was no chance of finding a second-hand pair of jodhpurs.

I was taken to Harry Hall, the outfitters, in London so that suitable riding clothes could be purchased. I was so excited when a pair of beige cavalry twill jodhpurs were produced for me to try on. The prospect of looking like a real rider meant that I scarcely felt their itchy roughness as the shop assistant helped me into them. The fashion then was for them to be cut very wide on the seams down the outside of the thighs which gave them a sort of bat-wing appearance. The fact that they were two sizes too large added to the balloon effect. Jodhpurs were supposed to be tight around the calves but these sagged into wrinkles from knee to ankle. The assistant noticed this

Riding in Hyde Park with Robert Barley.

and looked at my mother questioningly,

'Are they perhaps a little too big for your daughter, madam?'

'They'll allow for growing,' replied my mother firmly.

I held out my arms while the assistant slipped on a tweed jacket. That too enveloped me, the cuffs almost to my finger tips and its elegant cut was totally wasted on my child's figure. The assistant again looked doubtfully at my mother.

'She'll fill out soon,' said my mother confidently. 'Now, what about a hat?'

Hard hats – reinforced crash helmets as we have now – were not in general use then and most women rode bareheaded or wore a headscarf tied under the chin or a 'sensible' felt hat. After a quick look around, my mother chose one of the latter.

'Will you daughter be requiring boots?' asked the assistant hopeful of another sale.

'No. Her school lace-up shoes will do very well.'

There was a life-sized model horse to sit on to make sure that your new clothes were comfortable and fitted when you were in the saddle. There was even a mounting block so that you could easily climb on board.

'Can I sit on the horse?' I asked. Mother nodded and the assistant smiled. I sat there, preening myself and feeling supremely confident. I could hardly wait for my first riding lesson.

My mother and I went by bus to Kensington then walked to the Knightsbridge Riding School at 34 Queen's Gate Mews. Here, sixteen horses and ponies were stabled in four large stalls and four loose boxes intended for eight animals but the boxes were divided by swinging bales to accommodate two horses or three small ponies. Ponies were also put into every other available space. The system worked and they all looked well and had room to lie down.

A large white goat called Gertie was housed in a corner near to the entrance. She had enormous horns that curled backwards and malevolent yellow eyes. She butted me one day and I stayed well away from her after that. She was kept because it was believed that, in the case of a fire, the presence of a goat would calm the horses and enable them to be led out of danger.

I had my first riding lesson on a small pony called Brownie. I was taken onto Rotten Row by Robert 'Bert' Barley, one of London's last jobmasters. A jobmaster was someone who provided horses for all kinds of businesses for work in London. I was so fortunate that it was

Riding in Rotten Row, Hyde Park, in London. Saddle and bridle both made for a larger animal, but with all the horses and ponies out that Sunday morning, it was the only available tack.

with him and his instructress, Miss Dixon (whom he called Dickie and whom he married when he was about eighty) that I had my first lessons. They gave me a wonderful start and did such a lot to encourage me at this early stage of my life with horses.

He rode a large horse from which he led Brownie (and me) on a leading rein. It was usual to learn to ride in this way. There were very few indoor schools and pupils were taught the basics of riding by sitting on a pony and being led by the instructor, who told the pupil how to position body, legs and hands. Of course, a big disadvantage was that the instructor, being so close and somewhat above the pupil, could not see exactly how his charge was sitting. The leading rein would be lengthened so that the pupil gradually learnt how to control the animal and give the aids for changes of pace rather than relying on the instructor to do so.

On a busy day Dickie could have three pupils on leading reins at the same time: one on the left and two on the right-hand side. The leading rein of the outside pony would be extra long and threaded through the back of the noseband of its neighbour on its left and from there to the instructor's hand. Manoeuvring four animals through the narrow gateway into the road which led past the Albert Memorial on the way to Rotten Row took a great deal of skill on the part of Dickie and her pupils to ensure that no one banged their knees on the iron gateposts. Being the middle pupil meant that you were squashed, jostled and bumped from both sides. It was not, with hindsight, the best way of learning to ride.

I was told to sit up and straight at all times. To ensure that this was drilled into me I was taught the rhyme:

Your head and your heart keep up,
Your hands and your heels keep down,
Your knees keep close to your horse's sides
And your elbows close to your own.

At first it was hard to remember all this, let alone do it. When it was time to learn to canter Dickie said, 'Sit in the middle of the saddle and go with the pony. Slide your seat on the saddle in rhythm with his stride.'

Of course, I bounced around like a pea on a drum. It wasn't made

Riding in Rotten Row with Dickie. I am on the little pony, Cherry, on whom I first discovered how to sit down to the canter.

any easier by the then popular, flat-seated hunting saddles which, far from helping me sit down into the centre of the saddle, actually made me slip back. Eventually though, I began to get the hang of it and it all 'came together' for me on a pony called Cherry.

I rode once a week and was put onto progressively larger and more difficult animals but I was kept on a leading rein for about two years. I was supremely confident because nothing ever happened to cause me any fear. It was not long before I was bicycling from Chiswick to Kensington to spend weekends and school holidays at the riding school.

I am told that one day Bert asked me if he could have a ride on my fairy cycle. Apparently, I replied, 'Yes, if you pay me twelve and six-pence!'

One morning during the war when I reached the Albert Hall end of Queen's Gate on my bicycle, I found that the road was closed and there was utter devastation. Bombs had hit the houses and the buildings were still smouldering. I was told that I could get to the other end of Queen's Gate Mews by going back towards Kensington High Street and turning down the Gloucester Road. I had never been there before and it was with great trepidation that I set off on the new route. Eventually, I found the stables amid the chaos of the bombing raid and climbed through a small window at the rear. I accepted the destruction with the amazing resilience of childhood. Nothing mattered to me as long as the horses were unharmed.

Horses were becoming a way of life for me. On one occasion, Bert had an urgent call to take a vanner to a large bakery that was short of a horse for the following day's deliveries. A pony was put to a two-wheeled dog cart. I sat beside Bert and was told to hold onto the leading rein draped over the back of the seat. The other end was attached to the vanner which trotted behind the cart for several miles across London to our destination with no problems at all. He was left in a stall ready for the next day's work and we returned home in the dog cart. I was allowed to drive part of the way back. Bert had taught me how to hold the reins and whip correctly and he was very strict that they should be held in the traditional coaching manner – none of the milkman's 'one rein in each hand' methods were tolerated.

Bert frequently provided coach horses for films. Sometimes, a horse would come back from a day's filming work and would be hardly recognisable because white face markings had been added with chalk. It was not unknown for a horse to come back with injuries. There was a pair of superb brown carriage horses called Patience and Perseverance. One evening after filming, Patience came home with terrible injuries to her legs and she was off work for a long time. Bert was very upset. When she had recovered enough to be walked quietly Bert sent me out with her. He gave me a leg up and I sat on top of the jute roller that held her stable rug in place. She wore a plain snaffle bit that was smooth and comfortable in her mouth. I was told to walk her around the roads for half an hour, which I did. She behaved quietly no doubt because she was too sore and stiff to do otherwise.

On another occasion with a different coach horse I was not as lucky. Instead of maintaining a steady walk, for some reason our pace increased rapidly and we ended up galloping down Queen's Gate. I clung onto the rug until the horse turned sharply into the Cromwell Road, where he slipped and came down, sending me sprawling across the road. I scrambled to my feet.

'Are you all right, dear?' somebody asked me.

'Yes, thank you,' I replied, relieved to see that someone had caught the horse and was leading him back towards me.

'He seems none the worse,' said the rescuer. 'Are you sure you're all right?'

'Yes, thank you,' I said again. I was far more concerned that I would get into trouble for allowing the horse to gallop than I was about the odd bruise. Even so, I led him back to Queen's Gate Mews and on the way I met a fire engine and an ambulance that had been called out to rescue me. No doubt someone had dialled 999 on seeing a child being run away with along Queen's Gate. I was afraid Bert and Dickie would be cross with me when I told them what had happened but no one said very much at all. They were probably relieved that I was not hurt. Amazingly, the horse had not been damaged by the fall either.

A road coach, drawn by a team of four horses, was kept in the Mews and if this was taken out on a local business trip I was usually allowed to go along for the ride. On one occasion, I was told to clean the team harness. It had brown collars with black bridles and black pads in the traditional road coach manner. I had been given strict instructions not to alter any of the buckles. No doubt all the harness had been carefully adjusted so that it was ready for use once it was put onto the team. Bert would drive any team and, if he were short of a horse, I had known him put a riding horse that had not been trained for harness work into the lead. He got away with it. All horses went well for him whether in harness or under saddle.

★　　★　　★

One day Bert gave me a black mouse in a tall wooden cage with a glass front. I was devoted to Mousie as she was the first live animal I had ever owned. The affection which I had lavished on my toy donkey-on-wheels was now transferred to my mouse. I took her to school one day in the pocket of my navy school coat as I rode my bicycle from Chiswick to Hammersmith. No doubt Mousie enjoyed some crumbs from a penny bun that I had previously hidden in the same pocket.

I was not supposed to have had a penny bun in the pocket of my school coat because we were forbidden to eat in the street when wearing our school uniform which bore the St Paul's Girls' School badge on the hat. So, the solution, if you were very hungry on the way home from school, was to buy a penny bun at the bakery and hide it in your coat pocket. Small pieces of bun could then be pulled off inside the pocket and the forbidden meal could be consumed, bit by bit, without, you hoped, being seen. The fear of being summoned to the High Mistress's room made certain that you were never seen and reported by a prefect for committing this terrible crime. Dropping a sweet paper was also a cardinal sin and so we never dropped litter on the road. A 'talking to' by the High Mistress was the worst punishment possible and was to be avoided at all costs.

Later I was given a second mouse – a piebald with markings like a black-and-white Dutch rabbit. The idea was that he should keep Mousie company. It was not long before there were quite a lot of mice – they had to live in a glass aquarium in the garage.

At about this time, I was given a Scottish terrier puppy called Chops. I had seen a lovely tartan collar in Harrods that I wanted for him. But it was five shillings (25p) and I had only two shillings and sixpence (12.5p). I had an idea. Harrods sold mice in their Pet Department and I had a couple of very attractive young mice with red eyes. One was white and the other a kind of skewbald, being fawn and white. Although I was very fond of them, I put them into a box, mounted my bicycle and pedalled to Harrods in Knightsbridge.

I went up in the lift to the Pet Department and found an assistant. I hurried over to her and took a deep breath,

'Would you like to buy my mice?' I asked dragging out the box, lifting the lid and showing her the creatures. 'Only two and six,' I added hopefully.

'I'll have to ask the manager. Wait there,' replied the assistant and disappeared. I hung about for what seemed like ages. Then the assistant returned. 'All right. Half a crown it is.' She gave me the money and I handed over the box of mice.

The deal was done and I had enough money to buy the collar for Chops. In retrospect, I think the assistant felt sorry for me, purchased the mice herself and perhaps took them home for her own children.

I spent much time training Chops and we won several obedience classes at small dog shows but when I played with him I treated him like a pony. One day I decided to break him to harness. I attached him to a shoebox with some string for traces that I tied to his collar. I used to be given a penny for each box-load of stones that I picked off the flowerbeds in the garden. The idea was that Chops would pull my box

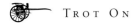

Sallie showing her
Scottish Terrier,
c.1947.

cart. It had not occurred to me that as the box got heavier the front would tear off when the willing little dog leaned into his collar. I was very disappointed when it didn't work.

A friend had a nervous red setter. I decided that we could pretend that he was a pony. We attached him to the wooden cart that was pulled by my toy donkey-on-wheels. It was too big for Chops but I thought that it would fit the setter. We fixed dog leads to the collar and tied them to the front of the cart. The setter was terrified and took off. He ran the length of the lawn and down a flight of steps by the rockery, where the whole lot overturned. This was my first runaway.

Back at Bert Barley's I was being trusted more and more, so that by the age of thirteen I was often sent across London, riding one pony and leading one or sometimes two, to the farrier where I waited until all were shod before returning. There were no mobile farriers in those days.

I also escorted American soldiers who wanted to ride in 'The Row' (Rotten Row). If anyone fell off it was my job to help to catch the horse and put the soldier back in the saddle again. Sometimes the riders dropped their whips or inadvertently pulled a ten-shilling note out of a pocket. It was my job to get off my pony and retrieve the object. Somewhat surprisingly, the soldiers did as I told them in spite of my being very young, very small and mounted on the tiny pony, Cherry.

Several well-known personalities also came to ride – actors Terry Thomas and Dennis Price and the concert pianist, Eileen Joyce – and I used to help them onto their horses.

On a few occasions I went to ride at the Seven Sisters Riding School in Hayes, Middlesex. It was on one of those trips that I saw a dun horse put to a phaeton. I thought it quite beautiful and I vowed that, one day, I would have a horse of that colour.

As time went on I was given more responsibility and by the age of

Sallie aged about fourteen, on the way to the farrier in London.

fourteen was teaching. I knew now that I was going make a career with horses rather than the alternatives of music or art. After seven years of weekly piano lessons I had reached Grade 7 and had competed in music festivals but had only ever achieved second place in these competitions. I had been presented with the school art prize on Speech Day but I knew my limitations and realised that with a career of either music or art I would never be 'the best'. I wanted to be 'famous'.

I decided that horses might satisfy my wish. I was, however, not going to be just a girl groom. Teaching was the best direction in which to proceed. My parents supported me but the High Mistress was not very pleased. It was not usual for a place to be taken at St Paul's Girls' School by a pupil who then decided to depart at the age of fifteen to 'play with' horses. It was expected that pupils would stay on and achieve great academic success.

Bert and Dickie employed me as a general helper and I was paid a pound at the end of my first week. This was great riches. One job, which was very hard work, was to turn the handle of the clipping machine that was used to clip off the horses' winter coats. Electric clippers did not exist then. The clipping machine's mechanism was supported on top of a metal stand about four feet high with three splayed feet as its base. There was a handle on the right-hand side of the top that you turned with your right hand whilst preventing the machine from falling over by bracing it with your left hand on its top and your foot against one of its feet. The flexible drive went down a tube to the clipper head that was held by whoever was clipping the horse. It was a very tiring job because the turning had to be kept at a steady rate so that the clipper blades cut properly. Also, you had to push the clipping machine with your foot to follow the clipping person around the horse. To keep the blades in good cutting order they were run through a mixture of oil and paraffin that was kept in a round saddle-soap tin.

If a horse objected to being clipped a front leg was held up to prevent his fidgeting and moving around. If a horse was really troublesome then a twitch was applied. This comprised a stout stick about one foot long and three inches in diameter with a hole drilled through the top. A short length of rope was threaded through the hole to make a loop. The twitch was applied by passing a hand through the loop, grabbing the horse's upper lip and pulling the loop up the nose. Someone quickly turned the stick to tighten the noose which pinched the upper lip. The horse then stood motionless and the job could be completed as soon as possible. I always disliked seeing a twitch used.

I later learnt that the twitch works because when that part of the muzzle is attacked it releases endorphins (Nature's sedatives) very quickly and hence the horse calms down. It is also said that if a lion attacks a zebra from the front it will grab the nose, thus releasing endorphins into the zebra's bloodstream, causing it to suffer less.

Bert used to go to the Elephant and Castle horse sale every Monday. It was a ritual and probably as much of a social occasion as a business one. I sometimes went to 'The Elephant', as it was known, travelling there on my own by underground purely out of personal interest. The stables at the sale yard comprised two storeys of stalls. When the lower level became full, the extra horses occupied the upper storey that was reached by a ramp. Carriages, harness, saddles, bridles and all kinds of equipment were sold.

On one of my visits I bought a double bridle. Although I had no pony yet, I intended to acquire one as soon as possible. I saved every penny that I was given and put it towards my dream pony. The bridle must have been very cheap and I imagined I'd struck a huge bargain. I was so excited! I was one step along the road to having my own pony.

Just then a man came up to me and asked if I was the girl whom

he had seen at Bert Barley's stable. I said that I was. He then asked me if I would ride a horse that he had just bought, back to Richmond Park for him where he had a stable. Naturally, I was very flattered and said that I would. I was then told that there was no saddle or bridle. Quite undaunted I agreed to ride bareback and use my newly acquired double bridle. I telephoned my mother from a call box to tell her what I was doing as I didn't want to get into trouble for being late home.

The horse was a rather thin, chestnut Thoroughbred-type mare. I was given a leg up and pointed in the general direction of Richmond. I can't remember how I found the way but can only assume that I followed the route as shown on the front of buses or the overhead wires of trolley buses! The mare jogged and bounced the whole way but somehow we completed the journey. Nevertheless, my bottom was rubbed raw by the time that we arrived at Richmond. I was then asked to ride her in the park so that some potential purchasers could see how she went. I demanded a saddle for I was so very sore. I was, however, given four shillings and sixpence and a new lip strap for my bridle because it had been sold without one. I was well satisfied.

After working for Bert and Dickie for about a year I felt that the time had come to move on. I desperately wanted a pony of my own and keeping one in London was out of the question. I also wanted to learn to gallop and jump. Galloping was not permitted in Hyde Park and there was nowhere to learn to jump. Bert and Dickie were very understanding and I am grateful to this day for the start they gave me.

CHAPTER 3

A Surrey Riding School

I HEARD THAT THE PROPRIETOR of a very small riding school in Surrey was looking for a working pupil. I investigated the situation and we agreed that in exchange for my working a seven-day week (I was so besotted with horses that I did not want any time off to do anything else!) I would be taught to jump, given a small amount of pocket money, my keep and that of a pony which I planned to get as soon as possible.

As it was too far to travel from Chiswick, I left home and moved into digs with a family who kept their son's show pony at livery in this yard. The son very rarely rode and never showed the pony because he had no interest in horses at all – something I found quite incredible! My transport to and from my work was my bicycle.

It was not long before two ponies arrived at the yard from a dealer in Ireland who sent them over, unseen, with a view to their being sold on. One was bay and the other was a 14.1hh blanket-spotted Appaloosa gelding – and he really was an Appaloosa. He had roan markings on his neck and body but his hindquarters were white with distinct black oval-shaped spots. I could feel the spots with my fingers because the black hairs appeared to be a little finer and shorter than the surrounding white hairs. He had pink pigmentation round his eyes, nose and sheath. His mane and tail were similar to those of an Arabian, being finer hair than would be usual on a pony of this type. He had plenty of bone and excellent feet. I chose him in preference to the other pony, a mare, because he was so friendly towards me and we seemed to hit it off right from the start. He appeared to like me and, of course, as he was to be my first pony, I already loved him dearly.

I spent nearly all my life's savings, seventy-five pounds, and had just enough left over to buy a saddle, snaffle bridle and a jute night rug with a surcingle sewn to the centre at the top.

I named my pony Mickey. He had a placid temperament, a natural aptitude for jumping and we learnt together, gaining confidence as the fences got higher. Mickey also acted as my escort horse when I taught both adults and children the elements of riding.

Mickey and I went to a few shows, either on the hoof if the venue was near enough or in a cattle truck driven by a man who came to collect us, waited all day while we were at the show then transported us home. Passengers travelled in the back with the ponies. In general, people did not have their own horse transport. It was more usual in those days to hire a lorry and driver whenever it was needed.

The highlight of these early days of showing was winning the trophy and red rosette for the Best Riding School Horse and Pupil when riding a horse that belonged to the proprietor's brother. Some time after the class an announcement over the public address called me back to the ring with the horse. I was convinced that the rosette was going to be taken away because someone had grumbled that I was not a true riding school pupil and that the horse was not a true riding school horse. It turned out that the then-famous 'Uncle Mac' of 1950s radio programme *Children's Hour* wanted to present his trophy to the winner. This large silver trophy was retained by the riding school proprietor and was displayed on the table in the saddle room before it had to be returned to the show secretary. I made such a fuss about not being allowed to have the big trophy that eventually, to satisfy me, I was allowed to keep, and still have, the small, solid silver replica that Uncle Mac generously gave me. However, I learnt that the rosette always stays with the horse, which, at the time, was hard to accept as I did so want a rosette.

A short time after I started work there, the riding school moved to

new premises but still in Surrey. I was put into digs with a retired working horseman and his wife. He gave me the set of horse brasses that he had had when he worked with heavy horses on the land. I still have them. The tops of the brasses are worn wafer-thin where they hung on the harness and swung against the horses as they worked all day in the fields.

The Old Surrey and Burstow Hunt were to meet near to my digs. The old horseman knew about the forthcoming meet because he often followed hounds on foot. He told me that I should have a day with hounds and so I took his advice and obtained permission to follow on Mickey when the hunt met nearby. It never occurred to me that fox-hunting was cruel. I knew that foxes were regarded as vermin and needed to be controlled. I had heard how, if you forgot to shut your ducks or chickens in at night they were likely to be killed by a fox, which would leave several headless carcasses and a few terrified hens

up in the trees too scared to come down. When I was following, hounds found a fox quite quickly and killed it. As far as I was concerned one moment it was alive and the next moment it was dead.

The huntsman, on seeing a new face out hunting and a youngster at that, came over to me.

'Have you been blooded?' he asked me. I did not know what he meant and said no. Whereupon he cut off one of the fox's forefeet at the knee. Then, much to my surprise he smeared the bloody pad over my face giving a shout and a whoo-oop as he did so. 'You're a true foxhunting person now,' he told me solemnly. 'Here, take this,' and he offered me the pad. 'Get it put on a plaque and hang it on the wall. It's a milestone in your life.'

'Thank you,' I muttered as I stuffed the precious trophy into my pocket. Today the pad hangs on the wall mounted on a wooden shield.

The smell of a fox has remained in my memory for the rest of my life. I can still smell a fox, if there is one anywhere near, long before most other people. The sight of a fox never fails to give me a thrill.

★   ★   ★

There was an old sidesaddle on a saddle rack at the stables and I wanted to learn how to ride this way. I was given a lesson, on the ever-tolerant Mickey by a lady who rode sidesaddle. She told me that the main requirements were a horse with a pronounced wither that would carry a sidesaddle comfortably and a rider who could distribute her weight evenly, otherwise the horse would develop a sore back. I was told to sit up straight and look squarely to the front by keeping my right shoulder back and my left hip forward. After this lesson I practised whenever I had the chance. One thing that always struck me was that when I wanted to stroke Mickey for being good, I had to lean down a long way before I could reach his neck because I sat much higher above him than in my usual astride saddle.

It was not long before the riding school moved again. I was now living in with the proprietor's family but Mickey, a couple of working liveries, and the other ponies were kept about half a mile away in a barn that was converted to accommodate them. There was no mains water and we had to carry buckets filled from a tank supplied by rain-water from the roof of a nearby building. Carting large quantities of water was an exhausting job – and the ponies in the fields seemed to drink an awful lot.

Neither was there any mains electricity and so we lit paraffin lamps once it grew dark. We warmed water for cleaning saddles and bridles in a small metal bucket kept on the top of a Valor paraffin stove in a shed. If the weather was cold, we would alternate the bucket with a saucepan of soup to warm us up. In another attempt to get warm, I would groom Mickey with a body brush so vigorously that I could see sparks of static electricity momentarily light up the dark stable.

A hay-cutting knife.

Because there was no water and no electricity we had to do every-thing by hand. It was hard work. For instance, in the early 1950s hay was cut from a stack with a hay knife. This knife had a large, broad, curved blade set at an angle to a wide wooden handle. You had to stand over the top of this and use your weight to saw through the hay. The blade had to be kept razor sharp or it was impossible to use prop-erly and I never became proficient at using it. Experts with the hay knife could cut out neat rectangular trusses that were bound with string to keep them together during transportation to stables such as the Knightsbridge Riding School.

After about a year and a half at the Surrey riding school I decided that I was not learning enough and was not progressing. The time had come to train for a British Horse Society teaching qualification. I began to make enquiries.

CHAPTER 4

Stocklands

I HAD HEARD ABOUT STOCKLANDS – a large residential riding school with an excellent reputation – in Petersfield, Hampshire. In 1953 I contacted the proprietor, an Irishman called Steve Gibson, who called me for an interview to be trained for the British Horse Society Preliminary Instructor's Certificate.

When I arrived at Stocklands I was very impressed as I went down the long drive past two houses and the grooms' chalets which took me into the smart yard. There was not a wisp of hay or straw to be seen and neither was there any sign of the muck heap. Steve Gibson walked out of his office to welcome and show me round.

A pair of beautiful horses' heads looked over the half-doors of two large loose boxes on the left of the yard. Next to these were saddle rooms full of immaculate saddles and bridles hanging on racks. The windows gleamed and the floor shone. Beyond the saddle rooms was a building that contained three stalls and a loose box. On the right of the yard were four big loose boxes housing high-class horses which I later learned were being prepared for sale. At the end of the yard was the entrance to the indoor school. The gallery door was on the right-hand side and it was through this that spectators unobtrusively entered to watch horses in the school without having to slide back the big doors that were opened when horses were led in and out of the school. This was a great boon for nervous horses being worked in the school for they frequently took fright if the big doors slid open.

The feed room, with all the feed charts on the walls, was on the left of the school and contained several enormous feed bins. Horses' feed bowls were laid out, washed and cleaned, in preparation for the next feeding time and a chaff cutter stood in the corner. At the back of the yard five loose boxes housed horses that were there for breaking in. Three small ponies stood in stalls next to them and the fourteen riding school animals were accommodated in stalls behind the long side of the indoor school.

There was a cinder-surfaced circular lungeing ring and beyond it, the grassland had cross-country fences enabling horses to be jumped from one field to another over a variety of obstacles. There was a row of brush fences along one side of the long field for point-to-point enthusiasts to gallop over.

After I had been shown all the facilities I was told to ride a horse in the school so that my capabilities could be assessed by Steve Gibson. The upshot was that Mr G, as we all called him, accepted me and I went, with Mickey, to be taught to teach riding properly. I took all the valuable instruction very seriously.

After a few weeks of preparation and practice I was examined at The Riding School, in Stanmore in Middlesex, because Stocklands was not an examination centre. I had to ride and jump unknown animals and complete a written paper. During the oral questioning I was faced with a huge selection of horseshoes. I was totally mystified by one which was a complete circle. Mr G had impressed on us never to admit to an examiner to not knowing the answer to a question. He told us to keep calm, think hard and come up with some kind of intelligent answer. I later taught my pupils to use the same technique when being examined.

After some thought, I replied that the shoe could possibly be used to help to keep a horse's foot together. The examiner appeared to be satisfied and I passed the exam, whereupon Mr G offered me a job. I accepted and was put in charge of running the section of the riding school devoted entirely to teaching children. I was to live in one of the chalets that accommodated some members of staff and young resi-

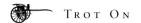

dential short-stay pupils. Other staff lived locally and came daily on bicycles or on foot. Some of the long-term pupils who were training with their show jumpers lived either with Mr and Mrs G or in a house adjoining the chalets. Adult pupils also lived in this house which was run by a housekeeper. At one time there were twenty-two girls on the premises and I, as the most senior, shouldered much responsibility when Mr G was away.

Mr G and I came to an agreement whereby Mickey would be kept here providing that he could be used in the school for teaching children under my supervision. In addition to my pony's keep I was paid a small wage and immediately put in charge of the fourteen riding school ponies and cobs.

The day began at about 6.30am when Mr G came round all the accommodation en route from his house to the stables. Once up, we all went to the saddle room where mugs of tea were waiting for us; at one time we were given glucose tablets to promote energy – not that I needed them for, at that age, I was not short of energy!

I would go to my stables and muck out all fourteen animals, separating the clean straw by pushing it forwards, away from the dirty straw and the muck, which I pushed backwards. Percy, the splendid yardman, brought a large, four-wheeled barrow to take all the muck away and swept up as he went. Later he would bring back the day's fresh straw and sometimes the hay. In the meantime, I picked out and checked feet for injury or loose shoes, then I quartered all the animals – giving them a quick brush over – and, as all but three were greys and skewbalds, I often had to wash hindquarters and tails. The other three were a dun pony, a black ex-polo pony and a bay cob called Pills. He got his name because he had belonged to a man to whom the doctor had recommended daily riding to promote good health in preference to lots of pills! Finally, there were the water buckets to clean and refill but, thank goodness, the tap was just at the end of the stalls.

By the time these tasks were done, the head girl would be putting the morning feeds together. Mr G would pin up a feed chart that stated exactly what each animal was to be given. Feeds consisted of oats, bran and chaff. Chaff was cut by hand using a chaff cutter. The hay would be pushed along a rectangular wooden trough towards two sets of teeth – you kept your fingers out of their way! These teeth

formed it into a tight bunch. Two sharp blades on the inside of a
wheel to which a handle was attached then sliced it. The operator
turned the handle in a steady rhythm to cut the hay neatly into small
pieces. Chaff cutting was always done the night before for the next
morning's feeds. The feeds were damped with a mixture of molasses
and water. At the cry of 'Feed up!' the horses neighed and kicked
impatiently at their stable doors while we collected and distributed
the feeds as fast as we could.

By the time all ponies were eating it was usually about 8.30am and
we all trooped in for breakfast that had been cooked by the housekeeper. We were then free until l0am when we saddled up whichever
horse we were listed to ride. These were usually those that were in for
schooling or for sale. Pupils who were there to train their own show
jumpers rode them.

Mr G instructed us, usually in the indoor school, and we learned
a lot. He was very interested in show jumping and his son competed
successfully in junior jumping competitions at the big shows. Mr G's
methods achieved good results with no hardship to the horses.

One day I was mounted on a huge horse and told to jump what
seemed to me to be an enormous fence that had been put up in the
school. It was over five feet high and I was told to jump from a trot.
The horse launched himself into space. It took forever before he
landed but we survived! I never did discover why I was told to do this;

there may have been a potential purchaser watching the lesson from the gallery and Mr G was proving the capabilities of this horse when ridden by a girl at a trot.

Sometimes I had to ride horses that bucked like rodeo broncos. I found that riding them in an Australian stock saddle was a great help. This stock saddle was not like the American cowboy saddle but more like an English saddle with a deeper seat and protruding pads in front of my thighs that were a huge help in keeping me in the plate when the horse's head disappeared between his knees! No doubt Australian stockmen found the design to be useful for the same reason and when a secure seat was needed when working cattle.

I wasn't the only one who had bucking horses to contend with. There were two lads who had worked at racing stables before coming to Stocklands. One was handsome, dark-haired and so athletic that on one occasion when he was bucked off a newly broken youngster in the school, he landed on his feet, and virtually bounced back on board before the horse even realised that he had momentarily dumped his rider!

After the daily riding lesson, which ended at about midday, we returned to whichever section of the stables was our responsibility, bedded down the horses and swept up so that there was not a straw out of place. I saddled my fourteen riding school ponies in readiness for the afternoon lessons. Then they were all fed and we went into the house for lunch.

I came out about 2pm and was helped to put bridles on all the ponies because, at 2.30pm the children would arrive. They came by coach from various schools nearby but, after the new horsebox was purchased by Stocklands, Mr G collected some children in this exciting mode of transport. At one time there were seventy-three children coming each week for lessons with me in the afternoons. Although I was teaching, Mr G monitored my lessons as I was, in turn, being taught to teach.

Mr G's wise words on teaching were: 'Explanation – demonstration – imitation' and they have remained with me throughout my teaching career. Later in life, when I began lecturing and public speaking, his equally valuable words that stood me in good stead were: 'Stand up – speak up – and shut up!'

In my early days of teaching at Stocklands one of my lessons involved instructing children to perform a half-turn on the forehand after riding around the track by the wall of the indoor school. I had omitted to tell the children to bring their ponies towards the centre of the school away from the wall. Consequently, on starting the half-turn on the forehand, the ponies' heads were almost jammed against the wall. Afterwards, Mr G quietly pointed out my error and explained what I should have done. I was very embarrassed that I had been so thoughtless to those long-suffering ponies and I did not make that mistake again.

In warm weather we would sometimes let the children sit on the ponies while they walked them round the field to cool off. On one such occasion the pupils were from a convent school and were accompanied by two nuns wearing habits. As we walked out to the field with the children I called to one of the two 'racing stable' lads as I had a job that I wanted him to do. (Mr G was away that afternoon and I was in charge of the yard.) A river ran beside the field and a path led into the shallow water. At first there was no response to my call although I knew the lads were around.

I was about to call again when a head broke the surface of the water quickly followed by the rest of the virile torso of the handsomer of the two. Around his chest was a bikini top stuffed with hay and the skimpiest of swimming trunks barely covered his nether regions.

'I'm here, Sallie!' he called innocently. I wanted to die with embarrassment. I could hear the girls giggling but I dare not look at the nuns. I could feel myself blushing and for a moment forgot why I had called him. I never did discover what the nuns thought but, judging from the excited tittering, their girls were delighted! I was terrified that the headmistress would be told and that I would be held responsible, but they all came the following week for their lesson so maybe the headmistress was never told about the incident.

Eventually, I was promoted from looking after the fourteen riding school ponies to four horses and ponies which were accommodated in the front yard. Talisman, an Anglo-Arab elementary level dressage horse, stood in the loose box. I rode him often and competed with him once. He was a good-looking horse and hence was used for promotion of the new horsebox. I was told to put on my smart jacket and

Sallie and Talisman advertising the new horsebox.

bowler hat and sit on him alongside the box for the brochure photograph, to give the impression that we had just arrived at a show having been transported there in the new vehicle. The horsebox was available for hire for, at that time, few people had their own private horseboxes or trailers.

I no longer looked after my own pony, Mickey, because he remained stabled with the riding school ponies. He was someone else's responsibility but I used to ride him in the evenings or in my lunch break, when I would sometimes take him into the field to jump just for fun.

'Open days' at Stocklands were when parents came to watch their children ride. It was on one of these open days that I noticed three young men, whom I did not recognise, sitting in the gallery of the indoor school. I knew most of the parents and assumed that these boys must be elder brothers of some of the girls. However, after the parents had gone, the boys remained and I went to the saddle room where several people were cleaning tack to find out if anyone knew them. They were, apparently, all staying on a week's course. I thought that the tall, dark, slim one looked the most interesting... I quickly found out that his name was Bill. Then I had an idea. The gears had gone wrong on my bicycle and so I sought out Bill.

'Are you any good at mending bicycles?' I asked him.

'Not bad. Why?'

'The gears have gone wrong on mine.'

'Shouldn't be too difficult,' replied Bill confidently.

'They're Sturmey Archer, hub-type, three-speed gears – the latest ones,' I told him proudly.

'I know the sort,' said Bill. I was impressed. 'I'll work on it this afternoon.'

And he did. Being mechanically minded, Bill quickly fixed the gears – and took me out for a meal that evening. We were immediately attracted to each other.

Bill told me that he had always had a pony, had hunted with the Suffolk Hunt for years and was starting to ride in point-to-points, but he had come to Stocklands because he wanted to be taught more about the finer points of riding. After that first evening together and when the serious business of learning and teaching during the day was over, Bill and I used to play with Mickey in the evenings. Much to everyone's amusement, Bill rode him sidesaddle and even jumped him, which I thought was very brave. Six years later Bill and I were married.

We girls were a great responsibility for poor Mr G. We used to sneak out in the evening, hoping not to be seen and would sometimes come home across the fields at night so that we did not have to pass his house. We must have been a real headache for him!

Mr G liked to bring a little entertainment into working with horses. At one time he decided that he would start a mounted band. He was always thinking up new ideas which we took in our stride. He

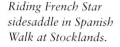

borrowed a few small accordions from a local music shop and organised musical evenings with himself playing the banjo. Having played the piano I quickly got the hang of the accordion but I was not sure how Mickey was going to take to being ridden with reins fixed to my feet in drum-horse style. Fortunately, the idea fell by the wayside. However, three of us did get together (without horses) and, with piano and drums to accompany my accordion, we played in a pub on a few occasions and once for a wedding reception in a village hall. We even got paid for our efforts!

I had been promoted again; I was teaching much more and taking greater responsibility in the running of the yard. Because of this I was now looking after just two horses, which were kept in stables known as the Front Two. These were large, imposing loose boxes and were the first to be seen by visitors. The horses wore smart rugs and their water buckets and feed bins were top quality. One stable housed an ex-dressage mare used for teaching more advanced movements to pupils. The other loose box housed a one-eyed chestnut Thoroughbred horse with four white stockings. He was called French Star.

As I mentioned, Mr G liked a touch of entertainment and one morning when the indoor school was free he called for me. I found him there, on foot, teaching French Star from the ground to perform the Spanish walk. He was teaching the horse to raise each front leg in

Riding French Star sidesaddle in Spanish Walk at Stocklands.

turn, up to elbow height, and proceed forward at each stride on command. He had placed the horse between himself and the wall and encouraged French Star to raise the front leg nearest to him when he touched it with a long training whip. My job was to grab the foot as it came up and to put it as far forward as I could so that he progressed up the school. French Star eventually grasped the idea. We repeated the process on the opposite side so that he learned to go in both directions. I had to be careful when I looked after him in the stable that I did not inadvertently give an unintentional signal that he might interpret as a command to execute a Spanish walk and strike out dangerously with a foreleg.

Another time Mr G had taught a horse to lie down to command. He called on me again explaining that, while the horse was lying down, I should jump onto its back. When he gave the command to get up, the horse scrambled up with me on board. I did as I was told and we came up together. I was amazed! It was another new experience and I kept learning all the time.

Mr G took advantage of the fact that I was the only person at Stocklands at that time who had ever ridden sidesaddle. French Star had been taught the movements of passage and piaffe and was improving at the Spanish walk and now it was time for him to perform them with me riding him sidesaddle. Mr G would sometimes have a visitor to whom he wanted to display the results of his teaching. I would saddle up French Star and bring him into the school wearing the sidesaddle and white buckskin double bridle with its curly-cheeked curb bit. I would don my habit and bowler and mount French Star. I usually started by cantering at almost walking pace. I then asked for a little passage and piaffe before finishing with Spanish walk. I loved every moment – and so did Mr G!

One Sunday afternoon I was told to put the sidesaddle onto a Thoroughbred horse that I had never ridden before and I was sure had never carried a sidesaddle. I saddled up, taking care not to tighten the balance girth too much because this might have caused him to object. The balance girth passed over the horse's ribs on the off side as it came up towards the rear of the saddle. I went into the school, mounted and put the horse through its paces. All went well – then my heart sank. The potential purchaser asked to see the horse jump some of the

cross-country fences outside. I had never got the hang of jumping sidesaddle and so I rode towards a tiny rail and popped over it. This seemed to satisfy everyone and, much to my relief, no further jumping was requested. A week or so later the horse was sold.

Inspired by Mr G's teaching of tricks, I taught Mickey to kneel down and bow. However, much later on I discovered the dangers of teaching such party tricks to horses. I taught my stallion, Ali, whom I had bought in 1965 and he seemed to use it against me, for sometimes he would kneel down if I wanted to trim his heels. It was, of course, impossible to trim his heels when he was kneeling down.

Party tricks and sidesaddle were fun but what I really wanted to do was to drive Mickey. I decided that I would start training him in preparation for the day when I might be able to afford some harness and a vehicle – perhaps a gig of some kind. I decided to begin his training right away.

The surface of the indoor school was harrowed on most days to prevent it from compacting and to remove the track made by horses as they were worked around the edges of the school. Pills the cob was used for this. He wore an open snaffle bridle and a breast collar with the traces fixed to a small harrow. I thought that Mickey could do this work and one day I put him to the harrow. Luckily, I got away with it. When I look back, I realise how foolish I had been to put him to without giving him any build-up training. I would not dream of attaching a horse to a harrow in this manner now. On reflection, I imagine that Mickey had been broken to harness in Ireland before he came over to England in 1951.

But the time had come for a change. I had been at Stocklands for about two years, I had learned an enormous amount but felt I was no longer progressing and I wanted to expand my equestrian horizons. My parents, who had moved to Felbridge near East Grinstead in Sussex, had heard of a local lady, Vivian Hurst, who was looking for a girl to help with her dressage horses. We met and she agreed to give me a job. We built a loose box in the garden of our new Sussex home for Mickey and I moved from Stocklands to live with my parents again.

CHAPTER 5

Dressage

Mickey provided my daily transport to my new employer's stables, a ten- or twenty-minute ride depending on whether I galloped or walked from my home at Felbridge near East Grinstead. Luckily, there was a good bridle path that ran from the end of the lane near our house to a road about half a mile from the stables. Sometimes the landowner put a rail at the entrance to the bridle path to prevent cars from using it as a short cut. Although there was room, to the side of the rail, for a horse and rider to get through, Mickey and I often popped over the rail for fun.

Once I had arrived at Vivian Hurst's yard (although she was always known in those more respectful times as Mrs Hurst), Mickey had to stand all day tied up in the open while I worked. I kept him supplied with plenty of hay. In bad weather I would put rugs and waterproofs over him, piling them high to keep him warm and dry. He was, thank goodness, totally uncomplaining.

The main stables were well constructed for ease of management. Four large loose boxes and a saddle room faced a spacious yard with a gravel surface beyond the concrete frontage. There was a wide, covered passage running along the back of the stables where the feed bins and hay were kept. Here, service hatch-type sliding doors gave access to the metal feed mangers that hooked into slots on the back wall of each loose box. Hay nets were also put through the hatches and secured to rings within easy reach but high enough to prevent a horse getting its feet entangled as the hay net emptied. Every net of hay had to be carefully weighed on a spring balance after it had been filled according to the instructions. Mrs Hurst always put the feeds into the mangers as only she knew, each day, exactly how she wanted each horse to be fed, as the work varied according to her other commitments. Boiled linseed was added to the feeds and helped enormously to keep a bloom on the horses' coats. A house cow was kept and surplus milk brought to the stables in a bucket for the horses – they loved it.

Other livestock included a couple of racing donkeys owned by the farm manager. He occasionally asked me to ride them after giving me the briefest of instruction,

'Sit further back than on a pony – nearly on its rump. Oh, and there's no saddle…'

Another row of stables faced the grass area behind the main stables. These housed youngsters and the donkeys. Close by there was an indoor school and an outdoor full-sized dressage arena. Low white fences decorated the edges of the arena to familiarise the horses with the sight of such fences when at competitions.

I was helping to look after two dressage horses, Playboy and Cavalier, which were being worked at Medium and Prix St Georges levels. There was also a grey mare of Lipizzaner type, the breed used in classical dressage at the Spanish Riding School in Vienna. Mrs Hurst did not compete with her but rode her for pleasure. I also looked after a retired show hack that Mrs Hurst used to work. I was also breaking in three youngsters under the direction of Mrs Hurst. One of them reached the level of jumping at a few small shows.

The four dressage horses had to be strapped for at least half an hour each day and, as a result, their coats gleamed. Strapping was hard work but at least clipping had become easier, for by now electric clippers had replaced the old hand-cranked variety. These made life so much better but, even so, clipping horses' heads could be tricky, for some were very sensitive about having clippers near their ears, eyes and throat. Somehow I had acquired a reputation for being able to clip horses' heads without too much fuss ('You can always do it better than me, Sallie' the farm manger would say ingratiatingly!) and so it fell to me to clip heads while he clipped the bodies. Twitches were never used.

Sometimes Mrs Hurst would work two or even three horses before going to work at the hospital where she held a senior post. She would tell me which horse she wanted, and when, and I would get it ready and lead it to the indoor school. At other times I would be told to come to the school to watch a certain movement being ridden. For instance, I would be asked to watch a pirouette then say where the hind legs had been positioned throughout the movement. This was valuable training for me as it taught me to watch closely and carefully and remember what I had seen. Spectacular action by the front legs was of little value if the all-important hind legs were not propelling the horse forward. I also learned to spot uneven strides, tilting the head or the horse bending to the wrong side. All this was very useful when, many years later, I judged dressage at driving trials.

Cavalier and Playboy competed in top-level dressage competitions. I accompanied them and learned a tremendous amount by watching experts working their horses.

For most dressage tests the rider had to memorise the sequence of movements. However, for some long and complicated tests the rules allowed an assistant to call out the next movement to the rider. Occasionally I was entrusted to do this. I would stand at the B marker half-way down one of the long sides of the dressage arena and command the movements from the test sheet which listed the sequence of movements. I was terrified that I would lose the place on the sheet and so, as I held the paper, kept my left thumb against each movement as it was performed. I had to give the command at exactly the right moment so that Mrs Hurst knew which movement was coming next in sufficient, but not too much, time. I then had to keep quiet so that she and the horse could concentrate.

Mrs Hurst would work in the horse before the test and then, about six or seven minutes before the time she was due to enter the arena, I would take off the bandages that were always worn to protect the horses' legs against any knocks and give the horse a slice of apple to get its mouth salivating to prevent it from becoming dry and unresponsive. I would then apply a little fly repellent and, last of all,

Mrs Hurst would hand me her whip because the rules stated that whips must not be carried unless the rider was riding sidesaddle. (There was, in fact, one rider who rode sidesaddle who competed at this level in the 1950s.)

After the competition the horses sometimes returned in the lorry in the care of someone else, while I travelled with Mrs Hurst in her car. We would discuss every movement of every test. Consequently, I continued to learn a tremendous amount and was very grateful for the opportunity to discover more about this high level of dressage.

Dressage experts used to come to advise Mrs Hurst on working her horses. If she were unexpectedly called away to work at the hospital while they were there, I was fortunate to be instructed by them.

One expert in particular, to whom I shall always be grateful, was Mr E. Schmit-Jensen even though I had only one lesson from him. I had watched his method of long-reining with great interest for he was the first person I had ever seen long-reining a horse on a circle. Up till then, the only long-reining I had seen had been with the trainer running behind the horse. As I have never been any good at running, this meant that all my long-reining had been at the walk. Mr Schmit-Jensen used a kind of small driving pad fastened over the top of the riding saddle of the horse he was training. The long-reins were buckled to the bit, passed through the terrets on the pad and then back to his hands. The weight of the reins alone gave enough contact with the horse's mouth most of the time. (No cruppers were used, as these dressage horses were unaccustomed to feeling something under their tails and would probably have reacted violently.) He would work the horses frequently changing pace by bringing them across the centre of the circle then turning them in the other direction; soon his pupil would be working at an advanced level at all paces.

I felt there was enormous potential, endless possibilities and many advantages with this method of long-reining, not the least of which was being able to see how the horse moved and where it was putting its hind legs. A high degree of obedience can be achieved with work on long-reins. The benefits of this training were proved to me in later years when, in two emergencies, my ponies responded to my voice when I was some distance away. I feel certain that their obedience was a result of years of careful training from the ground on long-reins.

I long-reined on a circle the three youngsters I was breaking. It was not as easy as it had looked. I was not allowed to use proper long-reins like Mr Schmit-Jensen in case I pulled too hard and made the horses overbend or spoiled their mouths. My long-reins were hospital bandages that broke if I pulled too hard! However, all three horses benefited enormously from the long-reining and developed light and responsive mouths.

Some time after I first met Mr Schmit-Jensen I persuaded him to come to a Pony Club camp for which I was organising the afternoon speakers. He generously agreed and used Mickey as his demonstration horse. By this time, Mickey was quite well schooled and towards the end of the demonstration, he placed Mickey alongside a wall and produced a couple of strides of piaffe. The wall kept Mickey straight while Mr Schmit-Jensen created plenty of impulsion but restrained Mickey with his light and sensitive hands. Mickey then elevated his legs in response. Mr Schmit-Jensen was indeed a very skilful trainer.

Gradually, I developed my own system of long-reining on a 20-metre circle based on Mr Schmit-Jensen's methods and have taught it to pupils all over the world. By methodical and careful training on the long-reins, which helps to develop the right muscles in the neck and quarters, even the most ugly horses can be made to look beautiful.

I was becoming very interested in dressage but Mrs Hurst knew that I was also keen on jumping and so a Grade C show jumper was bought for me to ride. However, I did not enjoy the training sessions to which I had to take him about twice a week. The standing martingale (which was almost de rigeur for jumpers at that time) was put on so tightly that it took two of us to buckle it to the noseband. Fences were large and the methods were rough. I was not tough enough for this level of jumping and I preferred the way Mickey and I enjoyed our jumping at local level and so the show jumper was sold. I did, however, learn a tremendous amount about the sport and was grateful for the opportunity that had been given to me in being taught by a top-class jumping trainer who produced many successful horses.

CHAPTER 6

Driving and Family Ponies

I HAD BEEN TALKING to Mrs Hurst's farm manager about wanting to drive Mickey. He knew of a vehicle for sale: an old governess cart with iron-shod wheels. One felloe had almost disintegrated, for that part of the wheel's rim had been standing, unmoved, for years in the mud and dampness had rotted the wood. There was also a very old set of harness with a full collar. Amazingly, it fitted Mickey's neck. I paid five pounds for the cart and harness. There were several pairs of lamps lying in long grass behind some buildings on Mrs Hurst's farm and I was told I could take whichever pair I liked for a pound. I chose the pair with the oval fronts, for I felt they would look so elegant when restored and I lost no time in rubbing down the metalwork, painting it black and polishing the brass until it gleamed. They looked wonderful and I still use those lamps when I show my gig today.

During one of Bill's weekend visits to Sussex from Suffolk we 'broke' Mickey to harness by putting him carefully to the governess cart. Mickey behaved perfectly and the next day we took my non-horsey mother for a drive. This confirmed my earlier suspicion that he had been broken to harness before he came over from Ireland several years ago. On another visit, Bill arrived at East Grinstead station in the evening. I took Mickey and the governess cart to collect Bill and

splinter bar   dashboard   lamp

mudguard

spoke

felloe

shaft   tug stop   breeching dee   mounting step

Pam Greene's Essex cart, shown here to identify carriage parts. (See also page 126)

his luggage. We drove back through East Grinstead to Felbridge in the dark. My carriage lamps, each lit with one candle, whose flame was reflected by the silver-plated side and rear panels inside the glass, provided a good glow to the side and a reasonable glow forwards to light our journey home. Tiny red lights on the back of the governess cart were the only warning of our presence to the following motor traffic. It was risky even then but we were young and had little sense of danger!

Sallie and Bill breaking Mickey to harness.

I was working six-day weeks at Mrs Hurst's but occasionally I had a whole weekend off. Sometimes I took Mickey to little local shows or I would visit Bill and his family in Suffolk. Bill rode in a few local point-to-points and I would go to watch him. He had won an Adjacent Hunts' race and had come second in another. We used to walk the course before he rode and I thought that the fences looked enormously wide. The water jump, in particular, with its brush fence on the take-off side looked impossible. Bill assured me that at the speed that he and Fish Hunter, his father's sway-backed chestnut horse, would be going, he would hardly feel the jump. I used to fuss about minor dips and humps in the ground, which with my dressage and indoor school background appeared dangerous, but Bill assured me that in point-to-pointing they did not matter and, of course, he was right.

On one of my visits we were going to the Suffolk Hunt ball in Bury St Edmunds. Before going to the ball we dined in the large, panelled dining room at Thorne Court, Bill's family home near Bury, where ancestral portraits stared down from the walls. There was a painting entitled *The Yellow Lady*. It portrayed an Elizabethan girl holding four hearts and wearing a pale yellow dress. Legend has it that she cursed the Walrond family so that the next four Walrond eldest sons would die before inheriting although no one seemed to know what they had done to deserve this. She would appear three times: the first time before selling family property, the second time before making an unhappy marriage and the third time before they die. Bill's great-grandfather is reputed to have said, 'I have seen that bloody woman for the third time.' In the morning he was dead.

I listened agog to this story. After the hunt ball I retired to my bedroom. I went up the wide staircase and turned into the long corridor that led off the landing towards my room. There were so many doors and I could not remember exactly which room was mine. Walking along the upstairs passage I saw 'The Yellow Lady' coming towards me. I was too frightened to scream in case I woke Granny or Elsie, who looked after Granny and had rooms here. I was more frightened of incurring their displeasure than I was of any ghost. I stopped. So did 'The Yellow Lady'. Neither of us moved. I turned my head slowly to look for my room door. So did 'The Yellow Lady'. Relief flooded over me and I wanted to laugh. This 'Yellow Lady' was nothing more than my own reflection in a huge mirror at the end of the corridor!

Bill, thank goodness, has never seen the 'real' Yellow Lady.

★   ★   ★

When I had been working at the Surrey riding school I had met the Parsons-Smith family. I had taught their daughter, Anne, to ride and she had kept her pony there as a working livery. Now, a few years later, I met them again and they told me that all five members of the family had become keen on riding. They asked if I would teach their two young sons, James and Nicholas, and resume lessons with Anne. I agreed to help whenever I had some free time while working for Mrs Hurst.

They lived at Roughets House, Blechingley – thirteen miles from Felbridge, so I needed transport. I had an ancient motorbike with a manual gear-change on the petrol tank. Its suspension was a series of small bars connected with nuts and bolts like a children's Meccano set but it wasn't reliable. I had also had a one-gear, stop-or-go Corgi motor scooter that was equally unreliable. So I bought a second-hand, pale green, BSA 125cc motorbike to take me to Roughets. This proved to be just as unreliable as the other two and let me down on several occasions. Sometimes a kind person with an empty van would stop, bundle my motorbike and me into the back and give me a lift. I can remember only too clearly how awful it was to have to push the wretched thing and how grateful I was for those lifts. Consequently, I always stop when I am driving an empty trailer or Land Rover if I pass some unfortunate person pushing a motorbike along the road.

I used to go, on my BSA motorbike, to Roughets in the afternoons and ride Mickey to Mrs Hurst in the mornings. Eventually, though, I left Mrs Hurst to work full-time for the Parsons-Smith family. Mickey was given a loose box and I was given a bedroom where I could stay overnight if we were very busy or had an early start. Mostly I 'commuted' between Felbridge and Roughets on the BSA but soon aspired to a brand new Francis Barnet 150cc motorbike which never let me down.

Some weekends the family and I would set off from Roughets to a small show. We put Mickey to the governess cart which we loaded with saddle, bridle, grooming kit and feed. Anne would ride her horse and perhaps lead one of the boys' ponies. One or both of the boys would travel with me in the governess cart. On arrival at the show we would enter for every class for which we were eligible. I would usually jump Mickey and he nearly always went clear in the first round but in the jump-off he would frequently tip off a pole with his toe, so we rarely won but were usually in the ribbons. Anne and the boys would compete in horse and pony showing classes. We would return home with lots of rosettes, if we had been lucky, but always feeling very happy.

★   ★   ★

The governess cart had served me well but I wanted a vehicle that had seats facing forward so that I did not have to drive from the sideways position which the governess cart demanded.

I heard of a suitable-sounding vehicle for sale in Blechingley and so I arranged to go and see it on my way home one evening. Despite its covering of dust at the back of the barn behind the hay, it was a beautiful black-and-yellow vehicle with two huge wheels and a forward facing seat. The asking price was eight pounds – quite a lot of money to me in those days. I dithered for a while wondering if I was doing the right thing. The vendor offered to deliver it to Felbridge for me and that clinched the deal. When it arrived my mother looked at it and asked incredulously, 'What did you want to buy that for?'

Soon after I bought the vehicle, Bill and I went to the Science Museum in London as we had heard that there were some carriages on display there and we thought that we might be able to find out what type of vehicle I had bought. We found a model in a glass case that resembled my vehicle and so decided that mine was a gig. When we took the wheels off some time later, we found the date, 1880, and the name Selby stamped on the axle. The vehicle proved to be a skeleton gig, so named because, unlike the model in the Science Museum, my gig had no boot under the seat. It was this feature which made my vehicle so unusual.

The skeleton gig lived under a tarpaulin by the side of our Sussex house. I painted the body black and the wheels and shafts a similar shade of yellow to the original paint. I was not, of course, sufficiently skilled to paint lines on the wheels, springs or shafts. My painting was mainly to keep the weather from damaging the wood because, unlike the governess cart, the gig was sound.

I was fortunate to obtain a lovely set of old but high-quality, black, polished harness with brass furniture. The bridle, which had the crest of a family unknown to me on the blinkers and face drop, was neatly designed and fitted Mickey's head. The saddle was an attractive shape and bore the same family crest. I did not realise, at the time, that I was not entitled to use this crested harness because I was not connected to that family. The breast collar was only just large enough and had to be used on the last holes of the neckpiece. There was no breeching, so I had a false breeching made by a local harness-maker as it was cheaper than a full breeching would have been. Luck-ily, the gig already had dees on the shafts to take false breeching. For safety's sake, I bought a new pair of reins. At first, I used a Kim-blewick bit that I had been riding Mickey in as I could not afford a stainless-steel Liverpool driving bit. The bridle had come with a nickel bit but I would never use nickel bits as I had seen them bend, crack and actually break.

Now that I had what I considered a smart vehicle, I was anxious to show Mickey in a driving class. At that time, about 1956, hardly any shows had classes for driving as there were very few private driv-ing turnouts. There was, however, a show fifteen miles away which had a driving class and a ride-and-drive class. It was pouring with rain when Anne Parsons-Smith and I set off very early in the gig and drove Mickey to the show, only to find the gates of the showground were still shut when we arrived.

I decided that Mickey needed a little feed after all his exertions. He wore a webbing halter under the bridle. I decided to remove the bri-dle so that he could eat better, the halter providing something by which to hold him. I then committed the crime of removing the bridle while he was still harnessed to the gig. Now, without the blinkers, he could see all around him. He looked back and saw the high, yellow wheels of the gig close behind him. Despite being a little tired from having been driven for two hours, he leapt forward in fear. Fortu-

Sallie and Anne Parsons-Smith with Mickey after a long drive in the rain to Carshalton show in 1956. The author, in her youth, assumed that the reins were meant to pass through the bearing rein drops on Mickey's bridle. She later learned this was incorrect. (Photo reproduced by kind permission of The Croydon Advertiser Group)

nately, I had only partially removed the bridle and Anne and I managed to slap it back on before he really set off. I would not have been strong enough to hold him in a halter. I had learned, nearly the hard way, that you must never take off a bridle while the horse is still harnessed to the vehicle. It does not matter how quiet the animal is, if he is not trained to be driven in an open bridle (one without blinkers), he is likely to run away under these circumstances. I believe the reason is that if the horse steps forward, he sees the tops of the wheels appearing to chase him. Natural self-preservation makes him run away from the 'predator'.

Despite the near mishap, we came home with a silver cup which we were given in the ride-and-drive class but were well beaten in the driving class.

★　　★　　★

The Parsons-Smiths became very involved with Pony Club activities and, inevitably, I was too, so much so that I set my heart on becoming an official Pony Club Instructor. I went on an instructors' course at the Silver Hound Riding School in Surrey, as it was one of the few places where one could go to qualify as a PCI. As part of the training we had to give lecture demonstrations with a mock 'pupil'. My subject was the rider's position when learning to jump. I began confidently enough,

'Before jumping, both horse and rider must be warmed up through some flat work.' My 'pupil' was walking her horse around the indoor school. 'Jolly good,' I commented, 'That relaxes the muscles and reduces stiffness. It's jolly good if you can manage half an hour but ten minutes will do. The rider should then stop.' I looked at the 'pupil' who halted on cue. 'Jolly good. Now, shorten your stirrups a couple of holes in preparation for jumping.' The 'pupil' did so. 'Jolly good,' I said. 'Shorten your reins, one hand on either side of the horse's neck, seat out of the saddle and lean forward. Jolly good,' I nodded enthusiastically. 'Maintain that position as you go into trot.' The horse trotted on obediently. 'Jolly good. The rider's centre of gravity should be directly above that of the horse – which is where?' I turned to my audience inviting an answer,

'Round about the withers,' somebody supplied.

'Yes, jolly good. The rider should aim to always be in balance with the horse,' I ploughed on, engrossed in my 'lesson'. My 'pupil' followed my instructions and trotted over a line of poles on the ground. 'Jolly good,' I congratulated. 'From there the rider can progress to a low fence at the end of the line of poles. Keep the impulsion, keep the rhythm!' I called to her, 'Now! Pop over the rail.' The horse jumped the tiny fence. 'Jolly good!' I said.

My demonstration over I turned to my instructor and could not help asking,

'How was that?'

'Jolly good,' he replied drily.

I had learned another valuable lesson: do not repeat clichéd phrases. From then on I made myself listen to what I was saying. Now, many years later, I become very irritated when listening to speakers who punctuate every other sentence with such phrases as 'basically', 'definitely' and 'you know'.

I was teaching numerous Pony Club children and naturally became involved with the running of Pony Club Camp. One camp was held at Lingfield racecourse. The racetrack itself was forbidden territory. Stephanie Dalton, who was in charge of the children, and I were sharing accommodation in one of the racecourse buildings. We were woken in the night by the sound of children's voices. Stephanie called across to me, 'Shall I go or will you?'

'I'll go,' I said, annoyed at being woken up and, at the same time, having horrible visions of them galloping their ponies all over the sacred turf. I emerged and breathed a sigh of relief as there were no ponies in sight – just a bunch of teenage boys and girls running around. When they saw me, outlined in the moonlight, wearing a pale pink diaphanous nightdress and gumboots, the voices stopped instantly.

'You are a bloody lot of children! Now go back to bed,' I yelled. And they did so without a murmur. When we faced each other the next morning for riding instruction there were a few knowing looks and some sheepish grins but mutual respect remained.

Anne Parsons-Smith had been competing in hunter trials and showing classes with a handsome grey horse called Mr Chips. They won consistently before Anne went to Lausanne in Switzerland for a while. On her return she proved she had learned some French by referring to Mr Chips as Monsieur Pommes Frites – I was very impressed!

Sadly, Mr Chips became incurably lame but there was a happy ending, as we were fortunate to find wonderful home for him with an elderly lady, who just wanted a good-looking horse that she could enjoy seeing out of her windows every day. Mr Chips filled the bill and was very happy.

Anne progressed to a bay small hunter called Royal Slipper. They competed in Pony Club one-day events and were always selected for the Old Surrey and Burstow Pony Club teams. Anne and I were both learning a great deal about eventing at this level which was a huge help to Anne in later passing both her BHS Preliminary Instructor's Exam and her Pony Club A Test – a great achievement. After her marriage to David Jacobs, she started the successful Shalfleet Connemara Stud on the Isle of Wight.

Her young brother, James, was taking an interest in foxhunting and so one day I took him, on a leading rein, mounted on his small

*Anne Parsons-Smith
competing at a Pony
Club event with Royal
Slipper.*

grey Welsh pony, Bossy. We followed the field at a distance in order to keep out of everyone's way. At one point we were faced with a small tiger trap jump comprising three rails, the highest in the middle. It was quite impossible for James to jump Bossy over this fence and so I popped Mickey over it and then, leaving James to hold him, I somehow got Bossy over the obstacle and put James back on. We were able to keep in touch with hounds and James was blooded after hounds killed. It reminded me of the time I had been blooded when following the Old Surrey and Burstow Hunt.

Taking children hunting was much easier when I rode in the Suffolk Hunt country. All the obstacles were ditches and a child on a leading rein could dismount if the ditch looked particularly frightening and the pony would follow my horse. The child would clamber down one side of the ditch and then crawl up the other side before remounting and carrying on. The pony that Bill hunted in his youth would, if the ditch was huge, slither down one side and run along the ditch until he found a suitable exit before taking Bill up the other side! On one occasion, so the story goes, Bill saw a scarlet-coated gentleman wallowing in the ditch that his pony was negotiating. On recognising who it was, Bill said,

'Oh, it's only Dad,' and galloped on his way after the hounds.

James eventually took his Pony Club D Test, the first and most

basic test. The examiner asked James what a curry comb was. James promptly replied,

'I don't know, Sallie always gets Bossy ready for me to ride.'

Despite his ignorance of stable management, he was a good rider and passed the test.

Dr Parsons-Smith, who had a practice in Harley Street, renewed his interest in riding again, so much so that he decided he wanted his own horse. Mrs P-S and I went to the Elephant and Castle horse sales to find a suitable horse for him. There was a handsome, brown thoroughbred-type of mare and we bought her for fifty pounds. At first we were thrilled with her for she was a lovely ride. But, within four days of her arrival at Roughets, she went lame behind. She was intermittently lame and her hind feet became very brittle. We had a dreadful time trying to keep shoes on her. She would become sound for a while and then, unaccountably, go lame again.

One or two people showed an interest in buying her but then she would fail the vet's examination. One dealer offered to take her and give us another horse in exchange but we discovered that that horse also did not have level action, indicating there might be some lameness problem. Six months later we returned the mare to the Elephant and Castle sales, looking magnificent with her mane plaited and wearing a smart summer sheet. No one was taken in by her appearance even though she was sound on that day. She just made her reserve of fifty pounds. She was probably well known by the regulars and was a classic example of 'Buyer beware' and 'No foot – no horse'.

The doctor now had a grey cob called Barney who seemed to get on well enough with the family's other horses and, despite their all being shod, they were turned out to graze at night. I learned at this point the dangers of turning a mare and a gelding out together. One morning I went to their field as usual to bring them in. They always came to the gate when I called. However, on this occasion the mare came but Barney stood in the middle of the field with his ears pricked. He looked quite normal but was resting a hind leg.

'What's the matter with you today, Barney?' I asked, giving his nose an affectionate rub. I liked Barney – he was a nice horse. He seemed perfectly all right then I noticed a small mark on the inside of the leg. It looked as though the mare had kicked him. 'Oh no!' I

Sallie on Barney and pupils on Twinkle and Mickey (in background) following the Old Surrey and Burstow hounds.

exclaimed as I saw what I thought was a piece of bone protruding alongside the little bloody mark. 'Wait there, Barney. I'll be back in a minute.' Barney stood there patiently. I tore back to the house and found Mrs P-S.

'Barney's hurt. I think he's been kicked,' I said breathlessly.

'How do you know?' Mrs P-S asked me.

'Actually,' I swallowed hard, 'I think his leg is broken between the hock and the stifle,' and I told her about the piece of bone.

She telephoned the vet and then we rushed back to the field with a bucket of 'goodies' for Barney. He ate quite contentedly and I waited with him until the vet arrived. He bent to examine Barney's leg then stood upright and shook his head,

'You're right. His leg is broken. There's nothing I can do, I'm afraid.'

Mrs P-S and I stood around disconsolately while the vet took his humane killer from his case. It was a terribly sad occasion as Barney had been loved by us all.

We had a number of ponies at Roughets and it seemed sensible, when the boys were at boarding school, to use the ponies to give riding lessons at weekends. These proved very popular with children of friends of the family who lived locally so that I was often teaching for five hours every day. A few other ponies, whose owners were at boarding school, were kept at working livery during term time. The weekend riding school work kept all the animals fit for the time when their owners came home for the holidays. Once the holidays began, everyone rode their own ponies and there were no 'visiting' pupils.

I was building up quite a business at Roughets. Horses and ponies also came in for breaking to ride or drive. Once we had a visiting donkey. He was quite easy to train but his bray terrorised some of the horses!

Each day on my way to work at Roughets I passed a field in which grazed a brown pony. The field was almost covered by yellow ragwort with barely a patch of grass to be seen. I became increasingly worried about the pony and would sometimes stop and get off my motorbike to have a closer look at him. I had always believed that ragwort was poisonous to horses yet this pony appeared to be fine. One day, however, we received a call from his owners. He was not well and could we help? We agreed that he should be brought to Roughets and he duly arrived. His coat was staring and he was very lethargic. We called the vet who came immediately. He was not hopeful but said he would come back in a few days. When he came the next time the pony was even worse. The vet shook his head and told us to lead the pony out of his stable into the yard but he was so weak that he could barely walk that short distance and his hind legs kept giving way. The vet had to shoot him. It was all very tragic – and could have been avoided by removing the ragwort from his field. The owners were devastated that their neglect had resulted in the death of their children's much-loved pony.

The event made a tremendous impression on me which has remained with me ever since. If I see any ragwort in my fields, I immediately dig it up and destroy it.

★　　★　　★

I took Mickey and the skeleton gig to Carshalton show in 1957 and was delighted to win a cup in the ride-and-drive class. Pam Stewart-Smith, one of the leading lights at the time, beat me in the private driving class driving her piebald pony, Whisky, to a lovely pony chaise. I shall always be grateful to her for coming to me after the class to tell me that I should enter Mickey for the prestigious Richmond Royal Horse Show next year. I was greatly encouraged and took her advice seriously.

I was beginning to realise that my gig was not smart enough in its present badly painted state and so I arranged for it to be painted by a professional coach painter. The bill for undercoating, top coating, lining and varnishing was £15 12s 6d (£15.62). The tyres were renewed for about £17 10s (£17.50) and to complete my turnout, I bought a holly whip for £1 7s 6d (£1.35). All this was a considerable outlay for me.

In 1957 the British Driving Society (BDS) was formed because it was feared that the art of driving was in danger of becoming lost. Sanders Watney, Colonel Arthur Main, Captain Frank Gilbey and

Sallie and Mickey at Carshalton Show in 1957, after winning the ride and drive trophy. (Photo reproduced by kind permission of The Croydon Advertiser Group)

No   14

THE BRITISH DRIVING SOCIETY

16 BEDFORD SQUARE,
LONDON, W.C.1.   20 / 19 58

RECEIVED from *Miss Susie Seaton.*

Entrance Fee   ...   .   10 .

Subscription   ...   .   2 2 .

Miscellaneous   ...   .

Received with thanks

Secretary   £ 2 12 —

Reg Brown who were all involved in four-in-hand coaching at the time, got together and called a meeting of enthusiasts. Unfortunately, I was unable to attend because it clashed with the day that Mrs P-S and I had taken the mare to the sale at the Elephant and Castle. I have always been disappointed that I am not a Founder Member of the BDS, for all those who attended that meeting were called Founder Members. Pam Stewart-Smith was entitled to this accolade, as was Bert Barley. I joined the BDS the following January and still have the receipt for £2.12s (£2.60) for my subscription for 1958. The Inau-

Pam Stewart-Smith with Whisky at the White City, about 1959.

Mickey at the BDS Inaugural Meet in 1958, with Mrs Gerald Parsons-Smith as passenger.

gural Meet of the BDS was to be held at the Royal Windsor Horse Show in May 1958.

Mrs P-S and I took Mickey to the meet. We assembled with other enthusiasts in a collecting ring on the showground before setting off in convoy on a drive around Windsor Great Park. On our return we paraded in the main ring in front of Windsor Castle and were presented with a beautiful mauve rosette to commemorate the occasion.

A few weeks later Mickey and I went to the Richmond Royal Horse Show. I was delighted when we were awarded third prize and a flattering mention in *Horse and Hound*. Also that year we entered the driving classes at the Royal International Horse Show which, at that time, was held at the White City. We came sixth in the private driving class. I was thrilled! However, it was becoming clear to me that if I wanted to win private driving classes I needed a horse with more spectacular action than Mickey.

Sadly then, the time had come to part with Mickey and I found a home for him in Northumberland. He was to travel the 200 miles or so by train (as many horses did in the late 1950s) and I wanted to go with him, so that if I did not like the new home I could somehow bring him back. His rail journey began at Redhill station, not far from

Driving Mickey at the White City in 1958, with Anne Parsons-Smith as passenger.

Roughets, where a railway container, designed especially for horses, was ready for him. He walked up the low ramp into the stall which was bedded with straw. There was a hay net and a full water container. The ramp went up and Mickey was on the first stage of his journey that would take him to King's Cross station in London. I did not accompany him for this short journey but had arranged to meet him there about midnight. He was very comfortably accommodated in the railway container which had been converted into a loose box so that he could move around and lie down if he wished. I sat with him for the journey to Northumberland and we eventually arrived at Belford station just before half-past two the following afternoon.

Mickey had been travelling for over twenty-two hours. His buyer met us; she had bought Mickey solely on his reputation but subject to his passing the veterinary examination. However, Mickey had been given a clean bill of health before we set off for Northumberland. We were taken to a huge farm where a palatial stable bedded deeply with straw, was waiting for him. All fears of bringing him back if I did not like the look of his new home were groundless. I saw immediately that this would be a wonderful home for Mickey and he was going to spend the rest of his days in luxury. I drove him and I rode him in order to show off what he could do. I stayed overnight and got up early the next morning so that I could go for my last ride on the pony whom I had loved for nine years.

I felt utterly desolate when I boarded the train for Surrey and cried all the way home. It was little consolation to know that I had done the sensible thing. Mickey gave enormous pleasure to the Northumberland family, he took all the children hunting and in winter he even pulled a sleigh. When I went back to see him a few years later he looked very contented.

However, he seemed not the slightest bit pleased to see me, which was disappointing, although he clearly recognised me because, just for fun, I asked him perform his party trick of kneeling down. He did so but grudgingly, scowling all the while. I think that he was far happier here than he had been with me where he had had to work hard at times teaching countless people to ride and drive. Sadly, he had to be put down at the age of nineteen. He had seriously damaged a leg by fooling around with other ponies in the field.

CHAPTER 7

Zapateado
(Thap-Ar-Tay-Ar-Doe)

I HAD BEEN TO SEE A COUPLE of young Welsh cobs but neither was what I was really looking for. One day at a show I was talking to Mrs K. Robinson, who was driving a show cob called Handsome on behalf of Mr H. Langdon Dowsett, a respected member of the BDS, and she said that she had a horse in her yard that might suit me – a grey, 15.2hh, six-year-old mare out of a Connemara by a Thoroughbred that had been very successful on the racecourse.

I went to see her and she was saddled and ridden so that I could see her spectacular action. She really was very exciting to watch and so I agreed to buy her. Bill and I decided to call her Zapateado after the Spanish dance of that name. We had seen the famous Spanish dancer, Antonio, on stage in London performing his magical and brilliant, heel-beating flamenco dance and we hoped that this horse would, in time, be equally brilliant. It was, however a difficult name for show commentators to get their tongues round and some referred to her as Zay-Potato! Years later, the well-known television commentator, Raymond Brooks-Ward, said, 'I had just learned how to pronounce the name of your horse and now you are driving another one!'

Z, as we called her for short, had had harness on but had not been put to a vehicle and so I started to train her for harness work. Pam

Stewart-Smith gave me a good set of old trade harness that was the same design and strength as that used at the United Dairies. As part of the initial stages of training, I use a weight to give the horse something to pull before it is put to a vehicle. Stupidly I used too heavy a weight at first and Z soon discovered that the best way to move it was to leap forward instead of leaning into her collar.

We had only my show gig and it was too small for her. The shafts were too short which meant that her hindquarters were too near to the dashboard. It was also too low so that the vehicle tilted backwards and needed big blocks to be put between the axle and the springs to heighten it. However, we chanced it and harnessed her to the gig. She kicked once and dented the wooden splinter bar below the dashboard.

Despite the slight hiccup on first putting to, Z, fortunately, had a good mouth and became an excellent driving horse. She was 100 per cent quiet in traffic and, being onward going and sensible, I drove her for miles.

Pam Stewart-Smith had heard about a barn full of vehicles that were being cleared out to make space for machinery. We went to see them and the contents were amazing. There was a Hansom cab, complete with lamps, for fifty pounds, and all kinds of four-wheeled vehicles such as broughams and phaetons but I was looking for a light two-wheeler that would be suitable for exercising Z so that I could keep my precious gig solely for shows.

Finally, I bought a vehicle that we called a speed cart although it could be called a road cart or a jogger. It comprised two wooden, rubber-tyred wheels, a forward-facing seat with an iron frame at the front that formed a rein rail at the top and a slatted floor. The draught was via a swingletree fixed by straps to the splinter bar. Two chains went from a ring at the centre of the swingletree to the axle, just inside the semi-elliptic springs. It was very light and ran well and I bought it for just ten pounds.

I rode Z from Roughets in Blechingley to Edenbridge and drove her home in the vehicle. Mrs P-S kindly gave me a bonus of ten pounds that week so, in effect, she paid for my new exercise vehicle which was very generous of her.

I discovered that the vehicle had been made by Offord – the high-class coachbuilders of London in the late nineteenth century. When, sometime later, John Mauger of Thimbleby and Shorland (auctioneers specialising in horse-drawn vehicles) looked at it, he remarked that it had all the signs of top craftsmanship, such as the curving finishes to the steps and the ironwork around the seat, that would have been the hallmarks of a coachbuilder such as Offord.

I had a new horse and my beautiful skeleton gig and so my thoughts were turning to showing Z. However, I had no suitable harness. Mickey's show harness did not fit Z but I was able to sell it to his new owners in Northumberland and use the proceeds to buy a second-hand set of show harness from Mrs Robinson.

In 1960 the Victory Coaching Rally was held in London's East End. Competitors assembled for judging at the Victory pub on Commercial Road in an assortment of vehicles both trade and private turnouts, made all the more colourful by their drivers and passengers in period costume.

I thought that it would be fun to drive Z on the hoof to London, three days beforehand then attend the rally. I contacted Bert and Dickie Barley, who had moved from Queen's Gate Mews to Elvaston Mews, about accommodation for Z and myself. With typical generosity Bert said that he would put Z in his stables even though, I imagined, it meant temporarily moving out a horse, and Dickie arranged a room for me at a nearby hotel in Queen's Gate. A friend, Freddie Turner, whom I had met at Mrs Hurst's, agreed to come with me, as he knew London well, and would show me the route to Kensington and then to and from Commercial Road.

I exercised, schooled and groomed Z with renewed vigour and polished the gig and harness until they gleamed. A few days before we were due to depart for London we reconnoitred the route by car. At the same time, we transported our equipment to Bert Barley's including all Z's food, our clothes to wear on the day of the rally and a saddle and bridle as I wanted to ride in Hyde Park again for old times' sake. Freddie and I set off from Blechingley at nine o'clock on the Thursday morning before the rally on Sunday with Z in the gig and arrived at Elvaston Mews just after midday. She behaved impeccably through all the London traffic, waiting patiently for traffic lights to change and seemingly making light of the twenty-five-mile journey.

She settled into her stall in Bert Barley's stables and felt relaxed and confident enough to lie down for the night.

The next two days I rode her in Hyde Park accompanied by Freddie on a horse borrowed from Bert. On Sunday we set off for the Victory Rally. I wore period costume comprising a long, striped dress with a lace jabot. We arrived at the Victory pub just before noon, found our parking place, on the road, among all the other competitors and waited for the judging to begin. Thank goodness the weather was fine and warm, for in my long dress and elegant hat, rain would have completely ruined the effect.

From time to time various people came to us, chatted then walked away. We had not given an individual show or even been asked to trot up and down the road but about two o'clock in the afternoon, much to my surprise, we were told that we had won the cup for the best single turnout and a shield bearing the words 'Pride of the Parade' for the best in show. And that was it! We had not even realised we had been judged!

On Cloud Nine, Freddie and I drove Z back to spend the night at Elvaston Mews. The next day we drove her back to Blechingley. She had not put a foot wrong.

On our return from London, I thought that it would be a good

Sallie receiving the shield for 'Pride of the Parade' at the Victory Coaching Rally.

idea to tether Z in the orchard at Roughets so that she could have some grass. I put a headcollar onto her and attached a webbing lunge rein that I tied to a tree, but within minutes she had caught her hind heel in the rein, tried to free it by pulling against the rein and incurred a terrible rope burn. She was lame for a long time and her heel always had hardened skin which I had to keep greased. I never again tethered a horse like that for I had learned a lesson the hard way. Years later, however, I discovered how Gypsies train their animals to be tethered.

In 1960 Freddie and I took Z to the Royal International Horse Show at the White City and she came seventh in a strong private driving class. I was delighted. Later in the show I competed in the Tom Thumb Stakes. This was an obstacle course against the clock and involved driving between H-shaped markers and even over a tiny jump between similar markers that swivelled on posts if touched by the wheel hub and lost points. There was a zebra crossing at which you had to stop to enable a 'nanny' pushing a pram to cross safely. We were beaten in our heat by Christine Mossman who later married Jon Dick. Under her married name she became one of the top British Whips and won the BDS show championship several times.

At the same show my former employer, Mrs P-S, rode her horse in the class for Riding Club Teams of Three. Much to my joy, as I had helped with some of the training, the team won.

I had been helping Pam Stewart-Smith with schooling her piebald pony, Whisky, using the Schmit-Jensen long-reining methods to improve his outline and paces. Pam wanted to drive a pair of piebalds to her chaise and she found a similarly marked mare which she called Splash. I broke Splash to harness and Pam and I put them into pair harness. We were desperate for expert help and wanted to read all we could on driving and harness work but, at the time, the only information we could find was from Morley Knight's book, *Hints on Driving*. It proved, however, to be a great help.

When Pam went on holiday she boarded Whisky and Splash at Roughets. Whisky, who was about 11 hands high, could not see over the loose box door but he soon worked out a method which would enable him to look at the outside world. He pushed his feed bin across the stable and turned it upside down. This gave him a platform on which he could put his front feet, enabling him to see over the door.

Pam Stewart-Smith with Whisky and Splash at the White City.

He did this consistently but Splash never copied his actions and seemed not to mind that she was unable to see out.

In June 1960 Bill and I were married and I moved into Thorne Lodge in the grounds of Bill's family home, Thorne Court, a large part-Victorian house, near Bury St Edmunds, in Suffolk. Z, of course, came with me. Bill had, apart from wartime breaks, lived in Thorne Lodge all his life. When Bill's grandmother died, his mother and father moved to Thorne Court leaving Thorne Lodge empty and ready for us when we married. Thorne Lodge is a sixteenth-century thatched cottage with ancient dark beams and two open brick fire-

Thorne Lodge. (Photo by Anne Grimshaw)

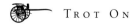
Thorne Court, showing the oval lawn, 2003. (Photo by Anne Grimshaw)

places. In Victorian times a semi-circular addition had been built onto the front. The brick-floored kitchen was added later and the old water pump and well remain as 'features'. More importantly, the kitchen houses the Aga which is wonderful for long, slow cooking: casseroles

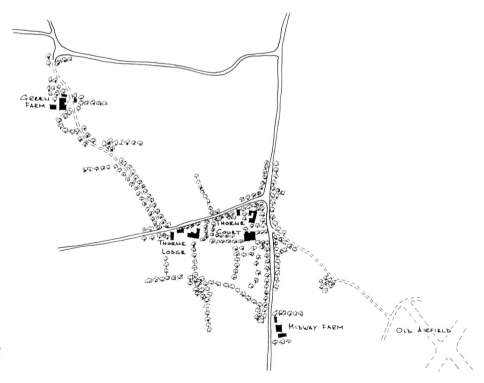

Thorne Court, Thorne Lodge and surrounding area

for us – and linseed for the horses. Thorne Lodge is very pretty and surprisingly easy to manage. Bill and I were very fortunate.

Z was accommodated in the stables at Thorne Court. Of typical Victorian design, they comprise three loose boxes and three stalls. Vertical iron bars divide the top halves of the substantial lower wooden partitions. Large brass balls top the pillars at the open end of the stalls.

After being harnessed, carriage horses would be turned around to face outwards in their stalls and pillar reins clipped from their bits to rings on the pillars below the brass balls. Thus they were tethered in readiness to be put to the carriage when the bell rang from the house alerting the grooms and coachman that the family was ready for the carriage to be brought to the front door. The oval lawn in front of the house was designed to allow plenty of room for bringing the carriage and pair round in position by the front door. The metal notice 'Please keep off the grass' is still in place, as are the large round stone balls which were put around the edges of the lawn to keep carriage wheels and horses' hooves off the neatly tended lawn which was the pride of the gardeners.

Another reminder of the horse-drawn era is the Wellingtonia tree by the back entrance. It has a crooked top which was, apparently, caused by daily damage from the butcher boy's whip as he drove his hackney to and from the back door when delivering meat to the cook.

Soon after we moved to Suffolk, Z needed to be shod. This necessitated a visit to the farrier's forge in Bury St Edmunds for there were few, if any, farriers with mobile forges in the early 1960s. I drove Z from Thorne Court to the forge to be shod, taking care to leave enough iron on Z's shoes to take us the eight miles along the main road. There were no grass verges or tracks to enable us to get off the tarmac. Fortunately Z had very good feet – such a journey would have been impossible if her feet had been poor.

This farrier told me a story about a particularly difficult donkey that he had to shoe. He had tied the moke's head down to an anvil to prevent it, he thought, from rearing. The donkey however, had the last word. It reared, lifting the anvil off the ground and deposited it on the farrier's foot.

The winter of 1962-3 was the worst for many years with huge

Zapateado in the Walrond sleigh. (Photo reproduced by kind permission of The Bury Free Press)

amounts of snow. Thorne Court, Thorne Lodge and the park looked beautiful, like something from a fairy tale. I was looking out across the snowy park one day when Bill's father said,

'There's an old sleigh in the loft above the coach house. Do you want it?'

'Oh, yes please!' I was thrilled at the idea.

'It'll probably need looking at. It hasn't been used for years.'

'It sounds fun. How are we going to get it out?' I asked.

'We'll manage,' Bill's father assured me and true to his word, the next day when I went to Thorne Court the old sleigh was being lowered on ropes from the doorway of the hayloft onto the stable yard.

'Shouldn't think it's been moved since before the first war,' Bill's father commented.

'It's all there, though,' I replied, noting that at least the shafts were there even though riddled with woodworm. 'I can soon treat those with Rentokil,' I said confidently but on closer inspection it was obvious that the draft of the sleigh was through the shafts, as was the steering, and so when any strain was put onto them they were likely to break. The traces fixed to protruding metal fittings. Nevertheless, I was determined to try it and got busy with the Rentokil.

The snow stayed long enough for us to use the sleigh but we quickly discovered the weaknesses of the worm-eaten wood. Bill renewed the damaged areas and was fortunately able to re-use the old steam-bent parts from the shaft tips to the tug stop areas. The body of the sleigh in which two passengers could sit, was set on runners. The coachman sat on a small seat behind them. The reins passed from the saddle terrets, over a very high rein-rail between the passengers' shoulders to the driver's hands.

When we first put Z to the sleigh I did not know what to expect but it ran very smoothly on the hard-packed snow on the lane and we drove through the village quite happily. George Bruce, the old gamekeeper who had worked for the Walronds for years and now lived in a cottage on the estate, saw us go by and came out to have a word.

'The last time I saw that sleigh must have been over sixty years ago. Yes, I remember now – it would be about 1900. I was just a boy then and at school – in the village, you know. I saw that sleigh coming, driven by Mr Bill's great-grandfather's coachman on the rear seat. Well, the schoolmaster said to us children, "Here comes the squire, now you boys, do you take your caps off and you girls do you curtsy." And we all did,' he said in a strong Suffolk accent. Then he paused and said, 'It's good to see the sleigh being used again. Reminds me of the old days.'

In 'the old days' of George Bruce's youth, the Suffolk Hunt used to meet at Thorne Court. Photographs on the next page show the family following hounds in the private omnibus pulled by a pair of carriage horses. In the summer the top used to be taken off this vehicle so that it was converted into a wagonette. The pulleys and rings that were used to do this are still in the ceiling of the coach house and the folding ladder used by ladies to climb onto high vehicles still remains in the corner of the building. Sadly, none of the carriages remain. They were rolled out of the coach houses to make room for

ABOVE: The Walrond family following hounds in the private omnibus, taken after a meet at Thorne Court in 1903. The rear-view photo above shows passengers inside as well as on top.

RIGHT: The Master arriving at a meet of hounds at Thorne Court in 1903.

motorised transport. George told me that the spokes from their wheels were used as replacement ladder staves. Some lamp brackets are still on the racks in the coach house. Everything else was burnt.

★   ★   ★

I hunted Z with the Suffolk foxhounds and on one occasion she fell into a deep ditch. I got off her, jumping into the freezing cold, dirty water and held her head above it. She made no effort to extricate herself and I began to think she might drown if I let go. I seemed to be hanging on forever when I heard hooves and saw the whipper-in. He jumped clean over us then pulled up.

'What's happened? Can you hang on?' he called.

'I'll try but I might need some help. She won't move.'

'All right. I won't forget.'

'Carry on,' I urged him but I felt better, for now at least somebody knew where we were and would come and rescue us. Vainly, I urged Z to move but she refused and I was worried in case she had hurt her back.

A few minutes later I heard someone approaching and was mightily relieved to see Gerald Hudson, our vet, on his horse.

'Am I glad to see you!' I exclaimed, momentarily forgetting how cold and wet I was. 'I think she might be hurt,' I ventured.

'We'll see,' commented Gerald and looked at Z. He knew her and she knew him. He cracked his hunting whip and bellowed at her,

'Get on outta there! Gerr on!'

Z made a supreme effort; lurching and floundering she finally scrambled out of the ditch. Gerald gave a quick inspection.

'She's not hurt. Just shaken up. She'll be all right once she's dry and warm.' He turned to me. 'Are you all right, Sallie?' Gerald asked, concerned. I nodded. I was shivering with cold and wet but at least Z was none the worse.

Another time out hunting with Z, I met someone who offered to lend me a four-wheeled American buggy. I was tempted because it sounded attractively different but I was reluctant to take it on loan in case it got damaged. Nevertheless, I went to see it. I did want it and asked the owner,

'Would you sell it to me?'

'I might.'

'How much?'

'A pound a wheel.' It was a ludicrously low price.

'No, that's too little. Will you accept ten pounds?'

'Agreed!' he said delighted.

I rode Z to the other side of Bury St Edmunds where the buggy was in a barn, harnessed her to it, put the saddle and bridle in the rear boot, then drove her back to Thorne Court.

The buggy's rubber tyres were of the 'wired-on' variety and were beginning to look a little shaky after this ten-mile trip. A split had developed in one tyre, revealing the rusty wire that ran through the centre of the rubber to keep it in the metal channel. I had heard that if a wire snapped the rubber would fly out of the channel. If this happened on a front wheel, the rubber would repeatedly hit the horse's hind leg as the wheel turned. The result did not bear thinking of!

Before the buggy could be used again Bill mended the tyre by tapping and dieing the metal ends of the wire and pushing the rubber over a connector in the gap. The mend worked for a while but the rubber moved again. The risk of an accident was too great and so I had the wired-on tyres and channels replaced with much safer iron tyres. In those days we could not get the narrow clencher channels and tyres that are a feature of American vehicles. The vehicle had a half lock as there was a perch, a wooden bar reinforced with iron running from the front axle to the back axle that formed part of the under-carriage, so, if you tried to turn too sharply, the front wheel jammed against the perch.

Some years later I saw this happen at a show: a horse in an American half-lock buggy started to turn and continued to come round until the spokes broke away from the hub under the pressure exerted by the horse. The vehicle had just been restored and the driver was getting ready to enter a Concours d'Elegance competition. I felt so very sorry for him.

The restricted lock of my American buggy sometimes caused me problems such as in the confined space of Thorne Court stable yard where I could not bring the horse round sharply enough. However, it was easily remedied, for I would go to the rear of the buggy and, because it was so light, I was able to lift the back across to wherever I wanted it to be!

Bill and I took Z to stay with Brian Shone, an old carriage-driving friend, who had three grey horses but needed a fourth to make up a team to pull his sporting break. We first put Z in pair with his existing leader then put her in the lead of unicorn (one leader and two

Z in the lead of unicorn, driven by Brian Shone.

wheelers) and all went well. We put her in tandem and Brian gave me a lesson in this form of driving. There were just so many reins! I felt as though I had eight reins in my hand not four.

After a few minutes Brian said, 'Turn left here.' 'Here' was a track that led through a brick-pillared gateway.

'I can't get through there!' I replied aghast and feeling what little confidence I had just gained in tandem driving had vanished.

'Course you can.' And he talked me through. My confidence was

Brian Shone's team, with Z in off lead.

coming back and I began to relax a little and negotiated a bend in the lane. I was beginning to really enjoy driving a tandem.

Then Z spotted a pig looking through a gate. She whipped round like lightning and the two horses stood side by side and head to tail like sardines in a can. Perhaps surprised to find themselves in this unusual position, they remained still for long enough for me to pass the reins to Brian so that he could unravel the muddle.

Despite that hiccup, we put Z in the lead of the team. With another leader to hold her straight, she was superb.

Z continued to be terrified of pigs and I wanted to cure her of her fear. As Bill's brother, Tim, a farmer, used to keep store pigs for fattening, I decided they could help Z overcome her fear. I put her into a loose box which had an opening like a service hatch through which she could see, smell and hear the pigs in the adjoining sties. Poor Z was so frightened that she ate hardly anything for three days. I left her to settle and eventually she would stand with her nose almost touching the pigs. She even began to eat normally. I was delighted and thought she was cured. But her fear never really left her, although she was better than she had been, and she was always edgy whenever she saw a pig while we were out.

I took Z to compete at the RIHS in London again to try to improve on our previous year's effort. The road drive, which in those days was called a marathon, was held around the roads of Wormwood Scrubs near to the White City. Competitors were judged along the route and on the concrete outside the entrance to the arena. They were told their placing before they filed into the arena for the presentation of the rosettes. I was thrilled when we were told to go in, in third position. We drove through the outer entrance then across the inner collecting ring where the show jumpers practised. The weather had been wet and the going was quite deep making the gig harder to pull. Z plunged into her collar and the right trace broke at the crew hole where the trace goes over the trace hook at the splinter bar. I told my passenger, John Stevens, to get down and tie the trace in an overhand knot through the breeching dee which was not in use. John quickly did this and we proceeded round the arena perimeter before lining up in third place facing the stands to wait for the judge and stewards to come along with the beautiful rosettes. I told John to stand with his

Zapateado – 1960, White City.

back firmly against the knotted trace and not to move under any cir-cumstances however ill-mannered this might seem. The judge pre-sented us with the cherished yellow ribbon and no questions were asked. I learned from this the importance of carrying a spare trace.

In 1964 we went to Hickstead for the British Driving Derby. After the preliminary judging in a side ring, our friends were congratulating us on our being placed first but I insisted that the ribbon was not yet on Z's head. As we went into the main arena, Z became very excited and the judge, quite rightly, relegated us to third place.

We took Z to numerous shows throughout the years and she was very successful.

I was then offered, by an elderly hunting friend of Bill's father, a three-year-old part-Thoroughbred mare which he had bred but for whom he now had no use. He generously said that he would give her to me. I planned to train her to ride and drive and so decided that the time had come to part with Z. I did not have accommodation for more than one horse and, in any case, could not afford to keep two.

I found a lovely home for Z in Surrey and delivered her in my Land Rover and trailer. I could barely see my way, for tears flooded my eyes for the entire journey. But Z was happy and she remained there for the rest of her life.

CHAPTER 8

Dolly

THE NEW YOUNGSTER, WHOM I CALLED DOLLY, was difficult right from the start. Whenever I tried to lead her into the old bullock yard at Thorne Court that I used for lungeing she would nap and jib back to the entrance rail. What was worse she would strike out with her near foreleg and bring it up over the lunge rein. It was obviously something she had learned to do before I started breaking her. It took a long time to get her going in a circle. She was touchy about being girthed and however gentle I was she hated the feeling of the girth against her.

One day when I put a saddle onto her she went down in the stable – just folded up and lay on the floor. I had never experienced a horse do this before but I persevered with her not realising that horses that throw themselves onto the ground usually have the last word. For a driving horse to lie down while in the shafts is very serious because of the damage to harness and vehicle. It is perhaps less so with a riding horse for there is only the saddle that might be damaged.

However, I could eventually hack Dolly around and decided the time had come to train her for harness work. She reached the stage of being put to a vehicle when one day, for no apparent reason, she folded up and went down, quite slowly, in the Thorne Court drive.

She got up and nothing was damaged and so we continued. I persevered and could drive her for miles with no problems but I always had the feeling that she might go down anytime it suited her. I was careful not to ask her to pull a load up a hill or through deep going but I never trusted her.

By 1964 I was the BDS Area Commissioner for East Anglia and had arranged a meeting at Thorne Lodge. The plan was to drive in convoy to a neighbour, Pam Greene, for some light-hearted competition. I put Dolly to the speed cart in the farm drive where other BDS members were harnessing their animals to their vehicles. Dolly was wearing my second best set of harness – highly polished black leather with brass fittings. I mounted the vehicle and prepared to lead the convoy. I told her to walk on. Dolly folded up, half-lying, half-kneeling between the shafts. She bent the hame and saddle terrets. She scratched the collar and saddle. She broke the left shaft. I had no choice but to take her out of the vehicle and remove my damaged harness. I took her back to the stable and I never drove her again.

I took her to a few shows and rode her in four-year-old hunter and small riding horse classes where she was always in the ribbons. After consultation with her breeder, I sold her cheaply as a riding animal, telling the buyer that she must never be driven as she clearly disliked harness work.

I offered to give the money from the sale to her breeder but he generously told me to keep it to help to pay for the repairs to harness and vehicle. I think that he probably felt very sad that she had not fulfilled my hopes and expectations as a driving animal. He may have known that her temperament left much to be desired and genuinely hoped that Dolly and I would get on well. However, I learned a valuable lesson: it is best to part with such an ungenerous animal at the first opportunity.

CHAPTER 9

Early Tandems

Wʜᴇɴ ɪ ᴡᴀѕ ᴀᴛ ʀᴏᴜɢʜᴇᴛѕ I put Nicholas' pony, Twinkle, and James' pony, Bossy, in tandem. I had broken Twinkle to drive using a small governess cart and a beautiful set of old, brown, polished harness with lovely brass furniture. She went so well that the children frequently used to drive her.

One day, I put a scratch set of lead harness onto Bossy and put him in front of Twinkle to give me my first try at tandem driving. We were lucky to survive. In retrospect, I realise how foolish I had been because, after all, Bossy had not been broken to harness. I had no experience of handling tandem reins and was too ignorant to realise how potentially dangerous this escapade was. It was lucky for me that Bossy did not turn round to face me then take off when he saw the vehicle behind him. Fortunately, Twinkle just got on with pulling the cart and Bossy kept walking ahead, in front of her. At the time though I realised what little control I had over Bossy if he decided to 'do his own thing'. Luckily for me, he was elderly and very well mannered and so I got away with it.

There was nowhere I could go to learn to drive a tandem and there was very little written on the subject. I had read the chapter on tandem driving in Morley Knight's book, *Hints on Driving* written in

1894, but had no other books on the subject. There had been nothing written in recent years about driving. I was very fortunate in that an elderly carriage-driving enthusiast by the appropriate name of Norman Hackney, had seen Z at the White City and had become interested enough in her to contact me afterwards. He abhorred the often-seen strong bits that made horses uncomfortable in their mouths and so had been pleased to see Z being driven in a mild Liverpool bit. He corresponded with me and eventually gave me his precious copies of four classics: *Driving* (one of the Badminton Library of Sports and Pastimes published in 1889) by Henry Charles Fitzroy Somerset, the Duke of Beaufort; the 1900 *Manual of Coaching* by Fairman Rogers; *Driving for Pleasure* by Francis Underhill (1898) and *Driving* by Francis Ware published in1904. I gleaned an enormous amount from these wonderful books and I practised handling four reins when exercising a ridden horse in a double bridle by pretending that the top reins were those of a leader and the bottom those of the wheeler. Of course, I held them in the classical coaching method in my left hand with my right hand in front in the classical style which no doubt looked very odd on a ridden horse!

The BDS was still in its infancy. Sanders Watney (or Sandy as he was known) was one of the founders and, with his wife, Biddy, did everything possible to encourage the younger generation in the art of carriage driving and gave me several reference books on the subject. Later, when I became BDS area commissioner for East Anglia and arranged a buffet lunch for my area members, the Watneys came to stay at Thorne Lodge to meet everyone. The event was very well supported by all the area members and was the first of many successful parties.

After this visit, and realising my interest in tandem driving, the Watneys invited me to stay with them at their home in Mortlake, London, so that I could go into Richmond Park with Sandy and his tandem of docked-tailed chestnut cobs, Acrobat and Annabel. (There were still lots of horses around with docked tails – docking became illegal in 1949.) With Acrobat in the lead we set off from their stables in Watneys' brewery in Mortlake where Sandy kept several horses and vehicles, including the Red Rover road coach. Sandy drove through Mortlake and into Richmond Park. It was early morning and there

was little traffic. He told me there was a large gravel car park where I could try driving the horses but when we arrived I felt it was a somewhat small car park with a large number of trees growing in it but, fortunately, no cars! We exchanged places so that I was sitting on the right. Sandy gave me the reins. The horses behaved impeccably and went everywhere that Sandy told me to drive them. I had a feeling that they could have done it all without me!

After a while, I drove them back through the park and was even allowed to hold the reins as we returned through Mortlake to the brewery stables. Those horses virtually drove themselves and they instilled in me an enormous amount of confidence. From then on I used to visit Mortlake quite frequently to go out with the teams of four horses put to an exercising break or the Red Rover road coach itself. I was usually allowed to drive when we reached Richmond Park.

I had met, through the Suffolk Pony Club, the Astley-Cooper family, who had a Connemara-type mare called Blueberry. They had asked me to break her to harness, which I did, then they drove her at a few shows and rallies in a spider phaeton. We thought that, as she was so quiet, we could put her in the wheel of tandem behind Z in my gig and perhaps take them to the Suffolk show. Full of excitement, they brought Blue (as she was known) to Thorne Court and we put

Blueberry to a spider phaeton.

her as wheeler to the gig with Z into the lead. Full of confidence, I picked up the reins, climbed up into the gig and settled myself on the seat.

'Walk on!' I commanded.

Z stepped forward immediately. Blue did not move – she was a slow thinker! Z was obviously puzzled as to why the gig did not seem to move and she stopped. By then, Blue, having worked out what was wanted, walked forward pulling the gig behind her. The shaft tip poked Z's stationary quarters. She kicked. Her hind shoe hit the ring on the hame chain on the bottom of Blue's collar and squashed it. Fortunately, Blue was not hurt. I, however, had to nurse my hurt pride and admit that I was simply not skilled enough to drive these two at home let alone at the county show, and abandoned the idea.

It was some consolation, therefore, when I had more success with helping Pam Stewart-Smith to get her piebald ponies, Whisky and Splash, going in tandem to a beautiful miniature gig. Bill and I went to stay with her at South Park Farm in South Godstone. We put the harness onto the ponies and I took up the reins and mounted the gig. Pam sat next to me. Bill ran alongside Whisky to encourage him forward, in the lead. The ponies behaved as if they had been driven in tandem for all of their lives. Eventually, Pam asked me to drive them at the Sussex county show. I readily agreed and went to stay with

Sallie driving Whisky and Splash with Pam Stewart-Smith as passenger. The vehicle is unbalanced – no wonder poor Splash is crossing her jaw. Also, Whisky is in too much draught.

Pam. Once on the showground we harnessed the ponies in an area covered in long, luscious grass. When all was ready I mounted the gig and sat down on the box seat. Pam got up beside me. There was a girl groom at the head of each pony: Whisky as leader and Splash between the shafts as wheeler. Everything seemed to be fine and so I confidently told the girls,

'Let 'em go.'

The girls did so, whereupon both ponies promptly put their heads down and started to eat the grass.

'Walk on!' I said. They continued eating. 'Walk on!' I raised my voice. Pam tried.

'Walk on!' she said sternly.

'Walk on!' I tried again but they didn't even flick their ears at my command, never mind stop eating. I touched them with my whip. They whisked their tails as if it were a bothersome fly and continued to tuck in. Try as I might I could not get their heads up however hard I pulled on the reins. I was utterly helpless.

'Shall we lead them?' ventured one of the girls. There was nothing else for it. The girls hauled the ponies' heads from their feast and led me to the main arena.

Once we were in the show ring, the ponies went beautifully and we began to enjoy ourselves. We were sent off in convoy for the marathon as the road drive was then called. Soon we came to a down-hill gradient where Splash began to slip. She was rapidly losing her footing and so Pam dismounted to lighten the load. In retrospect, I think that it was quite likely that, in my ignorance, I had not brought Whisky out of draught and poor Splash was being pulled off her feet. While trying to sort this out, the other competitors overtook us with much larger, longer-striding animals and we were left bringing up the rear. The drive seemed to go on forever and lived up to its title of marathon but we completed it even though, by the time we returned to the arena, the turnouts were being pulled into the final line up.

'Looks like we've had it,' I commented to Pam.

'You're probably right,' she agreed, disappointed. Then a steward came over to us,

'Have you completed the marathon?' he asked.

'Yes,' I replied.

'Just one moment,' and he went to confer with the judges. I looked at Pam,

'Perhaps all is not lost,' I said hopefully.

And indeed it was not for we were placed about sixth. We were delighted and Pam herself went on to drive them very successfully at numerous shows.

CHAPTER 10

A Gypsy Wagon

LESLEY AND SYLVIA WATKINSON lived about five miles from Thorne Lodge at Acton near Long Melford. Lesley was interested in Gypsy wagons and had bought a derelict Burton or showman's wagon. He spent a long time meticulously restoring the caravan to its former glory. The interior was refurbished to its original standard even down to the amber glass handles and knobs on the cupboards. The wagon's front door was divided across the middle like a stable door and entry was by way of curving steps which were positioned when the caravan was parked.

Inside, on the left and at the front, was a wardrobe and cupboard. Beyond was the stove used for cooking and heating with the airing cupboard above it. The stove was always fitted on the off side so that the chimney stack was as far as possible from tree branches that overhung the road when the van was on the move. There was a locker seat below the window. At the rear, below another window, was a double bed with sleeping space for children underneath. On the right side of the wagon was another cupboard, a chest of drawers and seating along the wall.

Lesley and Sylvia were moving house from Acton to Westhall near Halesworth about sixty miles away. They decided that the best way to

94

A Burton, or Showman's wagon, with Sallie, Anthea and Lesley. (Photo reproduced by kind permission of Anita Bradley, daughter of the photographer, the late Richard Burn)

move the wagon would be with a horse, by road. They bought a part-bred Percheron, Blackberry, and suitably strong harness. They made a few short trips to familiarise Blackberry with the caravan as well as themselves and me with the handling of such a massive and heavy vehicle. It weighed over a ton.

We planned the route from Acton to Westhall carefully to avoid hills wherever possible, for Blackberry was neither fit enough nor strong enough to haul this heavy wagon up steep gradients. Although East Anglia is basically flat there are a surprising number of hills which go unnoticed until planning a trip such as this.

Lesley reconnoitred the route and, wherever there was an unavoidable hill, he went to the nearest farm to ask if the owner would be prepared to help by supplying a tractor and driver on the particular day and approximate time when it might be needed. All the farmers along the route agreed that they would help out. He found suitable places, off the road, for lunch stops and to give Blackberry a rest and a bite of grass. He arranged safe overnight accommodation where Blackberry could be turned out to graze and the wagon stowed out of sight of the road. On the first two nights we planned to return to Thorne Lodge for dinner, baths and beds, being transported in the car by either Bill or Sylvia, and to spend the last two nights at West-hall. It was all very civilised and saved having to plan food and accommodation for the three of us.

I had asked a pupil, Anthea Jackson, from the Roughets' days, to join Lesley and myself as we needed three people to accompany the wagon. It was August when we finally set off. We drove at a walk all the time, taking it in turns to hold the reins while seated just behind the shafts on the left of the wagon as it is from here that the wind-on brake is operated.

When we arrived at our first hill, the pre-arranged system was put into practice. I sat with the brake handle between my legs and wound the brake so that the brake blocks were hard against the rear wheels. Lesley put chocks behind the wheels as a precaution against the brake failing to hold the weight of the wagon. Anthea took Blackberry from the wagon, leaving one chain trace behind, and led her to the top of the hill. Lesley then went to the farm and returned with the tractor and driver. The chain trace was fixed to the front of the wagon and to the back of the tractor. The shafts were lowered onto a stick, about a yard long, that Lesley laid over the chain and under the shafts so that he could steer the front wheels by holding the shaft.

On command from the skipper (Lesley), the tractor took up the weight of the wagon. Lesley retrieved the blocks from behind the rear wheels. I released the brake and the tractor towed the wagon up the hill. I dreaded that the chain would break and that I would not be able to get the hand-brake on in time. Luckily, the chain never did break and all was well. This drawn-out procedure made me realise why the pictures I had seen of Gypsies always showed a trace horse or, more commonly, a second horse put to a swingletree alongside the shaft horse, to help to pull the load at times like these.

Our average speed on this trip was three miles an hour and we covered about fifteen miles a day although this varied according to the overnight places which Lesley had arranged.

There was a huge amount of interest in this journey and the press had given it considerable coverage. This resulted in wellwishers lining our route in some places. However, in other parts, some people were less pleased to see us and suspected that we were real Gypsies. We could imagine them rushing home to lock up tool sheds or chicken coops for the night!

One day, at our lunch stop, a kind lady came up to us and remarked how well the horse looked. She admired the condition of the harness and the caravan and then she handed six eggs to us and said, 'Here you are, my dears, these are for your supper.'

We thanked her profusely and had not the heart to tell her that tonight's stew was already in the oven of the Aga at Thorne Lodge.

On another occasion, a lady asked Lesley,

'How do you folks earn your living?'

Without a moment's hesitation and keeping a totally straight face, Lesley replied, 'Oh, we make clothes pegs and sell them.' Anthea and I did not dare look at each other in case we burst out laughing. The enquirer happily accepted Lesley's answer and went on her way. When she was out of earshot, we doubled up laughing,

'You'd have been stuck if she'd asked to buy some!'

'Oh, I'd have said we'd sold out!' replied Lesley.

We finally arrived at Westhall with the wagon, horse and harness unscathed. It was a tremendous relief that we had completed the journey without any mishap. It was one of those experiences that I would not have missed for anything – but never want to do again!

CHAPTER 11

Ali

I KNEW EXACTLY WHAT SORT OF HORSE I WANTED: a three-year-old grey gelding about 14.1 hands that I would be able to ride and drive for the next twenty years. He had to be a spectacular mover with plenty of bone, good looking, full of quality and have a pretty head with big brown eyes.

Such a horse was advertised in *Horse and Hound*. I telephoned the vendor for more information and everything sounded very promising. I drove about 250 miles to North Yorkshire to see the animal. I turned the car into the vendor's stable yard and my heart sank when I saw a plain grey head looking over a stable door. Was this the horse that had been advertised? I could feel my face fall as the vendor confirmed that this was the horse she had for sale. I looked over the loose-box door and saw a short thick neck, a straight shoulder and piano-shaped legs. The owner brought the horse out of the stable and ran it up for me to see. It was patently not my dream horse and I told her immediately that I would not waste any more of her time because this was not the type of animal I wanted. She insisted that I should sit on the horse as it would give me a wonderful ride. I had my doubts but, to please her, I first saw her on board and then I got up and trotted it for a few strides. It was as I anticipated: its ears were nearly in my mouth and it was like sitting on a pogo stick. I dismounted and thanked her for her trouble. She was furious and proceeded to tell me in no uncertain terms that, in future, when I went to see a horse I should say nice things about it even if I did not want to purchase the animal. I had, in fact, not said anything derogatory.

I made the long journey home, all the time going over the acrimonious exchange and felt upset by her rudeness. I imagined an advertisement in the following week's *Horse and Hound* reading, 're-advertised due to time-waster'. I do not understand why people deliberately mislead in their efforts to sell a horse. It only results in wasting everyone's time and creates bad feeling.

There was another time later when I travelled over 200 miles to accompany a friend who was looking for a carriage horse. The animal had been advertised as a ten-year-old. As soon as we saw the horse I thought that he looked a great deal older than the alleged ten years. The vendor saw me lift the corner of the animal's mouth to see his teeth. I thought that he looked nearer to twenty and I asked how old he was. She replied that he was about fourteen years old. Already he had gained four years since he had been advertised the previous week. My friend drove the horse and liked it. I warned him that it was nearer to twenty than ten. We finally compromised and agreed that the horse should be vetted but if the vet thought that the horse was over fourteen years old then he should not proceed with any further vetting. The vet proclaimed that the animal was well over fourteen years old. This was another case of the time-waster being the seller and not the buyer.

I was driving along a main road in Essex one day when I saw a sign at the entrance to a riding school which said 'Horses for Sale' and although I did not expect that it would be of any use, I stopped and went in. I spoke to the owner of the stables and described what I was looking for. He thought for a while and said,

'No, we haven't got a gelding but I might consider selling my three-year-old stallion. He's exactly what you've described.'

'Thank you, but no. I don't want a stallion,' I said firmly turning to go.

'You just have a look at him while you're here. Not take a minute. Be a shame for you not to see him,' said the owner persuasively. I was

in no great hurry.

'Oh, very well,' I agreed.

'See him trot him up in hand. He's not broken to ride, you under-stand, but he's a grand mover.'

I was curious to see the animal. The horse was brought out in a bridle and run up the yard. He was, as the owner had said, 'a grand mover' – a spectacular mover would have been a better description. I fell for him the moment I saw him. He was my dream horse.

We agreed a price and subject to his passing the vet, I would have him.

'His papers'll follow. He has a Ministry of Agriculture stallion licence. It just says he's grey and was born in 1962. That's all,' his owner told me.

The horse was passed sound by my vet, Gerald Hudson, and I was assured that he could be castrated if he proved to be too troublesome.

When I went to collect him, it took three of us to put travelling bandages onto his legs. One person held up a leg, someone else held the headcollar rope and I applied the bandages as quickly as I could.

He was the most difficult, but the most brilliant, horse I have ever owned. He put me into hospital three times. Breaking him to ride was horrendous and to drive was even worse. But he did not kick, bite, rear or buck and he was not nasty or ungenerous. He was simply ter-rified of so many things. He had a small scar on the front of one hock that looked like a barbed wire injury and maybe had suffered painful injections and treatment. He always was extremely difficult to inject. His annual tetanus booster had to be applied in his hindquarters because he virtually climbed the stable wall if Gerald tried to put a needle into his neck. He could not even tolerate his mane being unplaited if shiny scissors were used to cut the threads that sewed the plaits and so I kept a rusty pair of nail scissors especially for this job. Even plaiting his mane using a shiny needle to stitch the plaits was dif-ficult and for years I had to start at the withers and work up towards the head, which was not easy. He was nineteen years old before he allowed me to clip the whole of his head. I never did manage to clip his ears. It might have been possible had I used a twitch on him but I was not prepared to do so.

I tried to trace his background and discovered that he had been

sold at Barnet Fair but had no pedigree or papers from his breeder – and no name. I was sure that he was out of a Welsh mare by an Arab stallion for he had the spectacular way of going and the courage of the best of the Welsh cobs and the bottomless endurance and fine mane and tail of the Arabian bloodlines. I called him Ali.

I started to break him to ride. The lungeing and long-reining were straightforward. Although he was frightened, there were no real problems. The time came for him to be ridden and so Bill and I took him to a small enclosed area of grass near Thorne Court. The plan was that Bill would hold Ali on a lunge rein. I would ease myself gently on board from a bale of straw I used as a mounting block and walk quietly round. Ali shot forward but Bill hung on. Ali swung round. I fell off. I got straight back on and we tried again. The same thing happened. And again. And again. Ali shot forward – or sideways. Bill hung on. I was catapulted out of the front, back or side door – whichever gravity dictated. I fell off six times in about as many minutes. We were getting nowhere. Disappointment flooded over me. I was not frightened just despairing.

Eventually, Bill and I decided to have a break and think what we should do. We were exhausted. We took Ali into his stable at Thorne Court and tied him up. We filled a sack with sand and left it tied to his saddle for half an hour. We then enlisted the help of Bill's brother, Tim, who is a typically strong farmer and does not let go of horses. The plan was that both Bill and Tim would hang on to Ali and I would sit on top. The three of us and Ali trooped outside once more. I got up onto Ali. He shot forward knocking Tim off his feet. Bill hung on, almost pulling Ali over. I fell off.

By now, I really was desperate. I wondered if I should send him to someone to be broken but did not want to because I knew Ali was scared stiff and it was fear that made him react as he did. I didn't want him to be knocked into submission. I wanted to build up his confidence in me. Also, I could not afford to pay someone else to break him. Besides, to whom could I send him?

It seemed that I had bought an unrideable three-year-old part-Arab stallion with no papers other than his Ministry of Agriculture stallion licence. It was unlikely, therefore, that I would be able to sell him easily. I could not afford to buy another horse. But I did not want to part with him. I just knew that if I could train him, he would have a great future. I had no option but to persevere and, somehow, get Ali going.

Bill and I discussed Ali at great length. Why was he so frightened? What could we do to gain his confidence? How could we convince him we meant no harm? How could we make him trust us?

'He's terrified of somebody on his back,' I sighed to Bill.

He frowned and then said, 'I think it's something to do with being held. Perhaps he feels he has no escape.'

'But we can't just let him run off.'

'I know that but how about trying him in a confined area – unheld. He can't go anywhere and if you fall off you're no worse off than outside,' Bill pointed out.

'It's worth a try. Anything's worth a try,' I nodded.

I bedded the floor of one of the big loose boxes at Thorne Court deeply with straw and banked up the sides as well. I put a straw bale on the floor to act as a mounting block so that I could get on board with the minimum of fuss. Bill stood in the passageway that ran the length of the building and watched through the upper railings of the loose box. I led Ali into the loose box and positioned him between the wall and the bale. I stepped up onto the bale and as gently as I could

I leaned over the saddle. Eventually, Ali relaxed a little and I put my leg over his back so that I was sitting on the saddle. After a while I managed to persuade Ali to walk round the loose box. He was very tense but did not shoot off as he had done outside. Greatly encouraged, I repeated the process later that day and from then on twice a day. Slowly, he began to trust me and, little by little, became less frightened.

One day I opened the door and rode him from one end of the stables to the other along the passage that I had also bedded deeply with straw. He tolerated this and I used to walk him backwards and forwards from one loose box to the other.

After several days of doing this, we ventured to a tiny barn which, again, I bedded deeply with straw. I led him into the barn then, while I erected a barricade across the entrance as there were no doors, left him to wander around on his own. I then mounted, as quietly as possible, from a straw bale, and rode around the barn. Sometimes, he would suddenly shoot forward. Eventually, I became quite adept at sitting back in the saddle as the wall at the far side came to meet us at great speed.

Despite these lapses, I was even more convinced that Ali would be a wonderful horse if only we could learn to work together. Even at this early stage he gave me a fantastic feeling when he walked for the length of the barn. There was enormous power which, even under these circumstances, made me feel strangely safe. He had a tremendous front and shoulder that resulted in the desirable 'uphill' ride so rarely found in ponies.

The next move was to hire an indoor school. I boxed him there daily and worked him in the school, first on the long-reins then under saddle, walking and trotting round without any problem. We were, at last, beginning to build mutual trust and we ventured outside. Ali was no longer frightened and, at last, I began hacking around at home.

One day I was riding on the disused wartime airfield at Lavenham across the main road from Thorne Court. All had been going well until our trot increased to an uncontrolled canter. In an effort to stop, I turned Ali into some long grass. He crashed to the ground, falling over a hidden log and the remains of an old plough. I saw his belly pass over the top of me as I lay among the rusting ironwork. He

scrambled to his feet and was off. I watched him as he galloped back towards Thorne Court. He crossed the main road and headed towards Bury St Edmunds before finally stopping to graze in a lay-by.

It was then the local lay preacher came along in his car. On seeing a loose horse he stopped, walked to Ali and took up the reins. He deduced that the horse might belong to a Walrond and, as he was so near Thorne Court, picked up the reins and led Ali back there. He told me afterwards that he had considered riding the horse but wisely decided that it might be safer to lead him!

By then I had staggered back to Thorne Court feeling very sore around the mouth and ribs. Bill was working in the stables. He took one look at my bruised face and broken tooth and rushed me to the hospital.

After a couple of months I had recovered enough to start working Ali again. I wondered if I might be back to Square One with Ali but we carried on as if nothing had happened which was marvellous. The experience had not set either of us back at all.

Having had such trouble in breaking Ali to ride, I wondered whether I would ever manage to break him to harness. I was very aware of the old saying: 'You tell a gelding, you ask a mare, you discuss it with a stallion.'

I had heard of an aromatic liquid called Pax. It was marketed as being able to cover the scent of fear which is transmitted to a horse from a nervous handler or spectator or if trouble is expected. Naturally, after all the problems I had experienced in persuading Ali to carry me on his back, I was wondering how I was going fare when I asked him to pull a vehicle. I needed all the help I could get and ordered a bottle. It had a quite pleasant smell: mainly eucalyptus but there was something else too – perhaps a secret aromatic ingredient! As instructed, I rubbed a little onto my hands and forehead. I applied a little each day before I started working Ali. My theory is that if the trainer is at all apprehensive, he or she emits a scent that is instantly picked up by the horse which immediately senses impending danger and prepares for flight. Nervous helpers can create havoc even though they may not even touch the animal.

Pax certainly worked for me. Simply knowing that any scent was masked by the aromatic, and hence Ali could not pick up any sense of fear from me, made me relax and that sense of calm was instantly transmitted to him further establishing our mutual trust. When, some time later, I showed him, I always used to apply a little Pax to his nose and chest. He was always perfectly behaved and could even be standing in the line-up next to an in-season mare and he would ignore her. I still keep a bottle of Pax in my horsebox and apply a little to the hands of all the people who are with me at a show or event. This ensures that the scent of any apprehension is not transmitted to my ponies. It is not necessarily fear but simply the excitement and apprehension of forthcoming events that can cause the problem. I receive letters from people all over the world asking me about the aromatic. Many want to know from where it can be obtained. It is, at the time of writing, available from Day, Son and Hewitt Ltd, St George's Quay, Lancaster LA1 5QJ, England.

The preliminary work for training Ali to drive went smoothly. I long-reined him for miles in all the harness before starting to teach him to pull a weight. For this I used a motor tyre which he dragged quite happily once he realised that it would do him no harm. Again, it was a question of building up his confidence. I thought, however, that once we had reached the stage of putting him to a vehicle there could be serious problems as he was likely to take off if he became frightened. So, Bill devised the Walrond wheel-less cart for this intermediate stage between pulling the tyre and being put to a vehicle. The 'cart' was constructed from elm suckers and held together with string and nails (see illustration). The rear skids enabled it to slide sideways so that Ali could be brought round if he tried to run away. It was almost a case of 'tie him in and cut him out' as we fixed the traces with string to the elm sucker splinter bar. However, it worked well and I

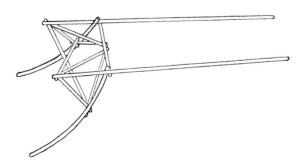

The Walrond wheel-less cart. Construction is of greenwood poles (elm suckers, 1–3 ins in diameter, are suitable) nailed together in the position shown. Joints can be reinforced by lashing with baler twine.

walked for miles with Ali harnessed to this contraption. Fortunately, he never kicked or attempted to lie down and accepted the wheel-less cart so the time came to try him in the speed cart. There were no problems. It took ten months before I could honestly say that he was acceptably broken to both ride and drive.

Throughout this period I was breeding from a couple of sows to raise money to pay for a set of new show harness for Ali. I had purchased, unseen, through *Horse and Hound*, a wonderful set of old black and brass, high-quality, tandem harness with two swept-back collars. One of these fitted the four-year-old Ali's neck and the wheeler saddle fitted his back so that it was used as a foundation for a new saddle to be made by a local harness-maker who made every strap of my show harness to my specification to fit Ali exactly.

The tenant, who had been farming the land around Thorne Lodge, retired. He had been using the large brick building, then known as the 'cow house', which was close to our cottage. This was fortunate for us as we were then able to use the land and the building. At one end of the building was an enormous loose box and the remainder of the 'cow house' became my coach house, housing ten carriages, but later, part of this was divided to accommodate a second horse in a smaller loose box.

So, I was now able to keep Ali at Thorne Lodge instead of at Thorne Court. He was stabled in the large box and, because he was on his own, Bill devised a toy for him to play with: a rugger ball hanging on a rope from a beam in the roof. Ali loved it and would bite and knock it around so that it swung violently. It quickly came to resemble a tulip with torn petals! So Bill replaced it with a motor tyre that he had sawn through and rolled up to look like the rugger ball. He ran a bolt through the tyre to keep it together so that it looked like a sausage roll and hung it from the beam by a chain. Very soon Bill had to protect the wood of the beam with a sheet of galvanised metal to protect it from the rubbing of the chain for Ali spent many happy hours playing with the ball. He would hit it with his teeth and send it flying into the air. He then cantered round the box and returned to hit the ball again. Sometimes, when I went out to the stables, I would hear him playing and I tried to keep very quiet. I would creep into the adjacent stable and go through a door that led to the corn bin. If he still had not heard me, I would climb onto the bin so that I could look over the walls and watch his game. Once he realised that he was being observed, he would stop and look up at me. He didn't seem to like being watched. Sometimes, when he came in from work or from being out at a show, he would give a little nicker to the ball as if it were a mare.

I started to take Ali out with the Suffolk foxhounds when he was rising four and very quietly followed for an hour or so to accustom him to the hunting field. He never gave me any trouble and most people did not realise that he was a stallion.

I decided to give up the pigs and keep a hunter livery to pay some expenses. One day, when I was out hunting, I asked a friend if she would keep her ears open for anyone suitable. Amazingly, that the same day, Martin Corke, chairman of the local brewery, Greene King, happened to mention to my friend that he was looking for somewhere to keep his horse at livery as he was finding it increasingly difficult to exercise in the dark mornings before going to work. He contacted me and we discussed the possibility of my looking after his hunter. In the end, I kept Martin's various hunters for the next twenty seasons.

The first one was a sexy chestnut Thoroughbred mare. I wondered what Ali's reactions would be to being stabled next to such a creature. I need not have worried because Ali was totally uninterested in the mare. I was able to ride and lead them for exercise every day and it did not matter whether I rode Ali and led the mare or rode the mare and led Ali. He was always a perfect gentleman and behaved like a gelding at all times. There were never any problems. Ali, apparently, did not find her sexy!

One day out hunting I was sitting on Ali next to our MFH, Paul Rackham, waiting for my next orders as I was usually sent 'on point' ahead of the huntsman and hounds to watch for foxes leaving a covert. We saw the huntsman, Tom Batterbee, trying to get his horse over or through an obstacle. It was unusual because nothing ever stopped Tom. He always went in a straight line after his hounds, however fearsome the barrier but this time his horse would have none of it. We continued watching for a while then Paul told me to go and give Tom a lead.

When I arrived beside Tom I saw a huge, gaping ditch that Tom's

horse was not prepared to jump.

'Do you want a lead?' I called to Tom and faced Ali towards the ditch and hoped for the best. Ali, however, had other ideas. A short distance away was a footbridge made from a couple of old railway sleepers that spanned the ditch. Ali spotted it and before I realised what was happening he headed towards the bridge and clattered over it to the other side.

Tom's horse was not prepared to follow suit, thank goodness, but, seeing Ali on the other side of the ditch, he finally jumped.

'Phew! Good job Ali didn't slip off and straddle the bridge,' I said.

'Not him – he's too clever to make that mistake, madam,' Tom replied. His faith in Ali was quite touching!

I started to take Ali to a few small hunter trials. When we set off from the start I always had to ride with great determination at the first fence but after we had cleared that, Ali would always look eagerly for the next fence. All I had to do was to point him in the right direction and sit still. He very rarely hit anything and never refused a fence. I think one of the reasons that he never refused was because I never over-faced him. He went on to win eight hunter trials.

On two occasions I scratched from a second class because I thought that a particular fence was too advanced for us. At one

Ali jumping a clear round at a hunter trial.

hunter trial, we had won our first class and when I walked the course for the next class, I saw that the coffin jump was just too difficult for us. The first rail had been raised and the rail after the ditch was too high. I decided that Ali would be overfaced and, rather than risk a stop, I withdrew. Eight others did the same and we watched the first competitor who, I believe, was connected with the organisation of the trials. We stood by the coffin fence and as predicted, the horse got into difficulties. It was not long after this that an announcement was made over the public address that there had been an error in the course building and competitors who had scratched could, if they wished, re-enter and go round the course. I did not go because Ali had been boxed up and prepared to travel. He had jumped superbly in the first round and won me a table-lamp which I still have. I preferred to take him home rather than ask him to jump again, after he thought that he had finished his work for the day.

★   ★   ★

In January 1967 it snowed heavily. We put Ali to the sleigh which he pulled with no problems and we had great fun. In readiness for the forthcoming show season that year the gig was repainted again to bring it up to top-class condition. It paid off because I drove Ali in it at a number of shows and won consistently.

That same year, at a BDS Council meeting, it was suggested that there was now the need for instructional slides to be made on harnessing and driving. As I had a suitable horse, a good set of harness and a newly painted gig I offered to organise a photographer to take the slides. As I had been instrumental in getting them done, I was invited to show them to the first audiences in Surrey and London. These initial showings eventually resulted in my being invited to travel to many parts of the world as I expanded the slide collection to cover vehicles and harness worldwide.

The following year, 1968, Ali and I were invited by Geoffrey Sparrow, the chairman of the Arab Horse Society Golden Jubilee show held at Kempton Park racecourse, to give a ride-and-drive display each day at the show. The purpose was to prove the versatility of horses with Arabian blood.

I was accompanied by Cordelia Hislop, a teenage daughter of some old friends. She had been learning to drive with Ali and came with me to shows whenever she could. She gave me tremendous support and we have remained great friends. We camped in a loose box next to the one where Ali was stabled. All our meals were provided by the show caterers so that it was like being on holiday! Once we had unpacked our gear and settled into our racecourse accommodation, we reconnoitred the arena and made all the necessary plans for the following day's performance.

I was anxious for the display to be both workmanlike and entertaining. It began with Ali, harnessed to the gig, entering the arena in his brilliant extended trot. I had no passenger or helper in the arena because I wanted to show the bond that had developed between us. After a couple of circuits in each direction, I brought him into the centre of the arena and took him out of the vehicle. He stood, on his own, perfectly still while I removed the driving saddle and put on the riding saddle. I exchanged the blinkered bridle for a riding bridle and took off the collar over the riding bridle. I mounted and showed his flat schooling through all the paces and a little lateral work which we had just begun.

There were no proper jumps available but a few chairs made a makeshift fence which he flew over without any problem. A narrow wooden garden seat served to show off the results of our training at home where I had been jumping him over narrow objects with the idea that he would eventually jump over a wooden sword stuck into the ground.

After going over the jumps, I sent him off into a gallop and laid the reins on his neck for a circuit of the arena before stopping in front of the audience. I then dismounted and asked Ali to bow. We both enjoyed every moment of our 'act' and we were invited to repeat the performance the following day.

★ ★ ★

I heard that Blueberry, whom I had tried to drive in tandem with Z, was redundant and thought that maybe I could drive her in tandem with Ali. After all, he had not been the slightest bit interested in the

Ali at the Arab Horse Show ...

... tied to the ground while he is being changed from a driving horse to a riding animal ...

... demonstrating the early stages of lateral work; the chairs in the foreground formed one of the jumps.

Bowing to the audience at the end of his display.

hunter livery mare so perhaps he would not be interested in Blue. I planned to put her into the wheel and I thought that Ali would make a wonderfully spectacular leader. So, I bought Blue and brought her back to Thorne Lodge on a cold and snowy February day. I turned her out in the field that adjoined Ali's stable. Ali took one look at Blue and promptly fell madly in love with her. It would have been madness to attempt to harness them and so, in May, Ali served Blue. The result was a grey filly whom we called Alibi. A year later he served Blue again and bred a dun filly – Razali. These two youngsters became my first proper tandem. Cordelia enjoyed driving Blue for a couple of years before Blue went to pupils from Wales where she remained for the rest of her life.

I took Ali to fifty-five shows between 1966 and 1971 and he was very successful. He won forty-six first prizes and a number of championships. Then in 1971, I took him to Hadleigh show. After entering the ring we were doing an extended trot down the long side of the arena. The last thing I remember was the commentator talking about the turnout behind us. It was a young horse and so I had agreed to go in ahead of it to give it a lead and also so as not to frighten it by overtaking if it hesitated.

I woke up two days later in hospital. Apparently, I had hit a dip in the ground and, because we were travelling quite fast, the gig overturned. I had been catapulted from my high seat in the gig and Ali had

Ali's trophies for 1968.

Sallie receiving a prize from Her Majesty The Queen at the BDS Show in 1970, with Ali.

galloped round the ring. He eventually freed himself from the over-turned gig and returned to his trailer. Fortunately, he had not hit any other turnouts and no one else was hurt or damaged. Ali was unin-jured but the gig was smashed and the harness broken. When I came back to Thorne Lodge from hospital, it seemed that there were bro-ken pieces of my cherished equipment wherever I looked. The whip was broken in two; the glass of one of the lamps was smashed; the shafts had splintered and the harness was scratched and ripped. It was a horrendous time and Bill was marvellous in putting up with my despair. Friends rallied round and everything was eventually repaired, renewed or replaced.

I expected that my nerve might have gone and I was quite pre-pared to have to give up my life of horses. I had seen people trying to ride and drive when clearly they were not enjoying themselves because they are so scared. I was determined not to join those ranks and so I decided that the best thing to do would be to drive a pair of horses that belonged to a friend and see how I felt. If I were frightened then I would take up some other interest. I got up behind the horses but did not feel the slightest bit of apprehension. So, thank goodness, all was well. I could carry on as before.

Ali, however, became very troublesome when I was out of action. He was turned out in the field beside his stable but he broke through substantial fencing to get to his yearling daughter who was grazing on

the next-door parkland. Alibi was turned out with one of Bill's brother's Thoroughbreds. Ali grabbed this horse by the throat – luckily the damage was not permanent – he then covered Alibi who, fortunately, did not conceive.

At this point, Bill and I decided that Ali should be castrated. He was clearly a very unhappy stallion now that he was out of regular work. Gerald Hudson, our vet, did a masterly job on the nine-year-old Ali, who recovered fully and remained the same bold and courageous horse and gave the same ride that he had when he had been entire. We decided not to show him any more. However, in 1972 there was a new ride-and-drive class at the Royal International Horse Show held at Wembley and Bill and I decided that we would take Ali. Although we had retired him from the private driving circuit, this was something quite different. We would be indoors and on our own so would cause no trouble for fellow competitors.

The format was that competitors drove a 'cones' course, going between pairs of cones without hitting any of them. This was against the clock and time was added for any cone displaced. The competitor then went into a marked enclosure where the horse had to be saddled and jumped over a course of fences. Again, time was added for fences that were lowered. The horse was then re-harnessed and the cones

Ali at Wembley in the ride and drive class in 1972.

course was driven again. The whole event was against the clock from start to finish.

We took the Norfolk cart which had quite a narrow wheelbase, making it easier to drive a clear round, as the width between the cones was standard for all competitors. We harnessed Ali with a full collar and his riding saddle under a driving saddle but used no breeching or crupper. The riding bridle had a steeplechase-type hood that I had had specially made in Newmarket so that Ali could see to jump but could not see behind when he was in the vehicle. Bill and I practised our changes from drive to ride until we had it down to a few seconds. In the competition we went clear in the cones course. As soon as we arrived in the enclosure, we both dismounted from the vehicle and took a trace off the hook as we went by. Bill undid the belly band, pushed back the vehicle and undid the girth. I unfastened the reins from the bit and ran them through the hame terrets while the other rein ends remained over the rein rail. I then removed the collar and Bill took off the driving saddle. I mounted Ali and jumped a clear round while Bill prepared the vehicle and harness for the final phase. We drove another clear round in the cones driving in good time and won our first heat of the competition.

A few days later in the final, however, we were well beaten on time

Ali completing a clear round at Wembley in the ride and drive class.

although we did have the satisfaction that Ali had gone clear through all three phases. It was the greatest fun and Ali was fantastic. It was the last time that he competed.

I continued to enjoy driving him at home, with friends, to wheeled vehicles in the summer and, when the weather permitted, the sleigh in the winter.

I hunted him for years and eventually he went on permanent loan to a friend, Margaret Collins. He was with her and wanted for nothing under her tender loving care. Margaret gave a party for Ali to celebrate his thirtieth birthday and I was invited. It was wonderful to see him looking so well and I rode him for a little while. He gave me the same fantastic feel that he always had with the wonderful 'uphill' ride. There will never be another horse like Ali. He died in Margaret's field at the age of thirty-eight in 2000. It was a very sad day.

Ali in the sleigh; Thorne Lodge in the background. (Photo reproduced by kind permission of the East Anglian Daily Times, Terry Hunt, Andy Abbott and Sharon Boswell)

CHAPTER 12

The 1966 BDS Show

THE BDS COUNCIL DECIDED that the annual show should be held at a different venue each year. The first show was held in 1965 in the New Forest. A local driving friend, Pam Greene, and I volunteered to run the 1966 show before it became too large for us to handle. We had run the area show for a few years. We were a committee of two, meeting occasionally to decide who was going to do which jobs, then got on with whatever needed doing.

The BDS Council was delighted to have volunteers to run the show. The site, a cricket field, was approved by Sir Dymoke White, a BDS Vice President, who, after meeting me, invited Bill and myself to go to his home in Norfolk for lunch and enjoy a drive with his coaching team. He even allowed me to hold the reins of his beautifully mannered team of bays.

Once the site was approved, the work began. Sandy Watney, and Bunny and Phyllis Candler, the secretaries of the BDS, were towers of strength to Pam and me. Schedules were printed and sent out to all BDS members. Area Commissioners were contacted and begged to persuade their area members to support this show. Advertisements were put into newspapers and magazines. We organised the Red Cross, Girl Guides, farrier, vet, water supply, litter bins and tents for

beer, lunch and secretary. Members' husbands and friends were enlisted to cordon off rings, paint notices to keep down costs and dig holes for lavatories as Portaloos had not been invented in 1966.

As some exhibitors would be travelling long distances, stabling was required. Portable stabling was not in general use then and so Pam and I contacted all our hunting friends who had stables near to the showground and arranged to use those that were empty because the hunters were out at grass. Eventually, about twenty loose boxes were prepared. (We also undertook to clean up afterwards although most people left the stables as clean as they had found them when they arrived.) We listed hotels and drew maps to show their location as well as the sites of the stables.

We enquired about caterers to supply lunch but costs were pro-hibitive, so the obvious solution was to provide the lunches ourselves. We asked the exhibitors to indicate how many lunches would be required when they sent their entry form to the Candlers so that we would have accurate numbers. Friends produced salads from their gardens and Pam and I cooked quantities of chickens and purchased items to provide a cold buffet. We ended up, on the day, by giving all exhibitors and grooms a free lunch and a glass of wine. We had over-catered and so an announcement was made over the public address that lunch was available to anyone who would like to come and eat it because we wanted it to be cleared up! People kept offering to pay

Roger Clark driving the Lancaster's donkey tandem at the 1966 BDS Show.

because they could not believe that there was, in fact, such a thing as a free lunch.

We had hired a 'cut price' marquee and we soon discovered the reason for the discount. In the afternoon the heavens opened amid a spectacular thunderstorm and the rain poured into the tent but no one seemed to mind.

There were two rings. The cricket field, with its fine turf and flat surface, was used for the showing classes. It was much appreciated and we received several 'thank you' letters from competitors stating that it was the finest ring in which they had ever driven. The second ring was used for the Golden Guinea driving competition which, as the schedule stated, was 'a competition to test the skill of the driver in negotiating various hazards'. There were H-shaped wooden markers (made by Pam) that swivelled on the top of a short post if the hub of the vehicle touched the arm. Five faults were added for every marker hit. Two rows of balls were laid on the ground and the right wheel of the vehicle had to be driven between the balls: one fault was added for every ball moved. The winner was the turnout with the lowest score in the fastest time. Pam and I made the rules and no one argued or grumbled.

Fifty-eight horses, ponies and donkeys came from thirteen counties and the day ran to time. Over 300 people paid two shillings (10p) each to watch the show. The date clashed with the finals of the World Cup football match when England was playing so it was amazing that the show received such good support from the general public.

However, we ran at a loss of £6. Our capital expenditure on items such as signs, markers and competition props was £10 but we still had those items for use at future BDS meets. So, if these were taken into account we could say that we actually made a small profit.

CHAPTER 13

Judging

In 1967 Sandy Watney asked me if I would like to be put on the BDS judges' panel. I doubted my ability but was assured that I would cope. I was fortunate enough to accompany Bernard Mills, son of Bertram Mills of circus fame, who was judging all the classes at the BDS show in 1968 when it was held at Stoneleigh, Warwickshire. I learned an enormous amount that day. One factor in particular remains in my mind: it is vital to take the whole turnout into consideration, not solely the horse. At this show, a great-going Welsh cob came into the ring pulling a beautiful spider phaeton. I fell for the turnout but Bernard, quite rightly, explained that although the cob was spectacular and the phaeton was superb, the two were not compatible as such a light and elegant vehicle needed an equally light and elegant horse, not a cob, however spectacular. I valued his knowledge and advice and listened to all that he said.

A few years later I was put onto the Coaching Club panel to judge teams of four put to private, regimental and road coaches and was fortunate to accompany Major Tom Coombs, a very experienced and knowledgeable coaching judge, when he was scrutinising the coaching at the Royal Norfolk Show. He taught me an enormous amount about this specialised form of judging.

Because of my dressage experiences in the 1950s, I was invited to join the combined driving (dressage, cross-country and cones) panel of judges and in 1971 judged the teams when these competitions were first held at the Royal Windsor Horse Show. I subsequently travelled all over the country and as a result was entertained, as were all judges, officials and competitors, in numerous wonderful places including Windsor Castle, the Palace of Holyroodhouse in Edinburgh and a marquee at Sandringham where, because I happened to be at the front of the crowd, I was highly honoured when Prince Philip presented me to Her Majesty The Queen. I was so overcome with excitement that I forgot to curtsy and only bowed my head.

One year, when I arrived to judge at the Brighton driving trials I was told that Prince Philip was judging instead of competing this year. He had been very successful driving The Queen's Fell pony team but was not driving on this occasion. When judging the dressage phase, judges work in panels of three: Prince Philip was to be on my panel – I was to be the President of this jury whereupon I became distinctly nervous, for it is the President who makes final decisions, such as errors of course and lame horses.

At the start of the competition, I drove my car into position at the C marker on the short side of the arena. Prince Philip was in his position at E on the long side. Normally, I would walk across and talk to the judges at B and E to clarify that we must not dwell because time was tight. I did not think that I could possibly approach Prince Philip but he made the decision for me by walking towards my car. Then, of course, I was able to go and meet him.

The class started on time and ran strictly to time with no problems. However, a competitor came in and I wondered if the horse was slightly lame behind. It was one of those cases where the animal was sound for most of the time but occasionally showed a little unevenness on a corner. I marked my sheet and commented accordingly that there were a few unlevel strides in order to cover myself.

As soon as the competitor had left the arena, Prince Philip got out of his car and walked towards me. Again, I went to meet him. He had seen the suspected lameness and asked me what I proposed to do. We called the judge at B who had also spotted the problem. We agreed that I would talk to the Technical Delegate, Richard James, then I would go to the stable manager's office when the class was over and find the competitor. This I did and had a long talk with the driver of the animal, telling him what we had all seen and that he was not to run the horse on the marathon the following day if he was unsound. There were long explanations and I concluded that the animal had probably trodden on a stone on its way to the arena.

The next day, Prince Philip asked what I had done about the problem and I told him. The horse was, in fact, sound and completed the marathon. The incident left me full of admiration for Prince Philip in astutely spotting the slight lameness: hind-leg lameness is much easier to miss than front-leg lameness and often goes unnoticed.

CHAPTER 14

New York

FOR SOME TIME I HAD WANTED TO SEE the Long Island Museum of American Art, History and Carriages at Stony Brook, New York. My mother was living in Florida and I was planning to visit her in the autumn of 1969. It provided a wonderful opportunity to combine seeing my mother with visiting the museum. I may have mentioned to Sandy and Biddy Watney that I was keen to see the carriages in the American museum because, in retrospect, I think that it was probably Sandy's influence that resulted in an invitation to stay with Colonel and Mrs Paul Downing at their home on Staten Island. Paul Downing was well known as the editor of the Carriage Association of America's quarterly *Carriage Journal*. I had been a life member of the CAA since the early 1960s and had all of the journals since it began in 1963.

I was met at New York airport by Paul and later taken the length of Long Island to the museum at Stony Brook village. Paul had a detailed knowledge of all the carriages and spent two hours showing me around them. They were housed in three large adjoining buildings and were beautifully displayed. Pictures and harness of all kinds lined the walls. In one part of the museum was a harness-maker's shop where a figurine of an old harness-maker was so lifelike that I nearly

asked him for his advice about some harness I had seen!

On the second day of my visit, I was taken to meet Commodore Chauncey Stillman at his home, Withersfield House, which was set among rolling hills in breathtakingly beautiful country. After a lavish lunch, we went into the garden to wait for the horses to be brought from the stables and, promptly at 2.30pm, up the drive came a phaeton drawn by a spectacular pair of bay hackneys in gleaming harness. Chauncey drove for two and a half hours along woodland trails and tracks. The horses were fantastic: perfectly mannered, working together as a pair, trotting in step most of the time in the slow cadence typical of superb hackneys. It was marvellous to view the beautiful scenery with the leaves in their wonderful colours of the American fall. I was thrilled to see Canada geese, a woodchuck (North American marmot) and a turkey buzzard.

After the drive, the horses were taken back to their stables and given a hot shower before being returned to join the numerous other hackneys in rows of indoor loose boxes. The harness was taken to the temperature-controlled harness room, where spotless, gleaming collars, bridles, saddles and traces hung from racks on the walls. The carriage was taken to the washroom where it was cleaned to keep it in show condition like all the others that lined the sides of the carriage house. Down the centre of the carriage house was a length of carpet with white ropes on either side. At the end of the carpet was a table where the most recent trophies and rosettes were proudly displayed. Shafts, poles and pictures adorned the walls. Palm trees, in the corner, completed the décor.

A chance remark from Chauncey has always remained in my memory. When we were returning from our drive we saw a gardener pushing a barrow containing an orange tree in a large pot. Chauncey said, 'I always dislike seeing the orange trees being brought in because it means that winter is on the way.'

CHAPTER 15

Books

In 1966 BUNNY CANDLER, the secretary of the British Driving Society, asked me to write an article about Ali for the BDS yearbook. I hesitated because I was not sure whether I was capable of producing an acceptable article. I had never been particularly clever at school, although I had always worked hard, and 'English' had not been one of my better subjects. However, I was persuaded to produce the needed piece. After this, I was asked to write a series of six articles for the magazine *Riding*. Again, I hesitated because I was not confident in my ability. However, the fee offered for these articles tempted me and Bill suggested a joint effort: I would produce the knowledge on paper and he would edit my words into a more acceptable form. Thus we worked together and the articles were completed and published.

Then, at a BDS Council meeting, one of the BDS Vice Presidents and Treasurer of the Society, Reg Brown, suggested that these articles should be published in the form of a booklet for BDS members to buy. I was thrilled and very flattered. I agreed but said that the BDS should retain all profits. Bill and I gave the booklet the title of *Fundamentals of Private Driving*. It was initially sold for five shillings (25p), was reprinted and continued selling successfully for the next thirty years.

After the articles had been published in *Riding*, the magazine's editor, Elwyn Hartley Edwards, invited me to write a book on driving for a series on which he was working. He explained how I must conform to the format, outline, style and length of content of the series and I agreed to write the book. Its title was to be *A Guide to Driving Horses*.

I was fortunate in that very little was being written about driving at this time and so I had gone into print when the subject of driving was still on the ground floor, so to speak. *A Guide to Driving Horses* ran to several editions as it passed from one publisher to another. There were also American paperback editions that remained in print for many years. It was also translated into German.

★   ★   ★

Pam Greene, with whom I had run the 1966 BDS show, visited frequently. She drove an Essex cart, a high, country-type vehicle which would have perhaps been used for taking chickens or piglets to market and the family to church on Sunday. One day we were standing by it when she asked,

'What are these called?' She pointed to the little uprights that went round the upper part of the body of the Essex cart between the top rail and the one below it (see page 53).

'I've no idea,' I replied, 'but I expect we can look it up.'

This proved more difficult than I had imagined for we could not find a reference to this feature of the Essex cart in any of my books. Eventually, we gave up and went into the kitchen for a cup of tea. Pam was leaning against the wall by the kitchen door, sipping tea from her mug, when she said,

'Why don't you just write an encyclopaedia so that we can look up things like that?'

'Me? Don't be silly!' I laughed, dismissing the idea as impossible.

After Pam had gone, I began to think about what she had said. Perhaps it wasn't such a crazy idea after all. I had always been a great admirer of the classic standard work, *Summerhayes' Encyclopaedia for Horsemen*, and I began to wonder if I could produce a similar work on carriage driving and related subjects. I had, by now, accumulated a sizable collection of old books on driving that had been given to me by elderly people who knew of my interest in carriage driving. The more I thought about the possibility, the more enthusiastic I became, However, it would be time-consuming and my time was well filled: in the winter I had hunters to look after and exercise, in the summer I had horses to break, shows to judge, and all year round I had a husband, house and garden to care for.

If I was going to do it then I must establish a routine for my writing. I would complete all house and horse chores by lunchtime. I would then sit at the kitchen table and write until 4.30pm when I would stop to feed and settle the horses for the night, then prepare dinner for Bill when he came home from his office where he worked in the family firm of solicitors. After dinner, Bill and I would go through my afternoon's work, which was all written in long hand, pulling it apart until we were both too tired to do any more.

When I started on *The Encyclopaedia*, as I referred to it, I assembled all the possible entries in a blank A to Z exercise book. I then went through every one of my carriage driving books and magazines looking for interesting items. Whenever I found something suitable, I would enter it under the appropriate letter and put the reference beside it stating the book title, page number and, in some cases, the line number. Some entries had references from several different books. Problems arose with multiple references when spelling and dates varied. I then had to decide which was most likely to be correct.

Once I had assembled enough entries to make a sizable book, I edited and refined the entries beginning with A after which they were typed by my friend, Cordelia Hislop, and the resulting sheets assembled into strict alphabetical order. I kept very quiet about my work on this book because I was afraid that if the idea became known someone else might start on a similar book and finish theirs before mine was ready for a publisher. I knew there were at least two people who could produce such a book. By the time I had reached the end of the entries for the letter C, I estimated the book was, at this rate, going to take five years to complete! I decided I must obtain a publisher because I did not want to do all this work without the knowledge that it was definitely going to sell.

One day after attending a BDS meeting at the Royal Mews in London, I mentioned *The Encyclopaedia* to John Richards, a fellow BDS member then later Chairman of the BDS and now a Vice President. He was also a publisher and had published Tom Ryder's excellent book, *On the Box Seat*. He agreed to publish my book providing it was completed in two years. We shook hands and the contract was sealed. The book was to be called *Encyclopaedia of Driving*. At the time it seemed pretentious to call it *The Encyclopaedia of Driving* and yet I didn't want it to be called *An Encyclopaedia of Driving* as it sounded as though it was simply one of many – which it wasn't.

I worked very hard and the book was published in 1974. A few copies were produced in magnificent leather bindings and I attended a signing session of these at the National Equestrian Centre at Stoneleigh, Warwickshire. To my horror, I signed one of these very expensive volumes at the back instead of at the front. I kept this copy for myself and have written in the back: 'Signed upside down in error at Stoneleigh'.

Eventually, *Encyclopaedia of Driving* went out of print but was taken on by the publishers of *Country Life* who asked for an enlarged edition. I had been keeping a file of possible additional entries against such an eventuality and so was able to update it immediately. The title did then become known as *The Encyclopaedia of Driving* because, by then, I knew that it was indeed the one and only encyclopaedia of driving.

Again, the book went out of print and Joseph Allen (always referred to as 'Mr Allen') of J.A. Allen, publisher of equestrian books and owner of the Horseman's Bookshop in London, agreed to take on the book. He asked me to produce more material so that it could be called an enlarged and revised edition. His editor, Caroline Burt, did a magnificent job on the book and the title was changed to *The Encyclopaedia of Carriage Driving* to differentiate it from the driving of motor cars when it was placed on library shelves or listed in catalogues.

I had tremendous help with the text of this edition from Sandy and Biddy Watney and Tom Coombs who had helped me in my early days of judging coaching classes and who themselves were, by now, successful authors of books on driving. They all read the copy before it went to the publishers and corrected any errors. I was extremely grateful to them.

While I had been building up my collection of vehicle slides for my talks both in the UK and overseas, I had had an idea for a book. It would be called *Looking at Carriages*. Bill and I went to visit carriage collections, stately homes and museums to obtain pictures and information about carriages. Sometimes, when I was abroad teaching or judging, I would see a vehicle of particular interest and I would ask the owner if I could have a photograph of the carriage for possible use in my proposed book. I obtained numerous excellent photographs in this way. Sometimes, I worked a barter system: professional photographers would take a picture for me and, in return, I would write an article on whatever subject they required for their paper or magazine. Neither of us charged a fee for our work and we both obtained what we wanted. Friends also gave me photographs of their vehicles and museum curators generously allowed me to reproduce pictures from brochures or slides on sale in their museums.

A trip to Brussels resulted in a number of very interesting photographs of vehicles from the carriage collections of Eric Andersen and the Baron Jean Casier. I was so fortunate that people were always very kind to me.

Eventually, I had enough pictures and accompanying information to complete the book. It was published in 1980 by Pelham Books under the title *Looking at Carriages* and I was thrilled that HRH The Prince Philip, Duke of Edinburgh, consented to write the foreword. It also went into a French edition. As with *The Encyclopaedia of Driving*, Mr Allen took the title when it went out of print and again I was grateful to Caroline Burt for suggesting that we should add a new section. This section described twentieth century carriages, built by the new generation of carriage-builders for both modern combined driving competitions that required robust rather than elegant vehicles, and along traditional designs for private driving. With this addition to bring it up to date, it could be called an enlarged edition.

I was then approached by Lesley Gowers, who was working for Pelham Books and whom I had met in connection with *Looking at Carriages*, to write a book about training horses for harness work. At that time, 1980, I had a grey Connemara pony called Cottenham Loretto and so I engaged a professional photographer for a day to take the pictures. The text was a simple matter for me because, unlike

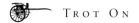

the last two titles, I did not have to do any research. This book, entitled *Breaking a Horse to Harness* went into three printings and when it went out of print with Pelham, Mr Allen took it. It again went out of print and Caroline Burt asked me to do the necessary work to produce an updated edition in colour for J.A. Allen. This title, in its black-and-white format, had become one of J.A. Allen's bestsellers and, in recognition of this, I was presented with an award in 1998 at a special lunch organised by J.A. Allen which was very exciting.

I went to work on the new edition and I asked the talented professional photographer, Anthony Reynolds, to take the photographs using my new dun Connemara pony, Scottsway Sunrise. The photography took two days owing to inclement weather but the text was quite straightforward. We kept the same title: *Breaking a Horse to Harness*. This title also went into a German edition.

In between these books, Lesley Gowers asked me to write a book entitled *Your Problem Horse*. Again, this was easy as I did not have to do any research. I just wrote down my experiences of troublesome animals and how I had dealt with them. This book was translated into French, German, Italian and Dutch and was reprinted several times.

Caroline Burt then asked me to write a book about judging carriage driving, which I was pleased to do, and again no research was needed. While I was working on that title Lesley Gowers invited me to produce three short books on driving for the Kenilworth Press Threshold series. Some of these have also been translated into French, German and Dutch.

When the *Guide to Driving Horses* went out of print, Caroline Burt asked me to produce an updated version. That too became another of J. A. Allen's bestsellers. Eventually, it went out of print and Caroline wanted a book that was similar in format to the colour edition of *Breaking a Horse to Harness*. Once again, Anthony Reynolds took photographs for the new edition entitled *Driving a Harness Horse* using Scottsway Sunrise as his model. We began at 8am under grey skies that threatened rain at any moment, then the sun would come out, then back would come the clouds – all of which made Anthony's task more difficult. We did not even stop for a cup of coffee and finished at 3.30pm. At 3.45pm the heavens opened.

This title has since been taken by an American publisher and hence is sold in an American edition – all very exciting. These eleven books have gone into a total of thirty-four different editions. It was a great thrill to know that my books were being read all over the world.

It has also given me great satisfaction that the High Mistress of St Paul's Girls' School has accepted several of my books for the school library. When I was there as a pupil in the 1940s I searched in vain for books about horses. I hope that my titles are giving pleasure to present-day pupils!

CHAPTER 16

An American Rodeo

WHILE VISITING MY MOTHER IN FLORIDA, I was fortunate to be taken to the Florida Cowboy Association State Finals Rodeo held at the Brandon Stadium near Tampa.

The sun blazed down, temperatures were in the 90s and the whole area surrounding the arena resembled a Western movie. There were hundreds of cowboys wearing traditional wide-brimmed stetsons, multi-coloured shirts and blue jeans held up by leather belts with large buckles. Horses wore ornate Western stock saddles, some of which were engraved with the names of winners of previous contests. All the horses wore long-cheeked bits; some worked purely on the horse's nose and curb while others had mouthpieces. Horses stood either 'tied' to the ground, to fences or to the sides of their trailers, which often displayed plaques indicating past successes. Calves, steers and bulls waited in pens for the afternoon's activities to begin. Small boys practised throwing lassos over posts or each other. One cowboy was sitting on his saddle on the ground earnestly swaying backwards and forwards.

'Excuse me, but why are you doing that?' I asked him.

'I'm rubbing my thighs against the saddle to work in the resin. See here, it's on my chaps,' he moved his leg so I could see the resin. 'Helps me get a better grip, ma'am,' he explained.

'Which event are you riding in?'

'Saddle bronc, ma'am,' and he continued to sway back and forth. The open stands filled with spectators while competitors worked their horses in the flag-bedecked arena before the rodeo began. Then, the sand-covered arena was cleared, a fire hydrant truck sprayed water to lay the dust and the rodeo began. The grand entry of the competitors, many of whom carried large flags, opened the proceedings. These men and women were competing for over $10,000 in prize money. Then the leading cowboys and cowgirls paraded and next came the 'pick-up' boys, upon whom riders relied for help to slide off their bucking broncs when time was up. This is a highly skilled job as these men have to be in the right place at the right time, yet never in the way. They also keep cattle away from fallen cowboys and drive both broncs and cattle back to their pens after each competitor. Next, the judges rode in wearing red shirts with 'Judge' written in large white letters across the back.

The first event was the bareback bronc riding. These horses were carefully selected and kept for this particular job. They were all in superb condition. The increase in motorised transport on ranches resulted in a shortage of suitable stock from which to find 'outlaw' horses that can unseat riders who, in turn, have become skilled at staying on board. Every year searches are carried out for such animals; the right horse could command a price over $10,000.

A top quality bucking horse was so treasured that an annual award was given for the bucking horse of the year, which cowboys elected as the one most difficult to ride. The bronc had a good life and was well cared for. His working year amounted to a few minutes and many lived well into their late twenties. Each horse in the bareback bronc riding wore a strap known as 'bareback riggin'. This resembled a stable roller with a suitcase-type handle on the top which the cowboy held with one hand. His other hand was held aloft as he must touch neither himself nor the horse during the contest or he would be eliminated. A flank strap was worn to encourage the horse to buck. This was of a quick-release variety and covered with wool or similar protective lining to prevent chafing.

Each bronc was penned individually and mounted in the chute by the cowboy who wore leather chaps over his jeans. His spurs must not lock nor have over-sharp rowels. As soon as the chute opened, the horse leapt into the arena in a series of enormous stiff-legged bucks and plunges. The cowboy's legs and body swung back and forth in rhythm with the bucks and his heels had to rake the horse's sides. The three judges awarded points: two gave marks for the rider and one gave marks for the horse. After eight seconds, a bell rang. The rider was then allowed to put his second hand on to the 'riggin' and the pick-up cowboy rode in to rescue him. The rider then slid from his bronc onto the quarters of the pick-up horse and from there to the ground. Of course, not all contestants stayed on board to complete the eight-second ride.

Calf roping came next. This was a timed event requiring a tremendously fast and obedient horse, usually a Quarter horse – so called because it is faster than a Thoroughbred over a quarter of a mile. A calf was released from a pen and galloped into the arena to be followed, a second or two later, by the cowboy, who had to throw a noose over its head. As soon as the calf was lassoed, the cowboy dismounted from whichever side was convenient and the horse stopped dead in its tracks. One cowboy shouted to his horse, 'Back up!' whereupon the horse reversed, maintaining the tautness of the rope holding the calf. The cowboy ran to the calf and threw it onto the ground. He crossed and tied three of its legs together so that it could not get up and flung up his arms as a signal he had completed the task. It took him barely ten seconds!

Saddle bronc riding followed. The horses used for this event were slightly heavier in build than those in the bareback event. They were capable of the most spectacular gymnastics. The horse wore a skeleton western saddle (minus the saddle horn at the front), a halter with a handhold and a strap round the flanks to encourage bucking.

The first horse to go was so anxious to get on with the job that he was not going to wait for the chute to be opened. It was quicker to come out over the top! However, he was pushed back, his rider mounted then, moments later, he sprang into the arena as the chute gate was flung back. His jockey bit the dust after the first buck. Charlie Driver won this event with a breathtaking display on what was considered to be the Number One saddle bronc.

In the next event, steer wrestling, the rider and Quarter horse left the pen at about thirty-five miles an hour a second or two after the steer was released. Once alongside the steer, the cowboy slid from his horse onto the steer, grasping its horns and twisting its head as he grappled it to the ground before it could reach the far side of the arena. Not all cowboys were successful – the steer would dodge, twist and escape unscathed leaving the cowboy in the sand.

Cowgirls had their turn with the barrel racing. This was a speed event with seconds added for dislodging a barrel. The girls galloped around three barrels placed in a cloverleaf pattern. The tight turns on both reins demand a well-schooled, supple and very fast horse. One contestant suffered a crashing fall by taking the last turn at just too sharp an angle.

Team roping was next on the programme. This involved two cowboys on Quarter horses and a long-horned steer. The steer was released from his pen. The cowboys galloped after him, one endeavouring to lasso the steer's horns and the other a hind leg. It required tremendous teamwork from horses and men, dexterity and accurate roping.

As a little light relief, children under thirteen were given arena time when they were let loose with ten calves which they tried to rope and throw. This activity must surely augur well for the future of rodeo as there must have been well over 200 youngsters chasing the calves.

Finally, came the bull riding. Cowboys tried to stay on board the large, humped Brahman bulls for eight seconds. A braided rope encircled the bull and had a handhold on the top similar to bareback rigging. Bells, like alpine cowbells, hung below the girth on a loose rope that came adrift as soon as the cowboy disembarked. A flank strap encouraged the bulls to kick even harder as they gyrated in furious twisting bucks that made their riders dizzy. Despite their size and bulk they leapt forward like kangaroos, their loose hides flapping and their bells clanking. Unlike bronc riders, bull riders were not required to spur their mounts during the ride (they had enough to do trying to stay on board) but higher marks were gained if they could do so.

When a cowboy had completed his ride, or more likely fallen off after a second or two, clowns ran in to distract the bull, enabling the cowboy to get up and run out of danger, for the bull was angry and wanted to vent his temper on somebody or something. While I was watching the rodeo, a row of cowboys were sitting on the arena fence with their legs dangling over the rails towards the arena. The bull, having dislodged his rider, dived at these men on the fence, ploughing along the barricade in a flurry of sand. But the cowboys knew what was coming. They remained sitting on the fence, lifting their feet in quick succession out of the way of the bull's horns as it charged beneath them.

I was lost in admiration for the skills of these cowboys. It was all so different from an English horse show!

The rodeo was an exciting event I shall never forget.

CHAPTER 17

Breaking

THROUGHOUT THE 1970S I was taking in horses to break for riding and driving but the numbers were limited, as I worked only one at a time and could have youngsters here only in the summer. The ground conditions in my outdoor arena made working outside in winter impossible and I did not have any facilities for working indoors. As a result, some people used to book their animals, as soon as they were born, to come to me for training in two years' time. This suited me because I was able to plan my diary well in advance.

My fenced 20-metre circle was ideal for lungeing, long-reining and preliminary training for riding and driving. The arena was only a few yards from the stables – not far to lead an unbroken or unruly youngster but there were occasions when even this short distance proved to be too far to take an unbroken horse.

I used to back animals as soon as possible after their arrival so that they did not become too fit or, in some cases, too cocksure of them-selves before I sat on their backs. I would lunge them to instil some respect and obedience then put on a saddle and bridle when I felt they were ready. This depended entirely on the reactions of each animal. Horses that had been bred by their owners and had been well handled since the day they were born were usually quite easy to break. They

were not afraid of anything and I was able to get them lunging happily in both directions and wearing a saddle and bridle within a couple of days. Providing that they were confident in me, I backed them on the second day.

I often worked youngsters twice a day giving them two very short sessions of perhaps ten minutes at a time. This way they did not get tired or bored. I always backed the youngsters in the stable where both they and I felt more secure than if I had tried to back them outside in the open. The youngsters lived in a loose box about four metres wide by seven metres long. When it was time to back them I bedded the box deeply with straw and used an upturned manger or a straw bale as a mounting block. I would shut the top half of the stable door and work alone. Bill was always within shouting distance so that in case of emergency he could come to help. I was delighted if owners wanted to watch but always insisted they were out of harm's way. They could climb onto a corn bin and look over the top of the wall that divided the feed area from the loose box and see all that was going on.

I always applied a little of the aromatic, Pax, before I backed the horse and I also applied some to any owners who were watching. I preferred them not to hold the animal as I wanted it to concentrate solely on what I was doing. Also, I did not want their apprehension to be communicated to the horse. I enjoyed backing youngsters and so did not feel nervous. I tried to read the animal's mind, partly for safety's sake and partly to avoid making mistakes with someone's much-loved youngster that they had trusted me to train.

In the first stage of backing a youngster I would lie across the saddle. If the horse humped his back or was frightened I would lie still for a few moments. Then I would try again and wait until the next session before I asked any more from the horse. If the horse was relaxed and totally unafraid, then I put my leg over his back and sat in the saddle for a few seconds. I always crouched and did not sit up straight on this first occasion because I did not want to frighten him by seeming to tower over his head. If he was very relaxed, I sometimes offered a titbit while I was on his back.

The methods were many and varied and depended entirely on the reactions of each individual horse. Once he was happy with me on his back in the small loose box, I then took him into my large loose box which is about twice the size of the small one. Here I was able to ride round, at the walk, in both directions. When the horse was happy with this, I would take him into my small, gravel-surfaced yard outside and mount from a mounting block. This yard is about twenty metres long by about four metres wide – an ideal size – long enough for a few paces of jogging. It is completely enclosed, having the stable wall on one side and post-and-rail fencing and gates on the other three sides. When the horse accepted this, I would open the gate and ride to Thorne Court along a woodland track which leads to the oval lawn in front of the house. This route is ideal as it gives a circular ride and is of just the right distance being about 1,000 metres in total which is quite far enough for these first outings.

I was breaking youngsters for a local farming family who had fields full of horses that they had bred. Some were kept and others were sold. One, in particular, was sent to me to break as the family wanted him as a hunter. He was very difficult to train. I remember his tearing round the small stable after I had just slid off him following my first attempt at lying across the saddle. He had arched his back in no uncertain terms so I did not try to sit astride. He flew round the box in terror and eventually put his face into the corner and nearly stood on his head! I was, after some time, able to ride him out but always had to sit tight. For some reason, I never fell off him – which was surprising.

Eventually, his owner came to try him and take him home but I was not at all happy about the horse being kept as a hunter. He bucked off his owner within moments of his mounting then cantered across the field, leaped over the high gate from the yard and galloped down the lane towards the main road. I checked that his owner was all right then went after the horse. He was grazing contentedly by Thorne Court. I brought him back and talked to the owner. We decided that the best thing would be to send the horse to the Newmarket sales in the autumn. However, just to satisfy myself, I rode him in the afternoon and he was fine. I think he was afraid of an unknown rider on his back.

Some time later I prepared him for the sales; he looked a picture when he went to Tattersalls. As I led him towards the inner sales ring

I saw some friends who were very taken by the horse's looks and interested because I had started him. I was concerned lest they bid for him for I knew his temperament would not suit their purpose of producing show hunters. However, I could not tell them at that time not to bid and so I looked them straight in the face and said in a loud voice,

'This horse is going to make a fantastic chaser. He could even win the Grand National!'

Luckily, they understood what I was trying to say and did not bid. He fetched a satisfactory price and went to a well-known trainer. It all ended happily for he had the right attitude to go over fences with a brave jockey on board.

I could usually tell, as soon as a horse walked up the yard, what temperament and aptitude it had. Chesnut, Arab-type mares gave me the most trouble when it came to harness work. They would ogle at everything with eyes out on stalks, walk up the yard with what I call the 'wet-knicker walk' – crouching down with fear and clearly terrified of anything new.

Not all the horses that came to be trained for harness work took to the idea of being driven but I would try. After a few days I would contact the owner and invite him or her to come and see the animal's progress. I would then explain that I did not think that it was going to make the kind of quiet ride-and-drive animal they wanted. In some cases, I broke the pony to ride and it was then sold as a satisfactory and much-loved riding animal so, all was not lost.

One pony arrived and behaved in the manner just described. I had a skilled teenage pupil (whom I will call Mary) here on a scholarship course. (The BDS awarded two or three scholarships each year to talented Junior Whips to enable them to have a few days' instruction with a recognised BDS Instructor.) While Mary was here she mentioned that she was being given an unbroken, three-year-old part-Arab. This worried me because Mary's non-horsey, although very supportive parents, had no facilities for breaking a pony to drive and ride. I said that she could come here for three weeks as our guest and that I would start the animal for her and teach her how to train it.

Before the pony arrived, the owner telephoned and told me that I must keep a headcollar on it in the stable. This seemed odd to me but I soon discovered why. When I went into the stable with the animal's food, it would bite and kick – with intent. I had planned that Mary would do all the stable work, mucking out, grooming, picking out of feet and such jobs and I would simply oversee the proceedings. However, it soon became clear that I was going to have to do everything. When I took the pony's feed to the far end of the stable, I had to bring the pony back to the door with me because if I tried to get past it while it was eating, I was very likely to be kicked. It had to be tied up during mucking out but I still had to be mighty careful. Picking up the feet was a highly dangerous business and brushing its legs was even worse.

I started to lunge him and got him going well enough for Mary to continue but as soon as she tried to work him, he flew at her with his teeth. So, I had to do all the lungeing and long-reining. He reached the stage of pulling the motor-tyre. One morning we were walking him along our farm track. There was a pony in a nearby field and, on seeing it, the youngster refused to go any further. He beat a tattoo on the ground with his front feet. He took off. I hung on and pulled him round into a wheat field. He became caught up in the traces and fell down. He lay quite still for a few moments with blood coming from his mouth. Both Mary and I thought that he was dying. He had, in fact, bitten his tongue. We unravelled the harness and he stood up unhurt. I sighed and shook my head,

'You really must not keep this pony, Mary. You'll have no pleasure from him. Contact the owner and say you don't want him,' I told her firmly. 'Blame me if you like. Tell her I say that the pony will never go well in harness.'

I was so concerned for Mary's safety that I wanted her to have nothing to do with that pony. So Mary's parents contacted the owner who arranged to come and collect the pony with her trailer. Before loading the pony some padding was needed for inside the trailer so I told Mary to go and get a sack from the area beyond the pony's stable. This entailed going past the pony and Mary was, not unnaturally, afraid of the animal by this time and hesitated.

'Tell the owner to go and get the sack,' I said, 'it's her pony and her trailer…'

Mary went to pass on the message and I saw the owner go into the pony's stable with Mary a few steps behind her. They emerged with

the sack and the owner took it to the trailer. Mary came up to me and with a grin on her face,

'He bit her!' she whispered gleefully.

The owner silently emerged from the trailer. I was tempted to ask, 'Everything all right?' but I didn't. She knew very well how horrible her pony was. No wonder that she wanted to give it away.

On another occasion, a three-year-old arrived, with his breeder and his teenage son, for me to break as a hunter. I had broken three horses for this farmer who had hunted them successfully for years. The horsebox arrived in the drive and the breeder, whom I will call Joe, said to me, 'Have you got a headcollar?'

'Yes,' I replied puzzled, 'but how come he isn't wearing one?'

'We had to drive him into the box behind my old hunter,' came the response. It did not bode well and so, instead of a headcollar, I brought out my heavy-duty breaking cavesson and went into the horsebox. In the restricted space the horse could not resist much and I managed to fit the cavesson on him. Joe led him down the ramp and into the yard towards the stable whereupon the youngster ploughed ahead, almost smashing his way through the substantial rail fence at the end of the yard. Joe managed to turn him and put him into the stable

'He's a bit of a handful, I'm afraid,' said Joe apologetically.

'A lot of a handful,' I corrected him. 'I really don't think I'll be able to do anything with him while he's so wild.'

Joe tipped his cap back and scratched his head.

'What are we going to do then, gal?' he asked me.

'If you can get him as far as my training ring I'll have a go at lungeing him. Wait and see how he goes. If I can get him going in both directions, I'll do my best to break him for you, Joe,' I told him.

'Fine by me, gal,' Joe agreed with some relief.

Joe and his strong teenage son took hold of the lunge rein and started to walk towards my training arena. The horse plunged forward and the men hung on. It flung itself around, charging everywhere and half-rearing until it fell over backwards. I heard a crack as it hit the ground. It lay quite still, sweating profusely and I was certain that it had suffered terminal damage.

'I'll ring Gerald Hudson – he's my vet,' I told Joe.

'No, not yet. The horse is probably just concussed,' said, Joe. 'He'll be on his feet in a minute.'

I wasn't convinced. I was sure the horse was never going to get up again and so I rushed into the house and telephoned Gerald. I told him briefly what had happened. As luck would have it Gerald was at home eating his lunch,

'I'll be right with you,' he said mid-mouthful. He left his meal and immediately drove the fourteen miles to Thorne Lodge.

When Gerald arrived the horse was still lying, alive, on the ground. Gerald, very gently, lifted the uppermost hind leg then put it down again. He lifted the front leg then put it down. He raised the horse's head – and the animal died. Gerald stood up and looked at us.

'Sorry,' he said quietly, 'nothing I can do.'

Poor Joe was devastated. He adored his horses and had bred and brought up this youngster with great hopes of its being a future hunter. It was a tremendously sad occasion for us all.

I telephoned the huntsman, Tom Batterbee, at the hunt kennels and asked him if he could come and remove the horse, which he did.

'When you get the carcase into the flesh room, will you let me know what caused its death?' I asked him. He agreed and rang back later,

'Looks like the horse had a broken bone at the top of his spine just behind his skull.'

'Thanks for letting me know,' I replied and put the phone down feeling physically sick. It was all terribly upsetting and I seriously wondered whether I had had enough of breaking horses for other people.

But, loyal as ever, Joe had another horse booked in for me to break. This was a five-year-old 17.2 gelding. His breaking had been left late as he had had problems with weak hind pasterns when he was born and Gerald (who was also Joe's vet) had advised that he should be given plenty of time to develop before he was worked. After the shock of the fatal accident with the other horse, Joe was adamant that the animal be well handled before he came to me for breaking. In due course the horse arrived and did not give a moment's trouble.

I still had my doubts about continuing to break in other people's horses. However, I had another horse booked to break but agreed to do it as I did not want to let the owner down. This was a three-year-old Anglo-Arab filly that had been bred by her elderly owner. She was, right from the start, very ungenerous. It took me three-quarters of an hour to get her going on the right rein on the lunge. She reared, plunged and tried to walk over me, making every effort to prevent my passing along her right side. She threw herself down in the stable on two occasions in spite of my being extremely careful when tightening her girth.

When I eventually sat on her, in the yard, she gave the feeling of 'disappearing' in front, behind and at the side giving the worst possible 'downhill' ride that I have ever experienced. When I told her owner how she felt, he said that he would like to sit on her in order to appreciate what I meant. She stood quietly while he mounted.

'What do you think of her?' I asked him.

'I've never sat on such an uncomfortable horse in my life,' he replied and got off. 'What's best?'

'Cambridge sales, I think,' I replied. 'Say she's the property of an elderly gentleman. She's young, sound and quite good-looking. Give her another chance with somebody else. Neither of us gets on with her, do we?'

The owner agreed and off to the sales she went. She was bought by a dealer, for which I was glad, as I had dreaded some teenager might have been tempted to buy her; she had been turned out to perfection and looked a picture at the sales.

I kept well away from her while she was being sold. I did not want anyone to connect me with such a horrible horse.

CHAPTER 18

Colorado and Wisconsin

As a result of publicity given to my books, my demonstrations on breaking and my showing of instructional slides, I was invited to speak at the 1973 conference of the Carriage Association of America in Colorado. I was very excited, therefore to receive an invitation to stay with Phil and Georgia Hoffman at their wonderful home in New Jersey prior to going to Colorado. Phil Hoffman's chauffeur met me at the airport in New York and drove me in a huge motor car to New Jersey. I received a marvellous welcome from the Hoffmans.

I had wondered what I could take to give as a present and decided that a 'coaching token' would be unusual and of interest. I had seen Sandy Watney's collection of coaching tokens; some of them were about the size of a 2p piece, others a little smaller and some bigger. They had been struck in the late eighteenth century as tokens of gratitude to John Palmer who had founded the mail coach system in 1784.

A coin dealer had a stall in Bury St Edmunds market and I had been fortunate to find two such tokens on his stall. I kept one for myself and gave the other to my host. The coin is mentioned in Fairman Rogers' *Manual of Coaching*. When I told Phil this, he immediately looked it up and was delighted to have such a token. I was equally pleased that my idea had been such a success.

After breakfast the following morning, we waited in the Hoffmans' kitchen for the helicopter to arrive. Soon we saw the leaves on the apple tree fluttering and a moment later the helicopter landed a few feet from the house. We ducked under the rotor blades and boarded. I had never been in a helicopter before and so this was a huge novelty. We flew to Trenton airport where Phil's private jet was waiting to take us to Colorado. I remember Phil remarking,

'I wonder what the pilots have fixed for our lunch?' and could not help but compare this with my experience of the usual airline trolleys with food in plastic containers. (I later sampled what the pilots had fixed for our lunch: delicious pumpkin pie, among other things!). Eight of us boarded the jet and after take-off we sat round a table looking at photographs of coaching and driving in general. The pilot was asked to fly low over the Grand Canyon so that I could see it from the air.

The final part of the journey was by car from the airport in Colorado Springs, at the foot of the Rocky Mountains, to the Broadmoor Hotel which occupies 500 acres to the south-west of the city. Its altitude of 6,000 feet above sea level took a little getting used to. My fingers swelled and there was so much static electricity that my shoes seemed to drag on the carpet of my bedroom. I got an electric shock when I touched a light switch or held onto the rail beside the escalator that took me up to my room.

The following day I was invited to visit the 18,000-foot mountain, Pike's Peak, but such a height can cause altitude sickness. As always, on trips like this, I was there to work. I was *not* on holiday and I had to keep fit and well at all costs. I declined the invitation and did not join the others of our group who went, one of whom subsequently spent the whole weekend in bed recovering from the experience.

The Carriage Association conference got underway with about 250 'buggy nuts', as the CAA members call themselves, registered as delegates.

After dinner on the first evening, I was asked to show the film of the BDS show at Smith's Lawn in 1972 and this was very well received. The following day I spoke about harness, vehicles and breaking and illustrated my talk with slides. I also showed films of Sandy Watney coaching in the New Forest and horses at the Royal

Mews being put to carriages for the State Opening of Parliament. These were enjoyed so much that there were groans of disappointment when the films ended.

In the afternoon we visited the Broadmoor carriage house which was adjacent to the hotel and it was here that I saw the small roof-seat break which later influenced my choice of vehicle for my pony team. CAA member, John Wort, kindly took photographs of a number of carriages in this collection which I used in my book *Looking at Carriages*. These included a massive covered wagon of the type used by pioneers in the opening up of the western part of the USA to white settlers.

The evening was taken up with a talk, dinner and an auction of numerous driving-related items including a cutter (sleigh) and a one-horse treadmill.

The next morning's programme included talks and demonstrations on carriage restoration, cane work, harness-making and the work of the wheelwright. After lunch, we went to the rodeo arena where I saw, for the first time, a covered wagon with a team put to. I found the owner, Lynn West,

'Would you give me a ride on the wagon, please?' I asked him.

'Sure, ma'am. Jump up here beside me.' I scrambled up onto the seat and settled myself, explaining that I was attending the conference of the Carriage Association of America. 'Well, in that case, how about you driving the team? Go round the track between the stands and the arena.'

I was thrilled! I took up the reins in my usual 'classical' style: anchored in the left hand with the right hand in front to guide and assist. When I was ready I spoke to the team,

'Walk on!' Nothing happened.

'Walk on!' I commanded again. The horses didn't even flick their ears in response. I could sense Lynn was amused as he said,

'Just what you doing, ma'am? They ain't gonna go anywhere like that. See here.' He leaned across me, 'Take the left reins in your left hand and the right reins in your right hand. See how the lead reins go down the insides of the wheelers? You just flap against the wheelers' sides. They'll move then.'

It broke every rule in book of classical driving! There was no way

Sallie driving a covered wagon at the rodeo arena in Colorado. (Photo used by kind permission of Western Horseman)

that I could possibly do this with all those buggy nuts watching and photographing me from the stands. I had been continually emphasising the importance of holding the reins in the classical style: anchored in the left hand and the right hand placed in front of the left to assist and support at all times. Fortunately, the team went forward on command from Lynn and we trotted happily round the track. I was really enjoying this novel experience! As we approached the entrance where we had begun our circuit I thought that the team might try to edge left-handed towards it. In anticipation of this potential problem, I put a little pressure on the off-lead rein. I underestimated their obedience for they assumed that I was asking them to turn right. The two leaders immediately turned. I halted them but by now the leaders were standing quietly at an angle to the wheelers. There were yards of loose rein dangling everywhere and Lynn and I were laughing as I tried to scoop up this 'leather spaghetti'. Later a photograph of us was published in the CAA Journal with a caption: 'Sallie Walrond from Suffolk, England, in an unaccustomed situation!'

Later that day I spoke on driven dressage with Phil driving a team through one of the tests. Then came a tandem and trandem (a three abreast) of magnificent greys driven by Evan Shaw and Harrison Cutler. They were followed by Mrs Paige and Mrs F. W. Insley's lovely

Saddlebred horse harnessed to a buckboard which they allowed me to drive. It was fascinating to experience the sprung wood of the buckboard.

The conference concluded with a banquet and more films of BDS shows. The next day we flew back to New Jersey and I was privileged to drive Phil's team of lovely Holstein horses. They were so obedient that they trotted happily along the left-hand side of the road.

'Sallie – you're in the USA, not England, now!' Phil remarked.

★　　★　　★

The following year, the President of the Midwest Carriage Association, Ann Friend, invited me to Wisconsin to conduct a seminar for the group's members. John and Ann Friend lived in a beautiful, luxurious house with a garden filled with such colourful birds as red cardinals and blue jays. Chipmunks ran along the garden walls next to the kitchen while we ate breakfast and skunks and racoons had made their homes in the grounds.

Barry Dickinson was in charge of the Friends' horses and carriages. He explained the intricacies of American stable management; I learned a great deal from him and we exchanged many views on

The trandem in Colorado. (Photo used by kind permission of Western Horseman)

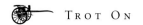

training and showing horses.

The temperature-controlled stables housed Saddlebreds which wore neck wraps all the time to prevent their gullets from coarsening. Their long tails were plaited to prevent them from being trodden on in the stable. Wire-mesh screen doors over the outside wooden doors prevented flies from entering the stables, yet maintained ventilation. About fifty vehicles were housed in another building.

A four-year-old Morgan horse was put to a quarter-lock runabout so that the owner could take photographs of me driving his horse for the Morgan horse magazine. I learned much about the American harness used with such a turnout.

Chicago Radio sent an interviewer to speak to me. I was glad I was given little warning of this because I had no time to be nervous. Just as well, for the programme was heard by about eleven million listeners!

People came from great distances to attend the seminar. I showed slides and the film of the BDS show before we harnessed a beautiful hackney horse called The Astronaut and put him to a Stanhope gig. I was told that it is traditional in this part of the USA for breeching not to be used with this vehicle. However, a kicking strap is obligatory as 'no gentleman would risk his neck by driving without one'. A long-cheeked, curb gig bit and bearing rein completed the picture.

We then put The Astronaut to a George IV phaeton. The bridle had a Buxton bit and a pulley bearing rein. Before I mounted to drive The Astronaut, I commented on the extreme length of the reins as I gathered them up in my hands. I was told that the reason for this excessive length is that if the lady Whip suspects impending danger, she can then hand the reins to the liveried groom who is sitting on the rumble seat at the rear of the phaeton behind the hood.

It caused great merriment when I remarked that the last thing that I intended to do would be to pass the reins back to Barry because I did not think that I would be able to let go for long enough if I were being run away with by The Astronaut. There was, of course, no 'impending danger' and The Astronaut behaved perfectly when I drove him.

I showed the vehicle slides after the lunch break. Ann and John Friend arranged with Barry for many of their vehicles to be photographed at a later date, so that I was able to add them to my collection and also use them in my book *Looking at Carriages*.

The following day I showed the slides on breaking. Then a pair of Tennessee Walking horses were put to a break, and later The Astronaut and a Saddlebred were driven in tandem so that this style of driving could be explained.

More movies were shown to complete the seminar and we all agreed that we had learned a great deal from each other in this exchange of views.

Ann Friend generously gave me a set of sleigh bells which I brought back to England to put onto my tandem.

CHAPTER 19

Pupils

By 1975, THE DEMAND FOR CARRIAGE DRIVING instruction was increasing. The BDS had grown and combined driving was becoming popular. I had used Ali for teaching a few pupils but he was not really suitable. He was too onward going and at times could pull very hard. He certainly could not be used for a nervous novice as he would have frightened them. However, his two daughters, Alibi (Libby) and Razali (Raz) were now five and four years old and both had very quiet temperaments, which they must have inherited from their mother, Blueberry. Fortunately, though, they had inherited some of Ali's action.

I was beginning to receive enquiries for lessons as a result of being seen with Ali at shows and travelling the country showing slides and films. I ran the BDS film library which by now contained a number of films made of BDS shows and meets. Area Commissioners who wanted to provide their area members with entertainment during the winter months could hire these. There had been discussions at BDS meetings about making a commentary to accompany the slides but I knew that this would not have worked because no two audiences are the same and a commentary that might have been suitable for one audience would not have fitted another. When I speak, I encourage the audience to ask questions as we go along while the relevant picture is still on the screen. Also, I was adding new slides to the few original ones almost weekly. It was far simpler for me to show the slides and give the talks, adjusting my commentary accordingly. Once or twice I sent the slides to someone else to show and they came back to me with some of the glass mounts broken having been damaged in the post. Another time, a hirer had wrapped them carefully in some kind of padding to prevent breakage. The tiny fibres from the padding stuck to the glass mounts and I had to take every single slide from its mount and clean it before remounting each picture. It was because of such problems that I preferred to keep the slides safely and show them myself.

On one occasion I was invited by the Duchess of Devonshire to stay at her home at Chatsworth House so that I could give a talk to the Shetland Pony Society enthusiasts. The Duchess was very interested in Shetland ponies and had a herd of beautiful black ponies. They all moved well and had pretty heads with big brown eyes. I was so impressed by her ponies that I was tempted to buy four youngsters to get a team going. Staying at Chatsworth was a memorable occasion and I felt very privileged to have been invited. Offers to unpack my suitcase and have breakfast brought to my bedroom were huge novelties and I left feeling very pampered.

Many people took me, as a complete stranger, into their homes and were so generous with their hospitality. I will always be grateful for the kindness I received throughout the world. This had all been the result of my early days with harness horses, being fortunate to be in the right place at the right time and being helped and advised by the right people.

★　　★　　★

When I began teaching carriage driving seriously, I would take pupils at Thorne Lodge for a half or whole day. I was fortunate to have access to a disused airfield a short distance away. Once over the main road, a country lane opens out onto miles of concrete airfield tracks on land owned by neighbouring farmers, who gave permission for us to go anywhere on the airfield, and so the routes could be many and varied. This meant that neither the ponies nor the pupils became bored. It was not long before I was taking residential pupils and so, if pupils were staying for several days, I would make a real effort to take them on different routes each time. With luck they lost their sense of direction, so never got bored with the airfield!

I used to give all pupils, regardless of their experience, a session with the reins attached to my weights and pulleys rein-handling apparatus (see the diagram below). I was fortunate to have been given this by John Maiburg who had come to Thorne Lodge from Holland to drive the tandem. He told me that he always used weights and pulleys to simulate the reins and their effect on the horses' mouths for teaching driving in Holland. He had a spare set in his car which he generously gave to me.

I would clamp them to the kitchen table so that the pupil could become accustomed to the feel and gain practice before trying the real thing on my ponies. It was much easier for pupils to understand the classical method of rein handling as they watched me demonstrate handling the reins attached to the weights. They could see for themselves how a slight turn of the wrist or movement across the body with the hands would put more pressure onto one side of the horse's mouth. Pulling on a rein raised or lowered the weight, proving that what I was saying was true, whereas the effect was not so obvious with a horse. Most pupils were surprised to see how much the weight

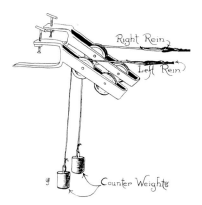

Driving weights and pulleys for single driving.

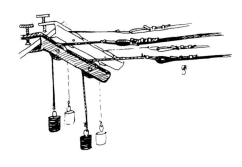

Driving weights and pulleys for tandems etc.

rose with what seemed to be a tiny movement of the hand. After all the explanations and demonstrations, pupils then practised the rein handling until they felt confident, and then did their best to apply the same techniques when driving the ponies. This was an excellent method of teaching and, generally speaking, pupils became very skilled at classical rein handling, which gave them a solid foundation for their future driving. This method also had the added benefit that my ponies' mouths remained light and responsive throughout their lives, as they had not been subjected to an unintentional roughness.

I quickly discovered that it was best to have one pupil at a time so that a one-to-one relationship could be developed.

In the early days of teaching, a family consisting of an English father, an Italian mother and their two children came for a day's instruction. They practised rein handling on the weights and pulleys before they took up the real reins after Libby had been harnessed to a light, four-wheeled dogcart.

I always drove until we reached the perimeter track of the airfield and the final leg home. One reason was that it prevented my ponies from being harmed by pupils because my driving for this distance at each end of the lesson kept my ponies going how they should. Another reason was the safety factor, especially crossing the main road, and the third reason was that pupils could watch my rein handling before taking the reins themselves.

For the morning session, the father sat beside me and the mother and children sat in the back watching him. Father drove quite well and appeared to learn much during the morning's drive. After the lunch break, all the family helped with the harnessing and putting to and the Italian wife sat beside me as we proceeded to the airfield. When we reached the perimeter track we changed sides and I passed the reins to her. I always kept my hand below the pupil's hands on the reins so that I had immediate control if there was a problem. To my horror, the wife took a rein in each hand, held them apart and shook the reins onto Libby's unsuspecting back and exclaimed, in a loud voice,

''ow do I make 'im go?'

I was furious but managed to contain my anger. Had she learned nothing from watching her husband that morning? Libby obligingly

stepped forward on feeling the strange 'aid' on her back but I stopped
her and carefully explained again everything I had taught during the
morning session.

I let each child take the reins for a short distance during the afternoon in order to encourage them. Later in the day, however, I told the
father that it would be better if he came on his own and I taught him
to drive then he, in turn, could teach his wife and children. I vowed
that I would never again take a whole family of beginners and try to
teach them all at once. It was just not fair on my ponies and I was not
going to have them ruined.

One of my earliest residential pupils was Minta Winn. Her parents
wrote to me from Co. Cork, Eire, where they lived in Kilbrittain Castle. As a child, Minta had shown an aptitude for driving and now that
she was in her teens wished to improve her technique. I somewhat
reluctantly agreed to have this unknown teenager to stay for about a
week. She arrived in a private light aircraft flown by her father. A few
years later, Minta herself would fly the plane with her father as passenger. They flew over Thorne Lodge at the agreed time. On hearing
the aircraft's engine, I went out into the garden and waved and they
headed off towards the airfield across the road. By the time I had
arrived on the airfield to collect Minta and her luggage, they had
landed on one of the runways.

*Sallie receiving a prize
from HRH The Prince
Philip at the BDS Show.
Minta Winn is the
passenger.*

Minta was a 'natural' right from the start. During the first week she progressed from driving Libby and Raz in single to driving them in pair and by the end of the week she was harnessing, putting to and driving them in tandem. Her father flew in to collect her and she came back later that year prior to driving at the BDS show where she was placed third in the Junior Whip class with Libby. Minta returned several times and she eventually progressed to driving the team. She then won the BDS Show Junior Whip championship with another of my ponies, Cottenham Loretto, who was only five years old. Minta's

Competing with Cottenham Loretto at Windsor in the Concours d'Elegance.

Minta's son, Rupert, with judge Audrey Sinclair. (Photo reproduced by kind permission of Kevin Stoddart)

achievements were many and included winning the BDS Show championship with a team, a pair and a tandem of ponies that all belonged to different owners. I am extremely proud that she was one of my pupils. She, in turn, is teaching her son, Rupert, to drive.

As the driving instruction increased, I stopped taking horses to break. I had neither the time nor the accommodation. People often brought their own horses when they came for instruction and they were housed in my only spare loose box. Some came with two ponies and we were able to divide the loose box into two little stables with a pair of swinging bales in Bert Barley fashion. There was adequate space for ponies up to about 12 hands and, as this arrangement was usually only for three nights at the most, it worked well. My animals were all accommodated in the large stable that could take four ponies tied up in stalls: three along one side and a fourth in one corner. Swinging bales separated the three and chains ran across behind them preventing them from backing into the fourth pony. They wore neck straps attached to ropes and logs that allowed a certain freedom of movement.

The system worked well and I could do all the early morning stable chores for the four ponies in about an hour. Mucking out was easy as the drainage ran behind the three stalls down a central gulley to the back of the box with a drain in the outer wall. Automatic drinkers

Early morning stables at Thorne Lodge, showing Libby, Raz, Loretto and Patrick. (Photo reproduced by kind permission of John Wort)

meant no carting water around or buckets knocked over. Quartering and grooming was minimal: I would pick out the feet of all four with a hoof pick, brush off stable stains before washing quarters and tails if necessary. All the hay and straw was stacked in the spare corner so as not to have to cart it each day. Feeds were put into iron mangers on the floor and hay was fed loose. There was never any wastage of the ponies' feed or my time.

Pupils were booked for a four-day course that proved ideal because they had time to settle into the routine. They departed having learned an enormous amount. It is mileage that counts towards becoming proficient in carriage driving and they certainly achieved that during the four days.

As teaching driving rapidly became a full-time occupation, I had to devise a routine for meals and catering. It involved being well organised months in advance. All the main courses for the meals were prepared at the beginning of the year so that they were in the deep freezer ready for use when they were wanted. Starters and puddings were prepared on Mondays when I returned from shopping so that the cooking time was minimal when the pupil was here. I was not Cordon Bleu trained but somehow the rumour got around that I was, which was very flattering. My cooking was, in fact, very simple. The Aga helped enormously because the kind of dishes I prepared just 'lurked' in an oven until required.

My daily routine was to go out to the ponies before breakfast and do all the morning stables. Then, at about 8am I would come back into the house and prepare breakfast for the pupil. I did as many household chores as possible until 10am when the instruction began. We would drive until about 12.30pm then return for a snack lunch in the kitchen after the ponies had been settled and fed. At 2pm we would go out again and drive until about 4pm. Once the ponies had been set fair we had a tea break. It was during this time that I usually tried to clean some of the harness that we might not be using again during the course.

I would then put the dinner into the Aga and go out to settle the ponies for the night. Bill would come home from the office and, after a bath and change of clothes, we would have dinner, which was a proper meal with wine, or whatever drinks the pupil chose. After

dinner, I showed slides to the pupil before finally staggering to bed.

Courses usually began on a Tuesday and finished on Friday after tea. After the pupil had gone, I then set about cleaning whatever harness had not been cleaned during the week, in preparation for the next course. A widowed friend, former guitarist and singer Elton Hayes, used to arrive at about 4.30pm on Fridays to help with cleaning the mountain of harness in exchange for dinner consisting of all the left-over dishes from the week! Pupils frequently offered to stay and clean harness after their course had finished but I did not think it fair to expect them to do this, for many had long journeys back to their homes. Of course, if they lived nearby and wished to stay then I was grateful for the help.

Pupils came from Australia, New Zealand and America as well as from all over Europe. One American lady telephoned to say that she was coming to Europe and therefore wanted to come to stay with us for two days. I imagined that she thought that once she was in Europe, Thorne Lodge was a short jump across the ditch. I booked her in for instruction and, as usual, did my utmost to teach her as much as I was able in the time available.

A number of pupils wanted to drive only a tandem and assured me that they had plenty of experience with singles. Even so, I used to give them a session in rein handling with the weights and pulleys, at the kitchen table, before we went to the stables. Then they drove both ponies in single harness before I let them handle the tandem reins. Once this was accomplished, they always agreed that it had been a sensible and safe approach because they had grown to know me and the ponies before they attempted the difficult art of tandem driving.

At the other end of the scale, I would have complete beginners of the middle-aged, rather nervous lady variety who really wanted a holiday that might introduce her to a new pastime. Usually, pupils who intended to drive only a single turnout would begin with Raz, who was a clockwork type of pony, and then progress to Libby. If all went well, and they were happy, they drove two more onward-going animals before having their last lesson with Raz, in order to send them home full of confidence. It was interesting how they nearly all remarked, during their last session, 'Raz seemed to go so much better than when I first drove her.' I would tell them that it was because they were now driving so much better than they had on their first lesson.

One delightful lady drove only Raz during her four days. I remember, on her last lesson when I was watching her put Raz to the vehicle, she held a trace end and said to me,

'I know this goes on somewhere. Don't tell me, I'll work it out for myself!'

'Oh dear,' I thought, 'I must be a pretty bad teacher.' It was the eighth time in four days that she had harnessed up and put to! I kept quiet and, sure enough, she did work it out for herself.

I often had enquiries from people who had ridden for years and wanted to see if they would enjoy driving. Such a 'taster' lesson was booked by Saskia Barker who arrived with her daughter, Catherine, then a tiny baby. I could scarcely conceal my horror but, because Raz and I liked Saskia, we did our best to teach her as much as possible under the circumstances. Saskia soon became hooked on driving. Catherine is now becoming keen and we have plans for Junior Whip classes in the future.

Saskia Barker driving Hazelnut to a governess cart, in front of the Royal Box at Smith's Lawn during the 2003 BDS Show, where they won two trophies. (Photo reproduced by kind permission of G. and C. Cook, Pleasure Prints)

One pupil brought two lovely hackney ponies that had been driven as a pair. She wanted them put into tandem. They were superb and gave no trouble. I drove them for miles on the airfield and enjoyed every moment. I was later offered them, on permanent loan, and I was

The late David Snowdon, aged thirteen, a talented pupil, driving Peanuts at the 1993 BDS Show, after winning the Junior Whip Championship. (Photo reproduced by kind permission of Hamish Mitchell)

very tempted. They stood about 12 hands, too small for me to ride, and I realised that I would be keeping them purely for showing. There was more to life than going to horse shows and winning prizes. If I took these ponies, I would have to keep them until the end of their lives and I already had enough ponies to look after. So, in the end, I declined the offer.

Some pupils brought horses or ponies with serious problems. I used to tell pupils to explain all their worries to me and I would do my best to help. I assured them that I would not tell anyone about things they told me, for trust and confidentiality were vital. Once they realised that their secrets would be kept, they revealed much. Such knowledge made my far job easier. I never gossiped because these confidences had to be kept. The driving world is a very small world and no one wants everyone to know about the problems they are experiencing. Indeed, some pupils preferred not to tell anyone that I had helped them. I did not mind at all because I obtained enormous satisfaction from watching a past pupil working a horse, in a corner of a field at an event or show and seeing it going really well in a superb outline and knowing that a few months ago it had been working with an 'upside-down neck' or an open mouth and hollow back. It was a real bonus to me when a past pupil was successful.

The 'downside' now is that my pupils frequently beat me! But after the initial minor shock, I feel very proud that I have been able to help and I genuinely feel great pleasure from the reflected glory.

★   ★   ★

For some time I had been teaching Chris Rushforth, who lived near Cambridge, to train and drive her Shetland ponies. Sometimes she brought them to Thorne Lodge, sometimes I travelled to her stables. It grew into a two-way arrangement: Chris helped me with the pair or tandem and I helped her. There was no financial exchange in either direction. I had reduced my teaching and cut down on taking residential pupils; hence I had more time and gained enormous pleasure from helping people with their own animals. I acted as her groom at a few shows and so was able to share some of the glory when she was successful.

In 2000, the magazine, *Horse*, ran a competition to find the most worthy 'unsung hero' and invited readers to submit their suggestions. I knew nothing about it until Chris telephoned me one day, to tell me that she had put my name forward and hoped that I would not mind.

Chris Rushforth accompanied by Andrew Derbyshire, driving Oliver and William at the 1999 meet of the Tandem Club. (Photo reproduced by kind permission of Andrew Crockett)

I was amazed and flattered that Chris should think of me in this way because I certainly did not consider myself to be an 'unsung hero'. The magazine was giving a wonderful prize of £250 of Mountain Horse clothing to each of the nominators and candidates who were featured in an article in *Horse* each month. This made the idea very attractive to us both!

Chris duly sent an article explaining how I had started teaching her to drive with Raz and how I had guided her through breaking and training her pony, Oliver. Her aim was to win the combined driving at the East Anglian Native Pony Show, which she did in 1998. Chris then trained a second pony, William, and drove at the Tandem Club meet to gain her membership and be awarded her tandem bars.

The magazine's reporter interviewed me and naturally asked me why I had trained Chris for no financial gain. The answer was simple. I had helped Chris because she was young, keen and talented. She always worked very hard and did most of the things I suggested in training her ponies. She usually achieved the results that we both wanted because she has a natural aptitude and ability for driving and handling her ponies. We waited to see if the magazine was interested and to our delight we reached the finals and received our prize. Chris and I went to the Mountain Horse clothing outlet and had a very enjoyable morning choosing clothes from this marvellous manufacturer.

CHAPTER 20

Lowther 1975

Up to 1975 no one had driven a tandem in a combined driving event because classes had been open only to teams, pairs and singles. In the mid-1970s I was on the Combined Driving Committee, as it was then known, under the chairmanship of Bernard Mills. I managed to persuade the committee that it would be perfectly feasible to complete a three-day event with a tandem. Several committee members expressed doubts but the organisers of the Lowther trials in the Lake District agreed to include a class for tandems providing that it was the last on the programme because of the possibility of an accident causing havoc with the timing. I did not disappoint them.

In February I began a programme to get Libby and Raz, then aged five and four years old, fit for the Lowther trials which would take place in August. I clipped each pony and rode her out for an hour on a couple of occasions with the Suffolk hounds when we mostly walked. The reason for this was that at two nearby meets, I knew that the likely draw contained a hard-bottomed and shallow river crossing. I asked permission from the Master, to bring out first one pony and then the next, on the same day and I was able to walk Libby through the crossing after the hounds had left the covert. I then took

Libby home and returned, 'in search of hounds' with Raz, later in the day.

This was the start of their water-crossing training. I continued the water training by boxing the ponies to suitable crossings and long-reining through the water before driving single then tandem. I enlisted the help of nearby friends who had water crossings on their land and would box the ponies to their homes, put to then drive to the water crossing where we schooled as needed.

I also accustomed the ponies to wearing the sleigh bells I had brought back from Wisconsin. The idea was that Libby, the leader, would wear them at Lowther as a warning to spectators of our approach as we sped along woodland tracks with blind bends.

In the spring, I was invited to give a driving lecture-demonstration at Anne Hammond's riding establishment at Stetchworth. I decided that, as a part of the ponies' fittening programme they should be driven the twenty miles, on the hoof, in tandem. They covered the distance in three hours on the day before the demonstration and it appeared to take nothing out of them. We gave the display the next day and returned home, on the hoof, on the third day. They met all kinds of 'horrors' along the route but nothing worried them. The worst hazard was meeting a tractor in a very narrow lane. It was towing a huge trailer stacked high with straw and as if that were not enough, on top of the straw stood a Border collie which barked at us from above as Libby went by. As leader she was perfectly free to turn round to face Raz and me but she never batted an eyelid.

In addition to getting the ponies fit and becoming accustomed to water and bells, I practised dressage in the arena at Thorne Court, set up a course of cones and devised hazards such as we might meet on the cross-country phase. Finally, the day of the Lowther event approached. The Barnard family, from Cambridge, agreed to take the ponies and myself in their lorry. Carl Barnard, then a teenager, accompanied me as groom in the dressage and cones driving. His father, Tony, was my navigator for the marathon and Sheila, Tony's wife, managed all the cooking during the weekend.

We were the only competitors in the tandem class but we took it all very seriously. We were driving a nineteenth-century Ralli car with elliptic springs, wooden wheels and shafts. Libby and Raz wore their highly polished, black leather and brass show harness and we wore 'private driving' type clothes with no crash helmets or racing colours as worn in such events today. We scored well on presentation (when the judges scrutinised the whole turnout for correctness and cleanliness) and in the dressage that followed. Next came the exciting crosscountry phase.

Tony sat beside me carrying a clipboard with copious notes about each hazard. We had reconnoitred the course beforehand, when all competitors had driven in convoy in the Lowther Estate's yellow Land Rovers to enable them to study, plan and make notes on how best to negotiate each hazard. There were two hazards we dreaded: the water crossing (despite our practice at home I was apprehensive) and a steep bank where the route lay between some very solid posts.

When our turn came we set off and the ponies were wonderful. They did not hesitate at the water and I was almost shedding tears of delight as they splashed their way across the river as though they had done this kind of thing hundreds of times. In fact, they had never been asked to cross a river of these dimensions before: all our training had been across small, shallow streams, as there are no rivers in East Anglia like those in the north. They were so trusting and obedient and I felt very proud of them.

Sallie, accompanied by Tony Barnard, driving Raz and Libby on the marathon at the Lowther Horse Driving Trials in 1975. (Photo reproduced by kind permission of Leslie Lane AIIP)

Then came the dreaded steep bank. The ponies took the gradient in their stride and wended their way between the posts, never touching one. I began to relax and felt sure that the remainder of the course was not going to give us any trouble. It was, however, a classic case of pride coming before a fall. We sped into the hazard where the route took a slalom course between a row of pine trees. Round the first tree we went, and the next, but I knew we were going too fast. I failed to hold off Raz sufficiently and the right wheel caught a projecting tree root. Very slowly but very surely we began to capsize. Tony did his utmost to keep us upright but gravity won and over we went.

Poor Raz was pulled off her feet and fell sideways, quite gently, with the left shaft under her side as the Ralli car tipped over. I heard the sound of splintering wood as the shaft and side of the vehicle broke. One quick-thinking person from the crowd sat on Raz's head to prevent her from struggling and hurting herself. Someone grabbed Libby and held her. I sat in the dirt, unhurt but furious with myself for being so careless. Tony too, was unhurt, thank goodness. I gathered my wits, got up and attempted to sort out the mess.

'Shaft's gone into her side,' I heard someone remark. I grew cold and hardly dared look at Raz, for I was sure to see a rush of blood appear from under her at any moment.

'You'll have to cut those traces to get her out,' commented someone else. I pulled myself together at last and said,

'No, the harness is far too precious, besides an ordinary knife won't go through it,' I weighed up the situation. 'Push the vehicle towards the pony to loosen the trace then it can be unhooked or unbuckled.'

A few shoves and the traces slackened. I undid the traces, the person who was sitting on Raz's head got up, and Raz scrambled to her feet quite unscathed apart from a minor graze on the side of her hock where the step had caught her. The shaft, however, was completely shattered.

The St John Ambulance crew, on seeing that I was not in need of their attention, then set to work on the shaft. They did a masterly job and their bandaging skills ensured that the break held for the remainder of the competition. Bernard Mills took charge of making the vehicle serviceable. Putting together my broken cart was a simple matter

The cones course at the Lowther Horse Driving Trials, with Raz and Libby being driven by Sallie, who is accompanied by Carl Barnard. The shaft is held together with the mend executed the day before by the St John Ambulance crew and the mudguard is missing after the turnover on the marathon. (Photo reproduced by kind permission of Leslie Lane AIIP)

after his years of experience overseeing the erection of the Big Top for his father's circuses. He took the thirty metres of washing line, which I had in my spares kit, and quickly bound the seat and the body together. It worked, although the balance was somewhat awry. Raz was put back between the shafts and Libby in the lead once more. I climbed up onto the seat with Tony beside me and was about to drive out of the hazard.

'Don't forget you've got to complete that hazard. You only went part way through it. You'll be eliminated for not completing the course if you don't,' Bernard reminded me. I had completely forgotten!

'Thanks!' I called in relief.

'Do you know which way to go?' he asked.

'No!' I replied in desperation.

'Follow me,' and Bernard set off purposely walking the route through the hazard. Libby and Raz simply followed him. After that we were on our way again. No one seemed to mind about this 'outside assistance' and we completed the course albeit twenty minutes late. When we drove through the finish we were greeted with cheers and hugs and kisses. It all became very emotional!

Tony did an excellent job with a hammer and nails to keep the seat

and body of the Ralli car together and regain its proper balance and the St John Ambulance crew's repair continued to hold the shaft together. The next morning the ponies were declared sound and later in the day completed a superb clear round in the cones course.

I could hardly believe that my ambition had been achieved as we lined up for the prizegiving: an engraved pewter tankard with the inscription 'Lowther 1975 Tandem Class' which, a year or two later, burglars stole from Thorne Lodge. We received a glowing report in *Horse and Hound* and tandem classes were included at horse driving trials from then on.

CHAPTER 21

Talking to the Gypsies

BILL AND I MET THE ARTIST, DORIS ZINKEISEN, and her twin daughters, Janet and Anne Grahame Johnstone, in the 1960s when we had all been invited to lunch by Norah Lofts, the novelist, who was a friend of Bill's mother, also a prolific writer under the name of Norah Burke. I had always been a great admirer of Doris's pictures of flamboyant carriage horses, so meeting her was a great thrill. Her daughters were also artists and worked in a similar style.

I had drawn the details of harness to illustrate *A Guide To Driving Horses* but the publishers had, quite rightly, tidied up my work to improve it for publication. I was not satisfied with my artistic endeavours and as soon as I saw Janet's and Anne's book illustrations, I knew that I wanted them to illustrate my books in future. I was working on *Encyclopaedia of Driving* and they agreed to do the line drawings.

One day I was returning home in the car from visiting them to discuss artwork when I passed some Gypsies camped by the roadside. Their horses were tethered by chains staked in the ground attached to neck straps so that the animals could graze without wandering onto the road.

I had been planning to drive Libby and Raz, in tandem, with Janet Johnstone as my passenger, from Thorne Lodge to Lincolnshire,

where a driving event was to be held later in the year. One of my quandaries had been about the lunchtime stops. It would be useful to tether the ponies to graze while we rested but I did not know how to train them for this. I had learnt, the hard way, when I had tethered Z after the trip from London that there was more to tethering than first appeared.

I turned the car round, went back to the Gypsy camp and walked across the grass to talk to the men. They were naturally very suspicious, at first, no doubt thinking I was perhaps a council official demanding that they move on or someone about to make trouble for them. When I explained that I had two ponies that I drove in tandem and I wanted to tether them during our lunch breaks on a trip to Lincolnshire, they grew interested and told me exactly how they trained their animals to tether.

'You want a strong strap to go round the neck,' one man told me.

'Will a headcollar do?' I asked. The gypsy shook his head,

'It 'll break,' he said simply. 'You want a long piece of heavy chain – not lightweight stuff, mind. Thick links that won't hurt the horse if it gets tangled. Then you want a weight. Heavy but not so heavy, mind, as you can't lift it. Know what I mean?' he asked. I nodded. 'Attach the weight to the chain. Then, you tie the horse to the chain. If the chain gets caught round a leg the horse'll try to get free – he'll panic a bit, like – but that weight'll move a bit – just enough to loosen the chain. See what I mean?' I nodded again. 'But 'cos the chain is heavy it'll drop away from the heel onto the ground – that's why you need a heavy chain.' The Gypsy warmed to his subject and continued, 'Once the horse had learnt how to get his leg free, he won't panic. He'll just lift his leg and shake the chain off. Soon, he won't even get his legs caught at all,' he grinned, 'they learn to watch where they're putting their feet. They become real experts!' he laughed. 'When he can do that then you can tether him to a stake in the ground.'

'That's marvellous. I'll try it. Thank you so much! I'm most grateful. Just what I need to know. Thank you again,' I said. I couldn't wait to get home to try it.

The Gypsies were quite right. It worked beautifully and I subsequently trained several of my ponies to tether using their technique. Although it worked with my fairly docile Connemara ponies, I would never have tried to tether a highly-strung animal like Ali. He would have been utterly terrified and galloped off in a panic.

Now that I had the tethering sorted out, I could plan for the Lincoln trip. I worked out the route and made preliminary arrangements for overnight stops with friends en route. Later, I planned to drive the route in the Land Rover, dropping off feed and equipment at all the stopping places. I also planned to note where all the telephone boxes were as, in those days, there were no mobile phones. I intended to obtain the telephone numbers of the nearest vets and farriers en route, in case of emergency. Bill made a waterproof map case and fitted it to the dashboard of the Ralli car. That way I could see the route marked on the Ordnance Survey for each day's leg of the journey and ensure I did not take any wrong turns.

Then the event was cancelled which was very disappointing. However, it had been thanks to this proposed trip that I had learned how to train horses to tether and very useful that proved to be, such as when I was competing with Raz as a single a few years later. It saved me a lot of time and effort after the marathon phase, when other people had to lead their animals about to cool them off, I simply tethered Raz – 'put her out to dry' – while I cleaned harness. She wandered around quite happily, on her tether, grazing and rolling, and cooled off very quickly. Sometimes she suffered from an itchy stomach and would sit rubbing her tummy on a hind fetlock. Then she would roll over to scrub the other side! In this contorted position she looked as if she were suffering a terrible attack of colic and passers-by were very concerned that some uncaring competitor had abandoned her in this state. If I saw such passer-bys I would call across to them to reassure them that all was well.

CHAPTER 22

Tandem Club

I<small>N</small> 1976 I WAS ATTENDING AN EVENT, on foot, and fell into conversation about tandems with Lady Vivian Cromwell, a keen tandem Whip who regularly drove her bay cobs many miles. We were joined by Richard James, another tandem Whip whose hackneys had recently won the private driving championship at the Royal International Horse Show at the White City. As the tandem talk progressed, Richard suggested that we should re-form the Tandem Club. This had originally been established in the nineteenth century to amuse young bloods in search of excitement but, inevitably with the growth of motorised transport and the decline of all forms of driving horses, had become defunct.

Vivian offered to host the inaugural meet of this revived Tandem Club at her home in Great Milton, Oxfordshire, in 1977 and I agreed to help with the organisation. All known tandem drivers were contacted and they showed considerable enthusiasm. Sandy Watney agreed to become the patron and eight Whips promised to bring their tandems. Vivian offered to accommodate my ponies for the weekend and so all the necessary arrangements were made.

I arrived with the ponies in the trailer the day before the meet and Vivian kindly offered a field which had recently been mown, hence the grass was not too lush, so that Libby and Raz could be turned out for an hour or so after their long journey. Vivian and I then went round the route of the drive. On our return we brought the ponies into the stables. People began arriving and settled their horses for the night.

When everyone was assembled we discussed possible rules for the new club. We decided to have no subscription, to eliminate administration problems and agreed to hold a raffle at each meet to cover costs. Drivers and all attending would be expected to provide good prizes and be prepared to buy lots of raffle tickets! This system has worked very satisfactorily ever since. It was also decided that the annual meet would be held in a different part of the country each year, enabling Whips from all over Britain to participate in due course. The qualification for membership of this exclusive club would be to complete the drive in a manner acceptable to fellow members.

After supper we retired to bed, despite there being one turnout short. We assumed they would arrive in the morning. A half-past two in the morning I was woken by the sound of hooves on the stones outside. My immediate thought was that it must be the people who had been due to arrive during the evening and I turned over to go to sleep again. The next thing I heard was an urgent knocking on my bedroom door.

'Sallie, are you awake?' called Vivian.

'Yes, what's the matter?' I mumbled.

'It's Libby. She's got colic.'

'Oh no!' I leapt out of bed, pulled on a shirt and jeans and rushed downstairs to the stables. Lord Cromwell, in dressing gown and slippers, was leading Libby around and trying his best to keep her on her feet but she kept collapsing in terrible pain. I rushed to my Land Rover for the colic drench that I always carried for just such emergencies. When I returned, Libby was on the floor making it impossible to administer the drench.

'I've rung for the vet,' Vivian told me, 'he'll be here shortly.' And indeed he was. He gave Libby painkillers and between us we got Libby on her feet and back to her stable.

'See how she gets on during the night. I might have to operate on her tomorrow if there's no improvement,' the vet told us. 'I'll start making the arrangements now then I can get on with it right away.'

I thanked him and he drove away. Meanwhile, Libby lay down again. I sat with my back against the stable door, and spent what was left of the night dozing fitfully and worrying. Libby passed a quiet night but her eyelids and joints were badly swollen where she had knocked herself as she had thrashed about trying to alleviate the pain. Early next morning the vet called again and decided that she was over the spasm and he need not operate.

It appeared that Libby had, in her pain, burst her way out of her stable. Fortunately, the gardener had heard hooves clattering on the stones outside his house and had alerted our hosts.

Obviously, Libby could not be driven and one of the other Whips, Bill Vine, offered to share with me the driving of his lovely greys to his high tandem cart but I declined as I did not want to disappoint Sandy Watney. Sandy was to have shared driving my tandem and so, as a compromise, we drove Raz, in her wheeler harness as 'half a tandem'! This was the only occasion when a single turnout has been driven at a Tandem Club meet.

At the end of the drive, over tea, it was agreed that all who had attended had qualified for membership of this re-formed Tandem Club of Great Britain. It was also agreed that, *of course* I had quali-fied because I had, after all, driven a tandem round Lowther a couple of years before. But I was adamant that I had not driven the route

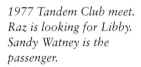
1977 Tandem Club meet. Raz is looking for Libby. Sandy Watney is the passenger.

with a tandem and therefore was not entitled to be a member. This proved a wise decision for, some years later when I was running the Club, I used to receive letters from drivers abroad, asking to be admitted as a member of the Tandem Club. These drivers wanted the badge that went with the membership of the club. They would tell me that they were the tandem champion in their country and therefore entitled to the badge. However, I always replied that they would be very welcome to drive at one of our meets to earn their badge and that I myself had not qualified in 1977 simply because I had not completed the drive on that occasion.

The question of a suitable badge had been discussed and I made enquiries from makers of badges but did not like any of the available designs. Then I had an idea. I drew the outline of the tandem bars (which fit between the leader and the wheeler) that I have in my collection and designed a miniature tandem bar badge. A friend, Deirdre Gordon, located a silversmith and persuaded him to make a few bars, by hand, for the club at an affordable price. They were beautifully made and hallmarked, and became very sought-after by tandem drivers. As the Tandem Club was growing rapidly I ordered a large quantity of bars to be made for future use of the Club. Tandem bars are now worn by over 300 tandem Whips, all of whom have earned them by driving in 'coachmanlike style' at one of the annual meets.

⸎❧ CHAPTER 23 ❧⸎

Channel Islands

In 1972 I was invited to go to Jersey and Guernsey to teach carriage driving and show slides to the many enthusiasts on these islands. As a result of this, I was asked to judge at a driving show on Jersey a couple of years later – a unique experience.

When I arrived on the showground it was raining hard and there was not a single turnout to be seen. I was assured that when the rain stopped, the exhibits would arrive, as they would all be sheltering in the potato sheds. I had been concerned that perhaps no one was prepared to exhibit under my scrutiny. I need not have worried because as soon as the rain stopped and the sky brightened, a number of very smart turnouts appeared for me to judge. In addition to the usual classes for private driving turnouts and classes for the best Whips, there were classes for Jersey vans. I had never seen these before and so I had had to do my 'homework' before I judged this class.

The Jersey vans are substantially built four-wheeled vehicles that were used for carting potatoes from the farms to the coast ready to ship to the mainland. The vans are now used for conveying tourists around the island during the summer. Because they are heavy vehicles they are pulled by a single or pair of vanner-type horses wearing strong harness with full collars which have wide bearing surfaces to

Judging Jersey vans.
(Photo reproduced by
kind permission of the
Jersey Evening Post)

spread the load well over the animal's shoulders. The harness is often decorated with brasses. I found this a most interesting and unusual class to judge and I learned a great deal about a vehicle I had hitherto known only from pictures. There was enormous enthusiasm among the competitors and the day was a very happy one.

A few years later, I was invited by the driving enthusiasts of Sark to visit their island and show slides. I flew to Jersey in a normal airliner and then from Jersey to Guernsey in a very small plane that seated about eight people. I then boarded the ferry to the tiny island of Sark – just 3.5 miles long by 1.5 miles wide. No cars are allowed on Sark and the only motorised vehicles are a few tractors and trailers to convey passengers from the boat up the long, steep hill to a café which seemed to be the focal point of the island.

I disembarked onto the dockside with my white suitcase, projector and slides, then clambered into the trailer fitted with bench seats behind the tractor. I was just about to load my suitcase onto the trailer when the driver said, 'You don't need to do that, missus. Leave it there and I'll bring it along later.'

'I can't just leave it here,' I said aghast at the thought of leaving my clothes and belongings to the mercy of anyone who happened to be passing.

'It'll be quite safe,' the driver assured me, 'all the tourists have

gone back on the last boat. There's only the folks that live on the island here now. None of them will pinch your case. Everybody knows everybody else – and none of them are thieves,' he smiled.

'Oh, I'm sure they're not. If you're certain…' I said doubtfully.

'Don't you worry. I'll bring it on to where you're staying,' he said soothingly. 'You could leave it there all night and it would still be there in the morning – not like on the mainland.'

And so I left it but secretly doubted if I would ever see my case again. It was really very strange to sit in the trailer and be driven away, yet see my suitcase sitting forlornly on the concrete of the quay-side. However, I clung to my projector and slides as these were vital for my evening slide show. All I had were the clothes that I stood up in, but at least I had my work with me and so would not let the audience down in the evening.

After a brief stop at the café for a cup of tea, my hostess walked with me along the unmade road to her home. On the way, we passed the building where I was to give my talk that evening. She stopped and said, 'Leave your projector here, Sallie, it's heavy and it'll save carrying it all the way back again.' I was quite pleased to put it down for a moment but, even so, most reluctant to actually leave it. 'Look, the window's open, just pop it inside.'

She opened the window still further.

'Are you sure it'll be here when we come back this evening?' I asked doubtfully.

'Certain,' she replied, 'we're an honest lot round here. It'll be quite safe.'

So I left my projector, again secretly wondering if, like the suitcase, I might never see it again. Even so, I was not trusting enough to leave my slides and carried them to my hostess's home, just in case people were not as honest as I had been led to believe.

Eventually we arrived at her house. After showing me my room and making me feel at home, she began to prepare an evening meal. The talk was not due to start until after nine in the evening, as this would give time for the islanders to finish their work. The time crept on and there was still no sign of my suitcase. I just knew my worst fears were about to be realised. I was sure somebody must have stolen my suitcase. Even so, I didn't want to appear to be accusing any islander of theft but I mentioned to my hostess that I needed to take a bath and change for the evening's performance.

She picked up her telephone and did not appear to dial a number but just said to someone that she was concerned about my white suitcase. Then she put the phone down,

'It's on its way,' she told me and resumed preparing the meal.

Within minutes I heard the reassuring chug of a tractor and the delightful, smiling driver, true to his word, appeared clutching my case.

'Oh, there it is!' I exclaimed. 'Thank you so much!' I almost wanted to hug him with relief and gratitude.

'Of course it is. I told you it would be quite safe but I know you didn't believe me,' grinned the driver. 'Like I said, it's not like the mainland here on Sark.'

I had a bath and changed my clothes. After dinner we walked to the venue for my talk. I was glad that I did not have to carry the projector – and that it was not raining. There was, however, a sea breeze which ruffled my hair. It was very strange to be walking outside wearing a long dress and patent shoes.

On arrival at the venue, I saw my projector exactly where I had left it, just inside the open window, several hours earlier. The tractor driver's words came back to me: 'It's not like the mainland here on Sark.'

No, indeed. It was not like the mainland at all.

We set up the projector stand and the screen, fitted the cables and tried the first slide. Everything worked and all was well when I eventually began about 9.30pm. The room was filled with a very enthusiastic audience – I had never imagined there were so many driving enthusiasts on such a tiny island! They were a most appreciative and interested audience which made giving the talk all the more rewarding.

The worst thing was the trudge back in the dark in my long dress and patent shoes. I would have happily settled for a tractor (even without a trailer!) or a horse-drawn Sark van but neither was offered.

I mentioned, during the evening, that I had heard about the famous Sark driving licence which is issued to carriage drivers on the island. Many of the Whips present drove the Sark vans that carry the tourists during the summer season. The Sark vans are smaller and lighter than Jersey vans. Their wheels have rubber tyres whereas some of the Jersey vans were iron shod. The rubber tyres give a more comfortable ride to the passengers and are less noisy, which makes it easier for tourists to hear the driver's commentary as he describes places of interest.

As my hostess and I walked back to her home after the slide show, I asked her about the possibility of my obtaining a Sark driving licence.

'You'll have to take a carriage-driving test,' my hostess explained.

'That's fine. I'm happy to do that,' I assured her.

'But you'll have to live on Sark for three weeks. That's one of the rules.'

'Oh, I see,' I replied disappointed. 'I really cannot spare that much time, I'm afraid.' So much for my dream of obtaining a Sark driving licence.

'Well,' said my hostess, 'that's a pity but there's a new horse just been brought over from the mainland. Would you like to drive it?'

'I'd love to,' I replied.

The next morning we walked to the dairy to collect fresh milk for breakfast. We took a jug, which we left for the following day's milk, and collected the fresh milk which had been left ready for us. It was a novel experience.

After breakfast, we walked to the farm where a bay cob was being put to a Sark van. I was invited to take up the reins and mount. I drove the turnout along the narrow lanes past small farms and fields. The horse was a sensible, strong-bodied sort, who knew his job well and so gave me no problems. After a while I was told to pull into a gateway and turn round, which I did, and we returned to the farm from where we had started the drive. I had thoroughly enjoyed myself, as it had given me the opportunity to see a part of this small island.

After this, we walked the length and breadth of Sark looking at carriages and visiting the homes of people I had met the previous evening. Many were anxious to show me their vehicles and to discuss finer points such as the doors on a Victoria or the seating in a brougham. However, there were no wheelwrights on Sark and so any maintenance work on wheels had to be done on the mainland when the tourist season was over.

The organisers of my trip took me to lunch at a restaurant and after the meal gave me a wonderful surprise. I was presented with a Sark driving licence! I had been, without my realising it, tested during the morning when I drove the cob. The licence resembled the old-fashioned British driving licence: a small, folded, orange-coloured cardboard cover. The insert states: '*No. H 81. Sallie Walrond of Thorne Lodge, Cockfield, Suffolk, is hereby licensed to drive a horse-drawn vehicle from 21.4.1979 until 31.12 1979. Signed by the Constable.*'

It is one of my most cherished possessions.

CHAPTER 24

Western Australia

I first met BDS members, John and Peta Horton from Perth, Western Australia, in the late 1970s at a show in the Midlands where Libby and Raz in tandem won a showing class. My *Encyclopaedia of Driving* had been published and reviewed in numerous equestrian magazines throughout the world and a few pupils from Australia had been to Thorne Lodge.

In 1979 I was invited by the Western Australian Harness Driving Society (WAHDS) to run a series of seminars and to judge at the Royal Show which ran for sixteen days, as this was the 150th anniversary of the founding of Perth. This was a wonderful opportunity to visit Australia and I accepted with enthusiasm.

After the seemingly endless flight to Perth, I was met at the airport by Midge Boag, the secretary of the WAHDS, and taken to driving enthusiasts Pat and Maiga Houlahan, where I stayed for about three weeks. Their property was right on the edge of the bush amid acres of wild flowers and home to hundreds of brightly coloured parrots and lizards that basked in the sun. But it was the 'laughing' of kookaburras and the chattering of black cockatoos as they knocked nuts from the gum trees that woke me each morning. After dark, small green frogs clambered up the mesh of the screen-doors in search of an easy

Ellmore Ballerina, driven by John Horton. (Photo reproduced by kind permission of Sandy Hannan and Hoofbeat Publications)

meal of bugs attracted there by the house lights but unable to get in. One evening, Maiga called me to see a large snake in the garden but it quickly slithered away so I never did see it, which was a shame.

Each evening Pat Houlahan and I went into the bush in search of kangaroos. I was anxious to see one in the wild. We would park the four-wheeled-drive Suzuki and proceed on foot through the bush. Pat would spot a kangaroo long before I did – they were well camouflaged and merged with the grey gum trees and beige parched grass. Pat, who was tall, walked ahead of me picking his way carefully from one rock to another so that he did not accidentally tread on a snake. I followed, literally, in his footsteps. He turned and whispered to me,

'Kangas ahead!' But it was too late – they had seen him and bounded away, and I never saw them.

We tried for several evenings and eventually Pat suggested I go first. I was terrified lest I trod on a snake and was bitten. I had the remainder of the show to judge and three three-day-seminars to run. I dare not risk being laid up in hospital suffering from snakebite. However, Pat assured me that, as long as I was careful and watched where I was putting my feet, I would be all right. I really *did* want to see those 'kangas'… so following Pat's instructions, I trod slowly and carefully from rock to rock, cautious over every footfall. At last, there they were! Fifteen kangaroos ahead of us. I was thrilled. All were browsing except for one sitting on its haunches and looking around

all the time. After a while, another kangaroo sat up and looked around and the previous one that had been 'on guard', began to feed.

'There's always one 'look-out roo',' explained Pat. 'It watches for danger while the others graze. Then they swap over. Clever, isn't it?' We watched them for a long time and Pat had pointed one out to me, 'See, she's got a joey in her pouch.' I could just make out the baby kangaroo peeking out of its mother's pocket. 'Watch them now,' Pat said and clapped his hands. Instantly, they bounded off into the bush, their huge, powerful hind legs propelling them effortlessly in a series of enormous leaps.

I missed the greenery of England even though I sometimes cursed the rain that made it so. Here the bush was tinder-dry and vegetation sun-scorched and brown. It was no wonder there was a perpetual worry about bushfires which can blaze for days once they take hold.

But I was there to work! Pat took me, each day, to the show where I judged some classes then returned to the Houlahan home. The Royal Show was held on a large permanent showground. It was enormous: the main arena alone was eight acres! On the first day, when I went to investigate the judging procedure, I was amazed to see that show jumping, two in-hand classes (known as 'led-in') and two ridden classes (known as 'horses in action', and 'hacking' when referring to children's ponies) were all being judged at the same time. The ring was divided into five areas by only a few small flags on posts but everyone kept to their allotted part. How different from British shows!

When the time came for me to judge my first class I was driven across the vast arena in a vintage motor car because judges were not expected to walk this distance! The first event was for hackney ponies. They could be driven to any vehicle but the cart and harness was not to be judged. At first I was struck by the length of the shafts on the two-wheeled vehicles. The Australians prefer the shafts to be long so that if the horse kicks the driver is less likely to get an iron-shod hoof against his shins. After a few days, I became quite used to these long shafts and when I returned to England, the shafts of my two-wheeled vehicles seemed very short!

It transpired that the pony I placed first was one whose ancestors were well known in Great Britain. His name was Rhyl Emperor P. and he belonged to Ros Budiselic. Harnessed to a Viceroy wagon, he was

Midge Boag competing successfully in the buggy class at the Perth Royal show, with Juliet, a part-Arabian mare, to a Whitechapel Speeding Buggy. (Photo reproduced by kind permission of Sandy Hannan and Hoofbeat Publications)

the epitome of a hackney: a combination of superb action, quality and a wonderful temperament. He later took the overall pony championship. I subsequently heard from Ros that that season he won just about wherever he went. The Budiselics showed another marvellous hackney pony with perfect conformation, bone, action and manners so superb that he was driven by the Budiselics' twelve-year-old daughter. He was aptly named Diplomat. I would have loved to have brought him back to England.

The classes for non-hackney ponies were held the following day. Again, the vehicles and harness were not to be taken into account. Welsh and Australian ponies predominated, being shown to sulkies (like our gigs), buggies (quarter-lock four-wheelers) and Viceroy wagons. I was strict on manners and asked the competitors to walk out of line when they went out to give their individual shows. This caused some difficulties and resulted in a shake-up of the form-book when some great-going ponies refused to walk and insisted on jogging in their anxiety to trot on. Each day after judging finished, press conferences were held when judges were invited to explain the reasons for their decisions and to give their views on the stock they had judged. I emphasised the necessity, on safety grounds, for harness

horses to have good manners – and I even gave two radio interviews on the subject.

Next came classes in which the whole turnout was to be judged. Separate events for ponies put to sulkies, buggies and Viceroys brought the same animals into the ring in different guises as the harness was also changed, in some cases, so that it was correct for the vehicle concerned. This enabled the first-prize ribbons to be spread around the different animals as there was so much more to be taken into consideration.

Ribbons were awarded instead of rosettes: long strips of felt bearing the name of the show and sponsor in gilt letters. They are tied, by the judge, round the animal's neck with a reef knot. Equal awards could be given if desired. The mounted steward, who escorted each class to and from their ring, would bring extra ribbons if required. The stewards also attended to all the judge's needs so that if I needed extra ribbons, I would give the signal – placing my hand on my head – and the steward would go for another ribbon. It was no wonder these mounted runners were called 'gofors'!

The class for period costume brought a large entry. Competitors went to tremendous trouble for this event and paid meticulous attention to detail, even taking off their digital watches and removing nylon ropes from their spares kits. They wore dress they considered appropriate to the style and period of their vehicle. I found the class almost impossible to judge because everyone was so eye-catching and I'm afraid took the easy way out by giving equal firsts, seconds and thirds so that they all went out of the ring with a ribbon of some kind.

Junior drivers came next and this class ended in a 'mini' driving lesson for each competitor. Fortunately, I was not under any pressure for time and so was able to spend as long as I wanted, within reason, with each child.

The class for the best adult driver produced a large entry. My winning Whip was the mother of one of the juniors who had received a 'mini' lesson in the Junior Whip class. This lady came into the arena holding her reins and whip in the traditional classical coaching method that I taught and she drove very well. The majority of the adult Whips drove with a rein held separately in each hand. Generations of Australian drivers have handled their reins by this method. It may have resulted from seeing American drivers of Concord coaches drive in this fashion when they arrived in Australia at the time when Cobb and Co. established a network of coaching routes between mining settlements near Sydney during the gold rush of 1851. These cumbersome coaches could not be driven using the British method of rein handling because the coach body swayed back and forth on the thoroughbrace suspension. (Thoroughbraces were made of buffalo hide and had a turnbuckle that enabled the braces to be tightened when the leather stretched.) Naturally, the driver's hands and body moved considerably to maintain contact on the horses' mouths. The driver's feet were well apart to brace his body and operate the brake. There was no ratchet on the brake and so it had to be held on by a foot stretched out to the side. It was understandable that Australian drivers followed the American method, hence it was not surprising that many Whips continued to use this method to drive their sulkies and buggies. However, the majority of the Australian Whips I met were anxious to learn and adopt the traditional British coaching method of handling the reins and whip, once it was explained that this method was really the best way in which teams and tandems can be driven successfully for long distances. A number of these Australians harboured ambitions to drive a tandem; inevitably, this was likely to lead to driving a team of four.

The classes for horses followed much the same pattern as those for ponies. The outstanding hackney horse was John Horton's Ellmore Ballerina. This beautiful bay mare went on to take the overall show championship. She combined spectacular action with impeccable manners and was always superbly presented with great attention paid to every detail of the turnout. Another outstanding animal was Keith Langan's dun stallion, Palthara Isabn. He was as near perfect a non-hackney type, as I was likely to see. He had quality and substance. He was light in my hand, obedient, and his beautiful manners made him a delight to drive. I was thrilled to see him win the ridden stallion class in the evening after I had awarded him the first prize in both the buggy and non-hackney harness horse classes.

Midge Boag, the secretary of the WAHDS, won three classes with her part-Arab mare, Juliet, whom she turned out impeccably in a series of different types of harness to suit her sulky, buggy and Viceroy as well as for the period costume class.

The Langan family with Palthara Isabn, in the period turnout class at the Perth Royal Show. (Photo reproduced by kind permission of Sandy Hannan and Hoofbeat Publications)

Keith and Marg Langan's part-Arab stallion, Palthara Isabn, driven to a buggy. (Photo reproduced by kind permission of Sandy Hannan and Hoofbeat Publications)

Some sets of harness had the traces, neck pieces, loin straps and reins made of rolled leather. The latter, I discovered, could sometimes give an uncomfortable feel in my hand. They vibrated where they passed through the saddle terrets thus preventing my taking a light contact with the horse's mouth. Some of the bits and buckles were gold-plated brass which, I was told, saved time in cleaning. I wondered, though, how long the layer of gold would last before it wore off through friction. All animals wore breast collars because full collars were, apparently, impossible to obtain in Western Australia at that time.

The three seminars I ran after the show were well attended and several people brought their own turnouts. The sessions followed the same pattern that I had developed over the years. They were based on what I had learned many years ago at Stocklands: explanation, demonstration and imitation. 'Explanation' took the form of slides and talk. In 'demonstration' I helped people with their own turnouts and 'imitation' was when everyone tried to put into practice what they had seen and been taught.

I used to sit beside each driver in his or her own turnout for a short time to help with the rein handling. I wore a stopwatch round my neck so that I did not run over time, as I often had many people to help. Some of the animals were less than perfect and, in a few cases, I did not even mount the vehicle because I considered it too dangerous. I would walk behind the driver and instruct from the ground for, at that time, vehicles did not have back steps for me to stand on from which I could easily dismount in case of trouble. I dare not risk an accident; I had to keep fit and well because I still had an enormous amount of work to do and could not let people down.

Some people just did not see the dangers of newly broken, nervous animals and ill-fitting harness. One pony was wearing a bridle that was so large that I honestly thought that if it shook its head the bridle might fall off. It was a lovely Welsh stallion of Section A type with a tiny head and little ears. The enormous heavy bridle bulged over the top of the pony's profuse mane and so I took a section of forelock and laid it over the headpiece before plaiting it back into the mane behind the bridle. Once I had secured the plait, and hence the bridle, with an elastic band, I felt much happier.

One elderly lady came forward for her teaching session with a brown but, going-grey-round-its-muzzle-with-age, pony. After I mounted and sat beside this lady I realised that the pony was eyeing me suspiciously through a gap between his face and the blinkers.

'Have you noticed how, if he looks back, he can see us? The blinkers should fit closely against his face so he can't see backwards. If he can see something behind him he could take fright and take off,' I explained.

'Oh, he often does that,' she replied airily, 'he is always running away with me. I just put up with it.'

She was a tougher lady than I and, I'm afraid, I didn't spend the full allotted time sitting beside her.

On the final day of the seminar, each member drove the advanced dressage test. Naturally, this took a long time and so we tried to involve everyone. One person sat beside the driver to act as navigator. This saved the driver from having to learn the test in a hurry and it also gave pleasure to the passenger. Everyone else, who was not involved with a turnout at the time, sat round me by the C marker on the short side of the arena. I judged out loud so that they could all hear my comments, and the reasons for the marks I allotted.

People took it in turn to be my writer (known as 'penciller' in Australia) and at the end of the test each Whip came to me and we discussed the performance. There were not enough ponies to go round and so some animals were used several times, which gave everyone the opportunity of driving a test.

At one point, proceedings were brought to an abrupt halt. Over to my right I could see a strange, black cloud making its way towards where I was teaching.

'It's bees! Get out of the way!' somebody shouted. Everyone ran out of the path of the fast-approaching bee cloud. I followed hot on their heels. We watched as the swarm buzzed over to a nearby tree where it settled among the branches.

'It's all right now. They'll stay there,' one of the locals assured me confidently. 'Come on, let's finish the tests!'

The locals took swarming bees in their stride, they were used to them. I had no choice but to follow suit and we continued as if nothing had happened but I kept a wary eye on the tree where the bees were. Apparently, there are about 4,000 types of wild flowers in Western Australia. Many people keep bees and site their hives in the bush so that the bees will collect the pollen in the spring to make their honey.

After a three-day seminar I always felt utterly shattered and asked, when arrangements were being made before my visits, for a day off to catch up with my washing and generally relax before going on to the next venue. Everyone understood and I used to enjoy my day off.

When I stayed with the Budiselics at their hackney stud, I was left to relax in their garden while they went off to the children's sports day.

'Would you just keep an eye on the pony, please, Sallie?' Ros Budiselic asked me. 'He might just try to annoy one of the hackney stallions on the other side of the fence. If he does, would you just catch him and put him back in his stable?' I agreed.

The elderly pony was blind in one eye. He was left to graze, wearing a headcollar, in the garden while I sat enjoying the peace and quiet. Then I saw him go to the fence and start making a nuisance of himself to the stallions. I approached him and attempted to catch him but he dodged away each time. Then, I had an idea. I would sneak up to him on his blind side and grab his headcollar before he realised what was happening. My plan worked. He gave in graciously, knowing his game was over, and allowed me to lead him to his stable.

One of the seminars was held near to a place where trotters were exercised. I was amazed to see four of them tied side by side to a rail on the back of a pick-up truck. The truck was driven slowly and thus they were exercised at a steady trot with no human effort at all and, apparently, no problems either.

I was taken to 'the trots', as harness racing is called in Australia, and enjoyed a fascinating evening. I was particularly interested in seeing the harnessing and general handling of the trotters in the areas behind the racecourse. I learnt a great deal – and felt very sorry for

Jenny Mackintosh driving Harry, a 17.3 Standardbred horse, who had won a few races on the trotting track before he was sold. He was later found by Jenny in a sad state and she bought him because she felt sorry for him. He is seen here, looking very happy, competing in the obstacle course at a seminar in Western Australia. (Photo reproduced by kind permission of Mike Mackintosh)

some of the horses, for they appeared so nervous that they were shaking as they were put to their light, two-wheeled, racing sulkies. It was interesting to see the harness in detail such as the straps that hang loosely around their legs to prevent them breaking stride and the bridles with the overhead checks.

I was taken to visit the spectacular show called El Caballo Blanco near Perth. Here, beautiful Andalusian horses performed classical ridden movements as well as work between pillars and in harness.

I was also shown a carriage collection belonging to Ray Williams, who ran the El Caballo Blanco display. It included a Cobb and Co. coach. On close examination, and seeing just how massive these coaches are, I could understand the reasoning behind the Australian method of driving with a rein in each hand. I obtained photographs for inclusion in my book on carriages of this coach and other vehicles in the collection including a Tonga, a covered, two-wheeler commonly used in India, and a karrozin, a four-wheeled, vis-à-vis vehicle used in Malta as a tourist carriage.

Before I came back to England, I was honoured to be made a life member of the WAHDS. I still look forward to receiving the newsletters and keeping up with the members' activities.

CHAPTER 25

The Team and Other Ponies

LIBBY AND RAZ HAD GIVEN ME SUCH PLEASURE in tandem that I now wanted to drive my own team. I had driven teams belonging to Sandy Watney, Sir Dymoke White and Phil Hoffman and any other team when the opportunity had arisen. I wanted a pony team. I had no desire to compete with a four-in-hand because competing would necessitate having two grooms. I would also need a large horsebox and portable stabling. Nor did I wish to drive for a sponsor. I neither wanted nor could afford to employ anyone to help. I always preferred to do everything myself. I had turned down offers to drive for other people in the past because I had not wanted to have to answer to anyone but myself if, and when, we did not do well.

If I were to have two more ponies, I must decide on the breed. I wanted animals that were registered with their breed society as they were more likely to be 'typey' than mongrel ponies like Libby and Raz who were of different colours and a hand apart in height. Also, I wanted foals so that I could, as with Libby and Raz, bring them up in my own way. I did not want a 'hairy' type, so dismissed Highland, Fell and Dales ponies. I considered Welsh cobs but thought that they would be likely to have more knee action than Libby and Raz who moved with longer, lower strides than many cobs. Exmoors,

Dartmoors and Shetlands were all too small and New Forests could throw back to all shapes and sizes. Of the British native pony breeds that left only the Connemara. I remembered the beautiful dun horse that I had seen harnessed to a phaeton at the Seven Sisters Riding School in Surrey when I was about twelve years old and I had set my heart on a dun foal.

In the end, I settled on a grey Connemara foal, Cottenham Loretto, bred by Sandy and Ann Macnab at their home near Cambridge. I went to see Loretto and liked him as soon as I saw him. I bought him and he came to Thorne Lodge in 1974. Like all my foals, he was put into a field that we call the three-corner field. It has the main road running along one side, a farm with livestock on the second side and a lane that is used by tractors and numerous farm vehicles on the third side. Six months in the three-corner field ensures that all of my animals are traffic, pig, sheep and cattle proof.

Loretto, or Retto as I called him for short, was no trouble to break because he had been well handled by Sandy and Ann and so had no fears. He became a great success and won on most of the occasions he was shown, including a strong class at the East of England Show and the Mountain and Moorland class at the BDS show in 1981. Minta Winn drove him when he was five and won the Junior Whip championship at Smith's Lawn. I used him, as the model, for the first edition of my book, *Breaking a Horse to Harness*.

Retto's dam was in foal again to the same stallion and so when Cottenham Lorenzo, another grey colt, was born, I went to see him and persuaded Sandy and Ann to let me have him. They had really wanted to keep him entire but eventually agreed to his joining his brother with me. I called him Ben for short.

I now had the four ponies for my team. I had team harness, part of which had been given to me by a friend and part of which was made to measure by Tony Russell, a harness-maker in Bedfordshire.

I had seen the wonderful roof-seat break in Colorado and wanted a vehicle like that for my team. The coachbuilder, John Gapp, agreed to build the vehicle to my specification. I went to his workshop in Norfolk for fittings so that he was sure that the legroom and height of the seat were right for me. He even made a cardboard replica so that I was able to sit in position before he progressed with the final

The pony team being driven to the roof-seat break. Anne Muir is sitting next to Sallie. Behind her is Deidre Gordon, next to her is Sandy Macnab with Fiona Gordon behind him, and June Hales on the remaining seat. (Photo reproduced by kind permission of The East Anglian Daily Times, Terry Hunt, Andy Abbott and Sharon Boswell)

wooden version. I was delighted when I went to collect the break and it gave me enormous pleasure during the years that followed.

When Ben and Retto were three and four years old, I travelled round the country with them giving lecture demonstrations on breaking a pony to harness. There were still very few people doing this kind of thing and so we had good audiences wherever we went. It proved to be a valuable education for the ponies. They learnt to box and travel without worrying. They accepted the noise of crowds and applause and seemed to revel in the attention they received. I always worked in an indoor school and would mark out a circle with cones and coloured tape in which to work the ponies. I would use both ponies, one at a time, to illustrate the various stages of their training. Whichever pony was not being used was tied in a corner of the indoor school, out of the way. There was no problem with this because they were quite used to being tied up in the stalls at home.

We were invited to give an evening demonstration to the members of the Civil Service Riding Club at the Royal Mews. Janet and Anne Grahame Johnstone, the artists, came with me from Suffolk to show

me the route across London with my Land Rover and trailer and help with the demo. It was early spring and the ponies still had their winter coats. By the time that we had arrived at the Royal Mews, after a three-hour journey, they looked distinctly scruffy and I felt quite ashamed of them. They had looked superb when we had left Suffolk.

The head groom showed us into the stables where several magnificent white-grey horses stood looking immaculate in their beautiful rugs. We led my scruffy, hairy, ponies into the two stalls that had been prepared for them. I imagined the resident horses wondering what on earth had been allowed into their home! We tied up the ponies with ropes and logs, designed so that the ropes and logs disappeared into wooden boxing below the mangers. But the ponies were less impressed! They could hear the logs clattering inside the casing but could not see them and became distinctly nervous.

I was afraid in case they broke loose and damaged a royal horse and was anxious about leaving them while we all went to get a bite to eat before beginning our demonstration. However, the royal grooms promised to keep an eye on them for us and, indeed, all was well when we returned.

The demonstration went without a hitch. When it was over the ponies were boxed in the mews' yard under floodlighting that threw frightening shadows into the trailer, but they never flinched. It had been a memorable evening for us all and we returned to Suffolk exhausted but elated.

With the six-seater, roof-seat break in the coach house at Thorne Lodge and the harness ready to use, the time had come to put the team together and take them for a drive. I enlisted five friends to help with the ponies. We harnessed the ponies: Libby in the position of near-side lead because I knew that I could rely on her to go forward off my voice alone (I doubted my ability to reach her with the whip without wrapping it round the other ponies!) Ben went into off-side lead because I did not want him to have to do any work as he was so young. He was also bomb proof in traffic. Raz was near-wheeler as she was tough enough to pull us out of the gutter and would simply get on with her job. Retto worked alongside her as off-wheeler.

Once we had put to, all passengers mounted and off we went. The ponies never put a foot wrong and we did not have a single problem.

On our return to Thorne Lodge, unhitching four ponies from the break was akin to an army operation. Each person went to a particular pony and did exactly as I commanded to enable each pony to be taken safely from the vehicle. Then all ponies were led to the yard and the gate was shut. Once again, each handler followed my orders, military-style, and all the harness was removed in the correct order to eliminate accidents and breakages.

We put the ponies into the stables, fed them, carried the harness into the kitchen for cleaning, put away the break and removed the cushions from the seats. After a snack lunch, we cleaned the harness. The whole outing made a huge amount of work, hence needing five people to help. Fortunately, there was never a shortage of willing hands.

In the summer of Ben's fourth year, he began to shake his head and sneeze continuously when the weather was warm and dry. He would sometimes even try to rub his nose against his knees while he was being driven. I thought, at first, it was all in his mind, then I began to wonder if he had a nasal problem. I sought the advice of Gerald Hudson, our vet, and the conclusion was, after numerous tests, that he was allergic to pollen. When I took Retto and Ben to shows in tandem, I always hoped for drizzle instead of sunshine. When the weather was damp, Ben did not suffer nearly as much as when the pollen count was high. I tried all kinds of nasal sprays on him and someone, who suffered similarly, suggested I give him antihistamine tablets as these had helped her and so I went to Boots and purchased some.

Before I took the ponies to the next show I read the warning on the packet: 'Do not drive or operate machinery' – that hardly applied to Ben – I noted that the tablets 'May cause drowsiness' but did not worry unduly. I gave him some of these tablets to ease the irritation in his poor nose. We put to and went to the ring. Ben wandered about in the lead of the tandem like a sailing boat with no wind! I managed to keep him going by applying the tandem whip, which Bernard Mills had given to me, when I hoped that the judge, Tom Coombs, was not looking. We lined up for inspection then, to my horror, Tom asked me if he could drive the ponies. Of course, I said that he could but poor Tom had a terrible time keeping Ben moving and I felt very sorry for him. I took up the reins again and before the final circuits of the ring, I pinged the lash against Ben's side to get him going forward enough for us to be pulled into first place. I never used the tablets before a show again.

I drove Retto and Ben at the Suffolk County Show in tandem and we were going steadily round the ring when a man driving an uncontrollable hackney horse ran the wheel of his vehicle into my gig almost knocking us over. Remembering my capsize at Hadleigh show with Ali, I clung on with my toenails! I managed to stop the ponies abruptly. Ben reared and plunged breaking the tongue of one of the trace buckles.

I then realised that one of the gig's wheels was not straight and so I pulled the ponies into the last position of the line-up. I explained to a steward that I was retiring but I did not want to leave the ring until the class had been judged because it might have looked, to spectators, as if we were bad losers. I cannot abide competitors who leave the ring in a temper when they discover that they are not going to win a class.

Once out of the arena, I surveyed the damage. The axle of the gig had been bent between the wheel and the spring. I had entered the ponies for Deeping show in four days' time: my gig was broken and so was my harness. However, coachbuilder John Gapp had been at the show and had witnessed the incident. He came to the trailer and commiserated with me then said,

'If you bring the gig to my workshop tomorrow I'll fix it.'

'It'll take you ages,' I replied.

'No, it won't. Go and do your shopping and I'll have it right for when you get back.'

I could have hugged him!

That evening I telephoned harness-maker, Tony Russell, and told him my tale of woe.

'Bring the harness in and I'll mend it in time for the Deeping show,' he offered.

'That's marvellous. Thank you so much!' I was delighted.

And so the axle was straightened on Thursday and the buckle tongue was renewed on Friday. On Sunday, the tandem won its class at Deeping and I was presented with a large trophy. It gave me enor-

Sallie, accompanied by June Hales, at Deeping Show, with Cottenham Loretto and Cottenham Lorenzo, winning their class. (Photo reproduced by kind permission of The Evening Telegraph, Peterborough)

mous pleasure to write and thank both John and Tony for their help. Without them, I would have had to withdraw from the show.

I struggled with Ben's allergy but, surrounded by fields of oil seed rape in spring and summer it was hopeless and I was going to have him put down to put him out of his misery. Then, a pupil who drove mostly in the winter, offered to take him. It seemed a good idea but, unfortunately, it did not work and he was sold to a family who lived by the sea. Apparently, he suffered less on the coast than he had inland.

After a few years I gave up driving the team. The work of cleaning all the harness and putting the team together was simply too much. I had, however, learned a great deal – and got the desire for four-in-hand driving out of my system. I had also taught a number of people to drive a team and so I was quite content to return to driving a tandem.

I was now looking for another pony to go with Retto as I wanted to drive a tandem of registered Connemaras. I spent an afternoon telephoning Connemara breeders in search of a dun gelding but ended up with another grey. He had been bought as a working hunter pony and was three years old. His name was Ironbridge Patrick. He

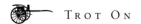

had a wonderful temperament and proved to be a huge success. I drove him in pair and tandem with Retto for many years teaching numerous pupils.

★   ★   ★

In 1980 there was a strike of steelworkers. This would affect the availability of horseshoes. It was vital that all four of my ponies were kept shod during the summer because I had pupils booked throughout the whole time. My farrier offered to purchase a year's supply of heavier flatter shoes and I was grateful. However, it may have been these shoes that caused or contributed to Libby's laminitis. I had always dreaded the disease and taken every precaution against it. One day Libby was perfectly sound but the next day she was very lame. Gerald Hudson was called and he diagnosed laminitis. I was devastated. Once a pony has had laminitis it is always susceptible to recurrences of this terrible foot complaint. To give her time to recover and yet to benefit from her being 'laid up', I decided to put her in foal to a hackney stallion that I had often judged and even made champion. He was superb and I had visions of breeding a world-beater with Libby's temperament and the hackney's action. This was a perfect example of 'fools breed for wise men to buy'. The foal, a filly, was a disaster. Within two days of being born, she laid her ears flat into her neck and threatened to kick me – and she meant it. I never trusted her because she delighted in trying to kick anyone who came near her. I sold her cheaply as a two-year-old.

Libby's laminitis was never going to be fully cured and, reluctantly I parted with her. She went to live with pupils, George and Lilian Bailey in Derbyshire, who had known her and learnt to drive with her. They loved her dearly and coped with her laminitis. She wanted for nothing and had a marvellous home with them. Many years later they sat with her holding her in their arms when she died.

One day when I was at Sandringham, judging the driving trials, I was approached by Anne Hammond (now Rolinson), who I had known for many years and who was looking for a pair of Connemaras for Phyllis Wyeth in Delaware, USA. She asked me if Retto and Patrick were for sale and I told her that they definitely were not.

Virginia Sirl, a pupil, driving Ironbridge Patrick successfully in the Junior Whip class at the BDS Show.

She asked me to think about the idea explaining that this would be a five-star permanent home with a lady who had become disabled owing to a car accident. Eventually, I was persuaded to let the ponies go to America. By then, Retto was twelve years old and Patrick was eight. I was keeping them purely for teaching which seemed silly as I wanted to cut down on teaching and I hardly ever showed them.

I felt terribly sad on the day in October 1985 when a smart New-market horsebox arrived with a uniformed driver, who was also their groom, came to collect them. I insisted that he took a whole bale of my best hay so that they would have their usual diet for the journey to Delaware. I was reassured when I heard that this man was going to accompany them for the whole journey. He fitted them with brand new headcollars and they boxed up without a murmur but a whinny from Retto as they were driven away down the lane had me in floods of tears. Phyllis telephoned me when they arrived and assured me that they were safe and well. They were a great success in America and Phyllis and I kept in close touch for years. She became keen to get a team going and asked me if I could find two more ponies for her.

I had acquired a young Connemara gelding, Watchover Cocktail, called Teddy for short, and was busy schooling him. It was partly

because of him that I let Retto and Patrick go. I had, by now, more or less stopped teaching pupils with my own ponies and taught only pupils who brought their own animals.

Teddy had an exceptionally quiet temperament. He was, in fact, too quiet. His dam was in foal again and I bought a filly called Watchover Christine whom I called Tina. Both Teddy and Tina went to shows as singles in the gig and won some classes. They were never going to be a matching pair for Phyllis Wyeth because Teddy was a grey and Tina was a brown roan. In any case, Teddy was not onward-going enough for Phyllis. He eventually went on permanent loan to David and Mary Roberts in Newcastle where he gave endless pleasure to the family and, because of his docility, was perfect for the disabled driving group they ran. He stayed with them until he died.

I was still searching for a dun gelding to drive with Raz. There were two advertised in the Connemara pony sales list and I went to see them. One was a pale dun that I feared might turn grey, but the other was a two-year-old golden dun with black points. He was a superb mover and had a pretty head with beautiful, big brown eyes. I was concerned about his feet which, when I first saw him, looked as if they had recently been trimmed. I assumed that this was because he had been prepared for me to see and decided that they were probably all right.

His name was Sandpiper. I bought him and he settled in well. He was easy to break to ride and drive but he was always very foot sore if the ground was at all hard or stony. I fitted him with equi-boots – a rubber version of the leather lawn-boots worn, in the nineteenth century, by ponies that pulled grass mowers to prevent their shoes cutting up the turf. They fitted over the whole hoof and protected Piper's thin soles from pressure of stones or hard ground when I long-reined him on walks around the farm. He was too uncomfortable without them for his feet were brittle and his shoes were forever coming off. I became quite expert at filling gaps in his feet, where the horn had broken away, with wadding covered with Stockholm tar and hoof oil. I tried every possible feed additive, supplement and ointment to persuade his feet to grow and strengthen but all to no avail.

I was offered a large sum of money for him by someone who had seen him at Smith's Lawn, winning a class at the BDS show and wanted him for their granddaughter but I felt I could not sell him. There were just too many problems with his feet. He was a classic case of 'no foot, no horse'. I struggled on with him for years because he was so pleasurable in every other way but, in the end, I gave him to a pupil, Brenda Waters, who adored him.

CHAPTER 26

Belgium

Eric andersen, a well-known belgian whip, had originally come to Thorne Lodge as a pupil. He was very talented and drove my tandem expertly.

We were in the kitchen at the end of his visit and I had put the kettle on the Aga to boil for tea. I always used to hang the metal teapot over the spout of the kettle so that it was warmed when the steam emerged as the kettle boiled. I poured him a final cup of tea before he left.

'Well, Eric, I hope you've enjoyed your visit to Suffolk but really don't feel I've taught you very much,' I said apologetically.

He replied, with a grin, 'You have taught me how to warm a teapot!' We both laughed. He put down his cup and said seriously, 'You must come to my house. You must see my collection of carriages. Yes, Sallie, you must come to Brussels and meet the Baron Jean Casier. He has a fine collection of carriages too – perhaps one of the finest private collections in the entire world. You would enjoy it, Sallie. He has vehicles made by Bugatti – famous now for their racing cars – but in the past…' and he continued to tell me of the wonderful carriage collection of the Baron before finally taking his leave and returning home.

Then, one day, Eric telephoned.

'Would you like to come to Belgium to give your talk? Illustrated with your slides of carriages, of course.'

I was a little taken aback – but pleasantly so – and hesitated whereupon Eric said, 'It is not far to Brussels – open your window, I'll shout and you will hear me!'

I laughed, 'I'd love to come, Eric. Thank you so much for asking me.'

The day I flew to Brussels was very hot and so I wore a sleeveless cotton dress. I was to show the slides in the evening and so I had packed my long dress for the occasion. I always used to take a soft hat that could travel in my suitcase without getting crushed and a pair of driving gloves in case the opportunity arose to drive someone's horses. Little did I know how vital these were going to be on this occasion.

Eric met me at the airport and took me in his car to the home of the Baron Casier – the imposing Chateau de Nokere, near Ghent. After my journey I felt very travel-weary and longed for a chance to smarten up and refresh myself but all I could do was comb my hair and hope I didn't look too untidy. On arrival at the Chateau in the morning, the Baron Casier and a large number of very smart driving enthusiasts greeted us.

We partook of the lavish refreshments before setting off to see some of the carriages. They were housed in numerous buildings and were all in superb show condition: the brass highly polished and not a speck of dust on any of them. There were about eighty and they were all different. The Baron Casier knew that I was working on the final stages of *Looking at Carriages* and he told me that he would supply me with photographs of any that I would like to include in my new book. I was extremely grateful to him for this generous offer and included a number of his lovely vehicles.

After we had seen the vehicles in the first carriage house, we returned to the harness room for more refreshments before looking at further carriages. This continued until lunchtime.

During lunch, the Baron Casier said to me,

'I've organised something different for this afternoon.'

'Oh?' I replied hoping it would include an opportunity to freshen up and change my clothes.

'I'm having a pair of horses put to a carriage,' he smiled, 'but there are deliberate mistakes…' I had a feeling I knew what was coming. 'I thought it would be most interesting if you could find the faults, tell us why they are faults and talk about the turnout.'

I felt it was not so much a request as a command. I swallowed hard.

'Of course, I'd be delighted,' I replied with more enthusiasm than I felt. No one had mentioned this, it wasn't in my plans and I felt decidedly apprehensive! What if I couldn't find anything wrong?

True to his word, a pair of beautiful bay coach horses attended by liveried grooms and harnessed to a break, were paraded for my inspection. I noticed, but at this stage did not comment, that the near-side hame strap had been put onto the collar back to front; the reins were tied to the splinter bar and a passenger was sitting on the box seat.

At least those mistakes hadn't been difficult to spot! The incorrect fitting of the hame strap is a common fault but not as unsafe as the other two which were highly dangerous. But there must be more. I began with bridles and made various suggestions which prompted much discussion. When I finally arrived at the hame strap, the Baron exclaimed, 'She has found the fault!'

I then pointed out the other two obvious – and dangerous – faults. The Baron beamed. I appeared to have passed 'the test'.

'Now, how would you like to drive the horses?'

'I would love to,' I said, just wishing yet again that I had the opportunity to change into clothes more suitable for such a smart occasion among such knowledgeable people. However, there was nothing for it but to don my hat and gloves and climb up onto the box seat wearing my sleeveless cotton dress. We set off down a narrow path between lawns and came to a bend where large stone balls, each about two feet in diameter, protected the edges of the lawn, just as at Thorne Court. A rear wheel touched one – I wanted to die with embarrassment.

After a while, the Baron Casier, who was sitting next to me, took the reins, although he was on the wrong side, and drove along paths and tracks before going through a spectacular water crossing of his lake! He skilfully skirted a deep dip on the approach, went through the water and expertly negotiated the tricky exit on the far bank exactly at the right angle. An inch or two adrift and we could have overturned. We returned to the chateau and consumed more refreshments before coming out again to find a team harnessed to the break and ready to go.

'For you to drive, Sallie,' offered the Baron. I climbed up onto the box and settled myself as much as I could, for it was very strange to be wearing a sleeveless cotton dress while driving. I had to turn the team in the forecourt before going out through the gateway. As we approached I could have sworn that the gateway was growing narrower by the second. But the horses were used to it and sailed through – I hardly had to do anything. Then we came to the path between the stone balls where I had scraped the wheel earlier. I concentrated furiously and took great care to hold the horses off the corner. There was no telltale scraping noise this time.

'Well,' the Baron laughed, 'she can drive a team even if she can't drive a pair!' Eventually, we approached the water crossing at the lake and I slowed the team. 'Go on, Sallie, take them through it!' the Baron urged me but I shook my head. I was not prepared to take any chances.

'There are far too many things that I might get wrong. It could be a disaster,' I explained as I held the horses straight and drove past the water crossing.

'As you wish,' the Baron sounded quite disappointed.

Later we came by the water crossing again. The Baron took the reins from his seat on my left and drove the team at speed into and out of the water, between trees and through bushes. He was an exceptionally skilful Whip.

At last, in the late afternoon, the horses were stabled and I was able to freshen up and change my clothes. What bliss to relax in a nice hot bath before putting on my long dress for my evening slide show. It was well attended and I greatly enjoyed giving it to such a receptive audience.

The following day, Eric showed me his collection of carriages and later arranged for photographs of several of them to be included in *Looking at Carriages*. He also took me to see yet more neighbouring carriage collections.

The visit to Brussels had been wonderful and given me so many memories. I had driven beautiful horses, seen marvellous vehicles and learned so much. I was very grateful to Eric for arranging the trip.

CHAPTER 27

Judging in Connecticut

In 1981 I received a telephone call from Frank and Jean Kinsella in Connecticut, USA, inviting me to judge at the Kent School two-day driving show not far from their home, to be followed by the Eastern United States pleasure driving championships which took place on the same showground. I accepted with enthusiasm because I had never judged in America and it was a chance not to be missed.

Before I went, I investigated what this would entail, as I had no idea of the differences between judging American pleasure driving classes and English private driving classes. I discovered that the pleasure classes at this show were to be judged on percentages: 50 per cent for the horse for 'manners in motion and at rest, way of going, condition, appropriateness, backing'; 20 per cent 'for the whip, contact (use of aids) posture'; 15 per cent each for harness and vehicle 'fit, condition and appropriateness'. I was not quite sure how I was going to cope with all this but I need not have worried because I was provided with a wonderfully efficient 'scribe' as the writer is called in the USA – a lovely lady called Janice.

The first day of my judging began with the open class for single horses in the Grand Prix arena. The ringmaster was the very experienced Robert 'Bob' Sorterup; dressed in a scarlet coat and black top

hat, he took complete charge. When all twenty-four exhibits were in the arena, Bob announced, 'Class in order!' which was the signal for the gate to the entrance to the ring to be closed, after which no more competitors were admitted. As a result of this discipline, no one was late. I had exactly thirty minutes to judge the class.

There were Morgans, Arabs, hackneys and crossbreds, and a wide variety of vehicles. I had to concentrate very hard to sort out this large number of turnouts in such a short time. I was also aware that, as I was judging the horses, the competitors and spectators were judging me! Bob commanded (at my request) that exhibits should work at the collected trot – and they all did. Then they progressed to working trot and extended trot, which was called 'trot on'. By now, a pattern of the placings was beginning to form in my mind. The class was then brought to a walk in preparation to change the rein or, as Bob commanded,

'Reeeevoice!' (reverse)

The turnouts then walked across the diagonal. Janice was at my side with her clipboard and pen and at this point I gave a mark for 'horse'. Having already placed the exhibits in some kind of order, the work on the other rein confirmed my thoughts.

The class then lined up for me so that I could inspect the harness, vehicle and Whip and Janice wrote down the marks as I judged each competitor. After I had seen each one I asked for rein back. They all did this faultlessly. Janice added the scores and the best seven were retained. I had to place six but an extra one was kept in reserve in case a horse suddenly did something terrible which would have forced me to put it out of contention. The remainder of the class were 'excused' which was a polite way of telling them that they had to leave the ring. No one grumbled or showed any sign of being a bad loser, which was most refreshing. The ribbons were pinned on in reverse order with each driver, on command from Bob, coming forward to take the prize. Finally, the winner was left to show a 'victory pass' (lap of honour) after he had taken his rosette.

The day continued in this way with single ponies, pairs, novices, road carts and juniors until the show finished at about 4.30pm.

Part-way through the show on Saturday evening, there was a book-signing session of some of my titles. This was followed by din-

Frank Kinsella, accompanied by Jean Kinsella, with their Lipizzaners to a Bennington Presentation Carriage. (Photo © Stan Phaneuf 05860)

ner and dancing. I greatly enjoyed meeting the people whom I had been judging and, even from those who had been well down the line, there was no grumbling and resentment.

The next morning I judged the junior obstacle competition when a number of children drove with great expertise, which, I felt, augured well for the future of the American Driving Society.

I then went to the start of the marathon course where all competitors were checked to ensure that they were carrying the specified spares before being allowed to start. These included a halter, a wheel wrench and a knife but many people carried extra items such as spare

Philip DuBois with Otter Brook Fleur tackling the water hazard in the Gambler's Choice class. (Photo © 1981 Sterling A. Steffensen, reproduced by kind permission of Lori Steffensen)

harness parts in case of breakages.

Later on, I was called to the ring to judge the draught horses.

'But I'm not a heavy horse judge,' I pointed out. 'I've no experience or training in judging heavy horses.'

'It doesn't matter. All the competitors want you to judge them,' I was told.

'Well, if you're sure,' I said doubtfully. And so, to please everyone, I judged the heavies. There were only three exhibits and the result slipped easily into place. I gave the first award to a magnificent pair of Belgians (very similar to the Suffolk Punches seen in England) that were drawing a Connestoga wagon – a bow-topped, canvas-covered freight wagon similar to but bigger and heavier than those used by pioneers during the opening of the West. I was even given the opportunity to drive the wagon – this was a new experience for me but I drove it with my usual classical method of rein handling. The horses were very obedient and responsive.

I later watched these horses pull a stone boat (a kind of sledge loaded with weights) then, after that, they manoeuvred between obstacles to win the handy horse class which was judged by a specialist in this competition.

I was next called to one of the dressage arenas to judge the singles and pairs for the advanced test when a reasonably high standard of dressage was expected. The arena was superbly set out, edged by white chains, decorated with yellow pot plants and matching yellow umbrellas to protect the judges from the sun. Throughout the two days of the show, five judges had worked in two arenas watching about 150 entries driving six different tests. I was pleased to see that a dressage test they were using was one I had written for the British Horse Society to use for driving trials in Britain.

While all of this was happening, a 'gambler's choice' obstacle class was taking place in the main ring. Here hazards were set for drivers to negotiate: the more difficult obstacles gained more points than the easier ones and drivers could choose the order in which they drove to include as many obstacles, and hence points, as possible before their set time was up. The hazards included negotiating a water crossing (which several horses jumped), driving past a hillbilly band on the top of a bank and turning, by means of an arm, a rotating carriage wheel that lay flat on an upright axle. My last class was the ride, drive and jump and I assumed, with not a little relief, that after this, my duties were fulfilled. However, I was called to the Grand Prix arena.

The show championship was determined by the number of points gained throughout the two days of competition. This explained why there were so many entries in each class: in order to gain as many points as possible, competitors entered the maximum numbers of classes for which they were eligible. The winner was Pat James, a BDS member, driving a lovely bay to an English Ralli car. She had travelled 3,000 miles from California to compete in Connecticut. Fortunately, I discovered these details after I had judged her and so felt I could not be accused of favouritism. There was a tie for the reserve champion award: a beautiful hackney gelding, Paladin, driven by Jo Anne Kellogg; a spectacular hackney pony stallion, Cassilis Last Chance, driven by Jennifer DuBois, and a great going palomino Welsh stallion, Turkdean Sword Dance, driven by Stephen Cody for Mrs Hope Ingersoll. These three exhibitors had all elected to be judged by me for the award and all were happy for me to drive their animals which, I was later told, was most unusual, as American judges rarely drive the turnouts. It was a difficult decision because all these turnouts were superb. They all gave me wonderful drives and I would have been proud to own any one of them. I finally chose the Welshman for the award.

The Eastern United States championship was held on the Monday following the weekend competitions. It was flattering to be asked to be one of the judges. All the competitors had had to qualify in that they had to have been placed first, second or third in at least two different shows under different judges during the past year to be eligible to exhibit. There were three rings and the other two judges were Deirdre Pirie and Colonel Donald Thackeray. In Ring One single horses, single ponies, pairs and tandems came before me to be judged before going, in turn, to the other two judges in Ring Two and Ring Three. The placings were confidential and the only people who knew them were my scribe and Frank Kinsella who computerised the results with those from the judges in Rings Two and Three. When the judging was finished, we were free to enjoy lunch. The results were still a closely guarded secret and I think that we judges felt just as nervous

and excited as the competitors. The awards were presented after lunch. In the single horse class, first prize went to Pat James from California, with Paladin taking the second award. The pony supreme was Turkdean Sword Dance.

It was reassuring that these results confirmed those of my earlier judging and I felt quite gratified. I was delighted too to be made an honorary member of the American Driving Society and given the badge, which I wore with great pride.

CHAPTER 28

Ireland

I WAS INVITED TO TEACH AND JUDGE in Eire and Northern Ireland on a number of occasions. In 1987 I flew from London to speak and show slides to driving enthusiasts in the Belfast area of Northern Ireland. The IRA was very active at that time and there had been instances of car bombs and incendiaries left in public places.

When I went through the security check at Heathrow, I was told that my slides would have to pass through the x-ray machines. I was concerned that the x-rays might adversely affect them and so the officials at the airport security were prepared to compromise and said that as long as I took all the slides from their cases, I could carry them, in my hands, but the boxes which had contained the slides would have to pass through the x-ray. I agreed to this but had nowhere to put all my slides. In the end, a kind person in the check-in queue went to one of the airport shops and returned with a carrier bag made of thin plastic. It was barely large enough to contain all my slides and threatened to tear when I put the slides into it. I was terrified that the bag would split and that I would lose a slide but all was well. Thank goodness that they were all in glass mounts that prevented their getting scratched or bent. They were also colour coded and numbered so that they could eventually be put back into their correct order in the slide

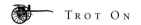

boxes the right way round. I was able to put them back into my hand luggage and there were no problems when I went through security at Belfast.

When I emerged from the airport I saw soldiers wearing camouflage-style uniforms and carrying guns. It was a sobering and somewhat intimidating sight. I was, however, met by a charming Irishman who reassured me that I need not worry. He took me to his family home where I was to spend the night after my talk. During the car journey, it emerged that he was a senior police officer.

When we prepared, later on, to drive from his home to the venue of the evening talk, he thoroughly inspected the area underneath his car before we got in. He was, I presumed, searching for any suspicious package that might have been placed there while we were all having dinner in his house. I was worried when he told me that the luxurious bedroom that I had been given for the night was, in fact, his and his wife's bedroom. They had moved out of their ground floor room so that I would be comfortable during my visit, which was very kind, but I was most uneasy and I kept the windows shut. I did not get much sleep that night. However, I should not have worried because the large audience who came to see the slides gave me a very warm welcome. I was assured that no one would do me any harm as I was a 'horsey' person visiting Ireland for a 'horsey' occasion. Even so, I wasn't convinced that either of the warring parties would know that.

I was invited to judge the prestigious Dublin Horse Show on several occasions. At one time when I was judging, during 'The Troubles' and security was tight, I had to fly back immediately after the show and had asked if I might leave my suitcase in the secretary's office for a quick getaway when I had finished.

Part way through my judging, a steward approached me in the ring, 'I'm so sorry to interrupt, Mrs Walrond, but the show secretary is most concerned because she can hear a noise coming from your suitcase.'

I could not think what this could possibly be but I could not leave the ring in the middle of judging a class to investigate.

'I'm sure it's nothing to worry about,' I replied, trying to sound confident but I was anxious. I knew my case was locked, but even so... Then I had an idea that cheered me considerably. 'It just might be my alarm clock. It's a wind-up one and the alarm catch could have turned, caught on something and switched itself on. Look,' I reached for my purse, 'here's the key. Go and open it and have a look,' and I handed the key to the steward. He looked somewhat relieved at this possible explanation and hurried off. He returned a few moments later with a smile on his face,

'You were right – it was the clock.'

We both heaved a sigh of relief.

On another occasion at the Dublin Horse Show, I was judging the driving on a very wet day. I had the class lined up for a close inspection. One exhibit was a chesnut horse with four white socks. It also had a strange, chesnut-coloured streak running down one front leg from knee to pastern. When I came to judge this turnout I looked closely at the leg but did not touch it. A large scar of a broken knee had been carefully camouflaged with brown dye which, unfortunately, was not waterproof. I looked up at the driver. He saw that I had 'rumbled' him. Neither of us spoke but we exchanged grins.

Later, I was enjoying lunch having, as I thought, completed my judging for the day when a steward announced that I was to judge the driving competitions in the afternoon.

'Do you have a plan of the course so I can learn the route through it?' I asked.

'It's not built yet. That's for you to do!' came the reply.

'Now they tell me,' I thought, but said, 'That's all right. I'll use the plan that I've used many times for disabled drivers. It is easy to build and I know that it drives well.' I gave it no further thought and enjoyed the rest of my lunch.

With the meal over a couple of stewards and I went down to the arena and began directing operations.

'Are you sure this is right, Mrs Walrond?'

'Yes, of course. I've done it lots of times before,' I replied. I really could not understand why they were querying it.

'You know it's a knock-out competition, don't you?' one of the stewards said at last.

'No, I didn't.'

My heart sank. This was a far bigger job than I had anticipated. It meant building two identical courses, one on each side of the ring.

Each course had to be exactly the same length as the other if the competition was going to work properly and be fair.

'We're going to have to measure the distance very carefully and make sure both courses are exactly the same,' I said.

Whereupon the steward replied, 'That's not a problem at all. You walk one and I'll walk the other and we'll both count our strides!'

I looked up at him for he was at least six feet tall.

'Your course will be twice as long as mine!' I said.

We compromised and, amazingly, the competition was a success. It did not appear to make much difference which course competitors drove. No one complained and they all enjoyed themselves.

CHAPTER 29

France

CHRISTINE DICKINSON, A HUNTING FRIEND of Bill and myself, had married Frenchman, Jean Bocquillon, and moved to his farm in Baron near Paris. Jean kept a pack of hounds with which he hunted the small deer in the 30,000-acre forest of Compiègne. I was invited to stay with Christine and Jean to enjoy a few days with these hounds. Most of the twenty or so mounted followers wore the long, dark green coats usually seen with this hunt, rather than the traditional scarlet, or black, so often seen in England. They kept together in a group as they followed the hunt in the forest.

I was keen to become more involved with the hound-work and so asked Jean if he would allow me to help on the basis that I always used to go 'on point' when hunting with the Suffolk foxhounds. I found hound-work most interesting and far prefer it to 'coffee housing' – which was just as well as my command of French was almost nil. I was to be mounted on an experienced hunter belonging to Jean's father. Jean gave me a small horn attached to a leather strap that enabled me to sling it across my shoulder so that it hung over my back.

Jean told me to go alone along the forest tracks and keep in touch with hounds by listening for them to give tongue. These large, black-and-white hounds hunted with a superb cry. I was to blow my horn if

I saw the hunted deer cross the ride. I was pleased to find that the horn, unlike an English hunting horn, had a reed, so no skill was needed to produce a note should I need to blow it! The forest has a mass of well-kept rides that criss-crossed each other and my horse was far too clever to let us get lost. Whenever we came to a 'crossroads' we stopped and we both listened then set off again in the direction of hounds. We proceeded, most of the time, at a slow canter. He was sure-footed and did not pull and so I was very comfortable and felt safe. He was also very fit and I got tired long before he did!

I saw a deer cross the ride just in front of us and blew the horn. Hounds came within a few moments, followed by Jean but – I had blown them to a new deer! Jean was very forgiving, which was most kind of him. He lifted hounds and took them back to the hunted quarry. Eventually, they killed the deer.

Once a deer was killed, hunting stopped and grooms appeared from nowhere to take the horses away. The deer was skinned and its carcass cut up while hounds were controlled in a pack. The deer's hide was swung over the carcass while Jean and other male followers blew musical calls on their enormous horns.

Suddenly, I was summoned to go forward. Jean took off his hunting cap and placed one of the deer's slots (feet) across the top of the hat. With great ceremony he presented this to me as guest of honour. It was later mounted on a wooden plaque bearing the words: *'Equipage Pic'ardie Valois, chevre-2h de chasse Les Honneurs à Mme Sallie Walrond 25 Janvier 1968.'*

The hounds were then allowed to eat the flesh before being taken back to the kennels. All the hunt followers went to a house near the forest for a meal. My dining companion was a delightful man and I felt I ought at least to try to converse.

'Parlez-vous anglais?' I asked hopefully.

'A leetle,' he smiled. At least that was a relief, I thought. 'Egg and bacon,' he pronounced firmly. I was somewhat puzzled as bacon and egg didn't seem the kind of dish we would be served during this meal but perhaps it was a post-hunt tradition in this part of France.

'Oh? Are we going to eat bacon and egg now?' I asked just to clarify the situation. He looked mystified. I reached for the dictionary to look up 'now'. 'Bacon and egg maintenant?' He shook his head.

'Non, non, pas maintenant.' So we weren't going to have bacon and egg now after all. My heart sank. I had a feeling it was going to be a long, silent meal. 'Shopping,' said my companion suddenly. 'Mark and Spencer!' he beamed. I stared at him blankly,

'Pardon?'

'Mark and Spencer. Shopping.'

'Yes, it's a big store where people go shopping,' I explained. He nodded and laughed, 'Anglais – leetle! You French?'

'A little,' I replied. Now it was his turn to sigh with relief. 'Cheval, reynard, fatigué,' I said the only three words of French that I knew. He looked at me expectantly. 'Cheval, reynard, fatigué,' I repeated. 'That's all.'

'More?'

'No.'

'Mais, madame, vous promenez à cheval, vous chassez le reynard et puis vous êtes fatiguée, n'est-ce pas?' he teased. 'Vous comprenez?' And I was surprised to find that I did!

It was not the long, silent meal I had anticipated. We got along famously and with the help of the dictionary, miming and dredging up some long-forgotten words from school French lessons, I even described foxhunting in England and how, unlike here, Suffolk Hunt followers jump huge ditches between fields to go from one wood to another rather than spending the whole time in one covert as here in Compiègne. He seemed to understand and when the meal was over and we parted company, he bade me au revoir, grinned and said,

'Shopping! Mark and Spencer!'

I hadn't the heart to tell him it was Marks and Spencer.

★   ★   ★

Christine began to take an interest in driving and it may be because of this that I was invited to judge the dressage phase of the driving pony championships that were held at Senlis near Paris.

I was met at the airport and taken to the venue of the competition. I was made very welcome, introduced to fellow judges and officials and given the paperwork and some refreshments for later. Fortunately, a bi-lingual dressage writer accompanied me, as my command of the French language was, to say the least, limited. I had taken 'extra French' at St Paul's Girls' School but the vocabulary had not included such phrases as 'falling in on the corner' and 'lacking impulsion'.

My writer and I took up our position at the E marker on a long side of the dressage arena opposite another judge at B. I looked around to check that all was in order but there was a marker letter missing on the opposite side.

'The P marker isn't there,' I pointed out.

'It does not matter because it is not – how to you say? Not needed for the test,' my writer informed me.

'There's a cable lying across the entrance at the A marker on the short side where the competitors come into the ring,' I drew her attention to this potential danger.

'It does not matter because they will come in at the other end.'

'But they start the test at A,' I objected.

'They will drive into the arena from near to C then turn down the centre at A.'

And, indeed, they did. The first few competitors came in and all went according to plan. I had to trust that my writer was correctly translating my comments and marks. Then, a competitor took the wrong course. The judge at the C marker, the President of the Jury, did nothing. It was, and still is, usual for the competitor to be stopped by the President and told to correct their course. The phrase 'error of course' is written on the dressage sheet and marks are deducted. To make sure I told my writer,

'Put "error" in the comments column.' The test continued with even more errors. 'Error of course,' I told my writer again – and again, and again. Finally, it became impossible to judge because the movements were being driven in all the wrong places but I gave a mark for the movement as it was being driven.

Eventually, the competitor left the arena and I expected the President to call the judges from the E and B markers to discuss matters but nothing was said and the next competitor came in to be judged.

When the class was over I went to the President to ask him about the test that had been full of errors. He looked completely blank and so I presumed that he had not been able to understand my poor French.

I then said how much I liked the chestnut Welsh cob that, in my opinion, had performed by far the best test of the class.

'Non, non, non,' said the President, and I gathered that he thought 'le petit poney noir' was the best – a little black Shetland which had executed a very ordinary test.

I flew out of Paris airport that evening feeling absolutely shattered. I had a raging headache and vowed to never again judge in a country where I was unable to express myself because I could not speak the language.

A week or so after my visit, I received a copy of the results and I was pleased to see that the chestnut cob had won the dressage so obviously the other judge had liked the test as much as I had.

Amazingly, I was invited to return the following year to judge the dressage at the French championships. I refused the kind offer, much as I would have liked to stay with Jean and Christine again in their lovely home.

CHAPTER 30

Driving Trials with Raz

I<small>N 1982 I WAS CONTACTED</small> by carriage driving enthusiasts from New Zealand. There was a possibility that I might be invited to visit both islands to judge and teach. It was an exciting prospect as I had always wanted to visit New Zealand. A keen New Zealand Whip, Humphrey Topham, was in England visiting relatives. He came to Thorne Lodge one weekend and drove the tandem and later came to watch me give a breaking demonstration.

Probably as a result of Humphrey's visit I was formally invited to teach and judge in New Zealand. There was talk about the formation of a New Zealand Driving Society and how funds were to be raised to finance this proposed trip. The drivers were keen to learn about the relatively new sport of driving trials and so I thought that if I were to teach them, I had better do some homework and put into practice what I preached.

I had, of course, driven my tandem round courses in the 1970s and had judged all over the country but I had *not* actually competed with a single pony. The best way of learning what I would be expected to teach would be to compete with Raz in the open single pony classes.

Throughout the summer of 1982, Raz and I, accompanied by

friends, June Hales and Robert Clinton, competed in the Windsor Park Equestrian Club events. We won the dressage phase on two occasions but we got lost on the marathon twice. This made me realise just how easy it was to take the wrong route, how carefully I must read the map and follow all of the directional arrows. We missed one such arrow because spectators were standing in front of it but, had we been following the map properly we would not have made that mistake and so it was entirely my fault. We gradually learnt how not to get lost and we ended the season by winning the overall championship at the Club and brought home a beautiful silver salver.

The following year, in the same competition, we came first in the dressage but in the cones section had dislodged one ball and incurred a time fault. When my passenger, June Hales, and I reconnoitred the marathon in the Land Rover, we made notes as we went round the course.

At one particular obstacle, comprising trees and bushes, we made a note: 'Can't see A on approach.' The 'A' flag, that indicated the first 'gate' of the obstacle, was hidden behind the trees and could not be seen from the approach track. Rather than helping us, this cryptic note hindered us because when we approached the obstacle at speed we did not know when to turn to find 'A'.

'Where's A?' I asked June.

Raz, on her way to winning an event, with Gill Hatley as navigator.

'Don't know,' she replied desperately searching for the flag marked 'A'.

'If we don't turn soon, we'll have gone past the obstacle area!' But we still could not see it.

Suddenly, I saw a red flag on my right and turned sharply to go round it.

'Are you sure you're right?' June asked me.

'Yes!' I replied.

'It might be the wrong course,' observed June.

'It's OK,' I said and urged Raz through the B, C, D and E 'gates' before going out of the exit. We continued and finished with a good time.

On our way back to the horseboxes, June and I discussed our score after the presentation, dressage and cones. We had twenty penalties in hand ahead of our nearest rival which was a comfortable lead, providing that we did not do anything disastrous. We knew that he could be very fast across country and likely to beat us on time through the obstacles. Just then we saw him and I called,

'How did you get on?'

'Broken a trace and a tyre came off the vehicle,' he replied disgruntled. When he had gone June and I looked at one another and grinned. It looked as though we had won!

We took the harness off Raz and tethered her to cool off while we loaded the vehicle in readiness for the journey home. We cleaned the harness and made some tea. I imagined that all that I had to do was to go to the secretary to pick up our red rosette and collect the trophy that we had brought back from last year. We were sitting on the ramp of the trailer, drinking our tea, when our rival came towards us with a broad grin on his face. I had a feeling that all was not well for us when he said, 'What happened to you then?'

'What do you mean?' I asked him.

'You've got the big E – eliminated!'

June and I didn't know whether to laugh or cry.

'You've won then?' I said at last.

'Looks like it!' and off he went.

'What on earth did we do?' I asked June incredulously and we went to find out. It transpired that we had gone round the red flag that indicated the turning point for the teams, instead of round the tighter turning point for the singles where there was a similar red flag clearly marked 'Singles and Pairs'. It led to the 'A' gate but we could not see it as we approached as it was partly obscured by the trees. So, we had eliminated ourselves… At least June had the grace not to say 'I told you so'.

I never made that mistake again and I learnt far more by losing this competition than I ever would have learnt by winning.

June continued to accompany me as passenger and together we took Raz to two national-level events in 1983 hoping that we might be lucky enough to qualify for the National Championships. The first one was at Brighton where I drove Raz to a weighty, modern Harewood sporting gig. We won the dressage, went clear in the cones and were second in the marathon in spite of the heaviness of the vehicle that Raz had to pull. We won overall which qualified us for the Nationals. We then went to Sandringham where she again won the dressage, went clear in the cones but came third overall as we were beaten on time on the marathon by faster drivers. I had, by now bought a lighter vehicle for the marathon phase for, strong though Raz was, I felt it a little unfair to ask her to pull such a heavy vehicle over an arduous marathon course. It was a John Willie cart with metal wheels and shafts and a light wooden body and was so much

easier for Raz to pull. We went to a few club events and Raz nearly always came first in the dressage but we were frequently beaten on time in the marathon.

At the National Championships at Windsor we were lying third after the dressage. We set off on the cross-country marathon course and all went well until we cantered towards the exit of the second obstacle where we hit a dip in the ground. The cart tipped up throwing us out. June landed balletically on her feet so luckily was not hurt. I was determined to hang onto the reins but when the wheel passed over my ribs, I let go. Raz cantered off across Smith's Lawn with the cart on its side. She did not gallop or kick or even appear to be frightened. She just kept going at a steady pace as though I were still driving her. I called, as loudly as I could,

'Raz... Waaaalllkkkk...' Much to my surprise, she began to turn in an arc, the canter became a trot as she began coming back to me in a wide circle. I continued, 'Raz... Waaalllkkk...' As she headed towards me at a brisk trot someone grabbed a rein and Raz stopped. Someone else began to undo harness.

'Stop! Leave the harness! I'm going to carry on! Help me right the cart!'

The cart, being so light, was quickly put back on its wheels while Raz stood quietly as though nothing untoward had happened. My spare equipment was littered over the grass and I gathered up as much as I could and put it back in the cart. Someone returned my whip, which had been found hanging over the exit flag. That confirmed my fears that we had capsized inside the obstacle area and hence incurred more penalties. The stopwatch on the dashboard had reverted to zero and so had the one that June wore round her neck.

We set off again and, after catching her breath, settling herself on the seat beside me, June looked at her wrist watch and said, surprisingly,

'We don't seem to have lost much time.'

'We must have!' I exclaimed.

'Not all that much, really.'

Consequently, I urged Raz faster and we flew round the rest of the course. As we approached the sand pit obstacle June said,

'We're only a couple of minutes late.' Indeed, it transpired that we

Raz competing at the National Championships after our turnover, which is why the trace is over the end of the shaft.

had lost only one minute and thirty-six seconds over the whole course!

Soon after the marathon finished I had to walk the cones driving course. I heard an announcement telling me to hurry as I had only two minutes to inspect the course. I could not hurry for I was so sore from the bruising of the wheels that I could barely stagger round the route I would be driving. Few people knew that we had turned over which was fortunate because if I had had any sympathy from my fellow competitors, I would have burst into floods of tears. The John Willie cart was now something of a parallelogram in shape but luckily we had the Harewood gig that we had used for the dressage. Raz went clear in the cones and we ended up sixth overall which was incredible.

I intended to compete in just one more driving trial before I retired from this form of competition. I entered for the Wyllie trials in October. It was, to say the least, uncomfortable competing with a broken rib and a sore back incurred when the wheel of the John Willie cart had run over me, but we survived. We came third in the dressage and went clear in the cones but were beaten on time in the marathon. We finished eighth out of twenty-seven starters.

By now I decided that I had learnt enough to be helpful to the drivers of New Zealand with their new venture of horse driving trials.

⊰⊱ **CHAPTER 31** ⊰⊱

New Zealand

THE NEW ZEALAND DRIVING SOCIETY was formed in 1984 and the following year I was officially invited to run three, three-day seminars and to judge at shows on both the North and South Islands. I accepted with great enthusiasm as this was a fantastic opportunity to see a country which I had heard so much about.

Brian and Chris King, the secretary of the NZDS, who had organised my trip were at Auckland International Airport to meet me and, by special permission of the airport authorities, John Quigley, President of the Auckland Driving Club, collected me with his horse and phaeton. (Never before, or since, had a horse-drawn vehicle been allowed on airport premises!) The flight arrived two hours late and they had all waited patiently for my arrival – as had press photographers and reporters. However, I declined to be interviewed by the media simply because I was so exhausted by the twenty-five-hour flight that even my speech felt slurred and I knew that I would be totally incoherent. I feared that they might think that I was either drunk or full of drugs. However, the photographers took pictures of my stepping up into the vehicle but after a mile or so of equine transport I was transferred by motor transport to the Kings' property in the north of the North Island. Once there, I slept for so long that Chris

Chris King in New Zealand. Her pony always wore an open bridle with no blinkers. (Photo reproduced by kind permission of Brian King)

told me afterwards that she had looked into my bedroom to make sure that I was still breathing!

The following day, feeling sufficiently recovered, I was interviewed by the press, who gave considerable coverage of my visit.

The first seminar venue at Rotorua was a long drive from the Kings' property. I wondered how I was going to have the time to give individual attention to the thirty turnouts. Brian and Chris, plus a friend of theirs, Jack Field, were among them and shared the transport of ponies and vehicles. I was surprised to see Jack's ponies were to be carried in an open-topped trailer. They loaded easily, one at a time –

Jack Field's ponies and gig in their open trailer, ready for travelling. (Photo reproduced by kind permission of Jack Field)

233

obviously very used to it all. Each was separated by a rail and stood looking over the side. Another three ponies were loaded onto the Kings' open truck and a trailer containing four carts was towed behind.

The convoy set off and arrived at Ngongotaha, on the outskirts of Rotorua, where I was to stay with the Barclay family. Their lovely home looked over Rotorua Lake. In a field adjacent to the house were Loma Barclay's small flock of Poll Dorset sheep. Loma had these sheep so well trained that they would go wherever she wished without the use of a dog. One morning, I helped her to move some to another pasture. They appeared to be very intelligent, had pretty faces and neat bodies and were very co-operative!

The Barclays also kept a few cattle and I helped to move heifers and an enormous red-and-white Hereford bull. I had great respect for him and kept my distance. I did exactly as the Barclays told me but the bull was very biddable.

Just before I was due to start day one of my first seminar, I was bitten on the hand by a sand fly and my arm swelled alarmingly. The Barclays knew exactly what to do and their first aid worked. As always, on trips like this, I have to keep on my feet come what may.

I began the seminar with slides, then put harness onto a single, a pair, a tandem and a team, to demonstrate and explain how the harness should fit. It was vital that I should impart as much information as possible for these keen people to put into practice. All the participants were extremely anxious to learn and very receptive, which made my job easy. I checked the harness on each of the thirty turnouts, then demonstrated the coaching style of rein handling. The vehicles varied from the basic two-wheeled, pneumatic-tyred variety to a few traditional European carriages. Brian King was, at that time, building gigs and so a few people were driving these. Horses and ponies ranged from small Welsh types to large Cleveland Bays and from crossbred heavies to hackneys.

I was invited to put four of Jack Field's ponies together as a team for the first time. However, I discovered that the leaders' reins were not long enough. I could only hold them if I knelt on the floor of the vehicle rather than sitting on the seat. As this was decidedly unsafe we joined some more pieces of rein to lengthen the leaders' reins and that

enabled me to sit on the box. The ponies went as if they had been driven in a team for all of their lives. It was hard to believe that this was the first time that they had been driven as a four-in-hand. They were a credit to their owner as they had such trust in him and because he sat beside me they felt fully confident.

Jack Field's team put to for the first time, driven by Sallie in New Zealand. (Photo reproduced by kind permission of Chris King and Jack Field).

In the evening I showed films and spoke about showing.

The second day's morning session began at 8.30am and went on until 1.30pm. During that time I sat beside twenty-seven Whips. That meant that each one had eight minutes of going round the field and between a few cones. After a brief lunch break, I showed more slides and gave talks on driving the cross-country phase of an event and how to drive a cones course.

The evening session comprised watching a video of Raz taking part in the Sandringham trials and a talk on how to drive a dressage test. Everyone was given a copy of the test to learn overnight so that they could drive it the next day.

When judging them all driving the test, I made sure that everyone could hear my comments and remarks, which were recorded by my writer for future reference. Everyone was here for pleasure as well as to learn and so I had taken some tri-colour rosettes to award. These, I felt, would give some sense of purpose to the tests. I divided the Whips into three groups so that three different people were able to win a rosette.

Contestants then drove the cones course. Again, there were three different winners of my rosettes, which the New Zealanders loved as

they were so different from the strips of felt or ribbon they normally received.

Jack Field drove three of his experienced ponies harnessed abreast – a trandem – to a pneumatic-tyred, two-wheeled cart and he flew between the cones at a canter. The outer ponies were brilliant, nipping in and out to avoid hitting a cone and they easily won their phase of the competition. Jack's harness was a good example of New Zealand enterprise: it worked superbly and was very simple. It comprised breast collars and breechings on the two outer ponies, with no pads or cruppers, simply some straps to hold the traces and breechings in place. Jack allowed me to drive the trandem. The ponies were a delight to handle, being very responsive. No doubt, this was why, when we put the team together, they were so good.

In the evening, and to conclude the seminar, I showed the slides of carriages. I was made an honorary member of the NZDS and given one of their solid silver swingletree badges to wear.

With the first seminar over, I took a day's rest to relax and catch up with washing and ironing. During my 'time off' I was taken to a local tourist attraction called the Agrodome where I saw a remarkable display with sheep. One at a time, nineteen rams came into the arena, and stood on pedestals of different heights arranged to form a pyramid. Each ram was rewarded with a bowl of food when it reached its platform whereupon it stood quietly until all nineteen were in position. A sheepdog then came in and ran up and over the backs of the sheep until it reached the top of the pyramid where it balanced triumphantly on the back of the topmost ram. The whole spectacle was most unusual and hugely enjoyable.

I was also taken to visit Rainbow and Fairy Springs, near Rotorua, another tourist attraction comprising a farm, a trout hatchery, and plants and wildlife native to New Zealand. Half a million gallons a day of crystal-clear, pure, spring water bubbles naturally into the Rainbow Spring and here swim the most enormous trout I had ever seen. Some weighed up to fourteen pounds. Every winter wild Rainbow trout from Lake Rotorua swim upstream to Rainbow Springs to spawn. (I had to remember that 'winter' here was from May to September.)

After the trout we went to a darkened aviary to see the flightless, nocturnal kiwis, the national bird of New Zealand. I was very privileged to be taken behind the scenes and actually allowed to hold a kiwi. A rota system operates so that each bird is not subjected to public viewing, which is stressful, for too long. I was concerned that my handling the bird would cause it distress but was assured that it was all right. The kiwi was a very strange creature. Contrary to popular opinion, it has wings but they are too small to support it in flight; its feathers are like fur, it sniffs for its food with nostrils at the end of its long beak and has whiskers like a cat!

Next we visited the famous hot springs of Rotorua, created during volcanic eruptions millions of years ago. Underground thermal activity made geysers spout high, thundering fountains of hot water from warm pools rich in minerals. Lakes of mud bubbled like huge pots of brown boiling marmalade. But there was a dark side to it for notices warned spectators not to stand too close to the edge of the pools. There have been horrible deaths due to people falling into the boiling mud.

All this was set in a Maori village. The seminar participants had had a 'whip round' to raise money so that I could attend a 'hangi', a traditional Maori feast. I enjoyed a most unusual meal that had been cooked by steam in a hole in the ground. I asked how and was given instructions – in case I wanted to try it at home!

1. *Dig a hole in the ground at least 40 centimetres across and 'quite deep'.*

2. *Make two wire baskets with handles.*

3. *Put some rocks on a wood fire and burn for one and a half hours.*

4. *Prepare the food (meat or fish and any kind of vegetable).*

5. *Drag the rocks into the hole and splash with a bucket of water to make steam.*

6. *Place the food in the wire baskets on top of the hot rocks, with the meat and fish at the bottom, the root vegetables in the middle and the green vegetables at the top. Place a wet cloth on the top and cover everything with a layer of earth to prevent the steam escaping.*

7. *Cook for three hours.*

Somehow I didn't think I'd be trying it at home...

As this particular 'hangi' was being served at The International Hotel in Rotorua, I had my doubts about whether this method of cooking had been used! The food for the feast was spread out on a central table in the middle of the dining room and guests sat at long tables. When the time came to eat we were invited to help ourselves to whatever we wanted. There were masses of salads and fresh fruit as well as lamb, chicken, venison, fish, sweet corn, potatoes and carrots. There were two things that I had never eaten before: mutton bird and raw fish. I took a teaspoonful of each so that I would be able to finish it even if I did not like it. The mutton bird tasted like fatty mutton and raw fish tasted of, well, raw fish. I will not be eating either again.

After dinner we were entertained by colourful Maori dancers and singers. The Maori warriors, huge fellows with painted faces, stomped their feet and shook their arms in the furious rhythm of a traditional dance. I was glad it was a display for they were really quite frightening, especially when they flashed their tongues. A group of Maori girls sang and swung colourful pom-poms round their heads, their bodies swaying gracefully in time with their singing. What a memorable party it was!

But next day it was back to work and Chris drove me to my next venue, Fielding, on the south-west side of the North Island. We went through the Kaingaroa State Forest to Lake Taupo where we stopped for a picnic and I collected some pumice stones, created during volcanic eruptions, but which now floated in the water of the lake. From there, the road wound between an active volcano on one side and ice-topped mountains on the other side. We continued through the Tongariro National Park and across the Rangipo Desert to Taihape, a town of wooden houses grouped around a narrow gauge, single-track railway. Finally, we arrived at Fielding where I stayed with the Hodders, relatives of Eric Bolstad, the President of the NZDS. They lived in a neat little suburban house that Grace (Mrs Hodder) kept spotless. I was looked after very well and wanted for nothing.

I was taken to finalise the arrangements at Fielding racecourse where the seminar was to be held. I looked over the areas set-aside for dressage and cones driving, inspected the hall where I was to show the slides and checked that all the equipment, including blackout material for windows and extension cables, was ready.

Next day the judging began at 10.30am. Classes were divided by the sizes of the animals, beginning with the smallest. Each size was judged first on 'turnout' then on 'style and manners'. Championships were awarded to ponies and to horses. There were two similar classes for heavy horses as well as a heavy horse championship.

I was interested to see, during the show, that a number of the animals were wearing rugs, despite a temperature of 70 degrees. I learnt that they were to prevent the sun from scorching the animals' coats. The next classes were for 'reinsmanship' and Whips were divided into novice and advanced. There also classes for novice and advanced horses and ponies. Obstacle driving and scurry classes were popular and included four classes for juniors and one for pairs. There was also a class for vintage vehicles. So, the organisers really did do their best to put something on for everyone.

The second seminar followed a similar programme to the first one. There was a sprinkling of barely broken animals and much of the harness needed attention. I sat beside most of the drivers and did what I could to help. The dressage judging was recorded so that members could watch the videos and listen to my comments later at a Society meeting. On the last evening, one couple asked me to harness their ponies as a tandem after having driven them only as a pair. There were no problems and the owners were delighted.

The next day it was time to move on again and Humphrey

Topham, whom I had met in 1982 and who had been instrumental in my being invited to New Zealand, collected me from Fielding to drive me south to Upper Hutt, where I was to have a break before flying to the South Island. He had been competing with his horse, Cannon, and he collected me with his truck pulling a trailer containing Cannon and his vehicle.

It was a very long but interesting journey to Humphrey's family home at Upper Hutt, not far from Wellington, New Zealand's capital city.

First the road took us along one side of the spectacular Manawatu Gorge; the railway runs along the other side and the river flows through the bottom. It follows a mountain range where the sheer rock walls that towered above the road were covered with wire mesh to keep them from crumbling and prevent rockfalls onto the road.

We arrived at a place called Masterton where we dropped off Cannon and his vehicle, for they were competing in a show there the following Saturday and it would save the horse unnecessary travelling. We continued along a winding road for miles and miles, past the Rimutaka Mountains, through farmland with rolling hills and pastures full of Friesian cattle, deer and angora goats but whose fields were scorched by the sun. Finally, we arrived at Upper Hutt where I stayed for a couple of days' holiday.

Humphrey had done an enormous amount of work on the New Zealand combined driving rules. He had written them, with amendments to the British rules, to suit the conditions in New Zealand and was anxious for my comments. We discussed them at great length.

He had built his own vehicle and showed me an equirotal version (wheels all the same size) that he had also devised in his carriage-building shed. The rear half of the vehicle was hooded and joined with a ball hitch to the axle of his gig to form a four-wheeler, rather like an equirotal Victoria. It was an imaginative carriage and typical of New Zealand ingenuity.

★　　★　　★

A couple of days later, I flew from Wellington to be met at Christchurch in the South Island by Lucy Giles and driven to the home of Audrey and Bill Ellen, who have a stableful of lovely hackneys. When we arrived, a friend, Nola Wallace, who drove the ponies, was busy plaiting four of them in readiness for the following day's show at the Kirwee showground nearby. Gladys Dale, a BDS judge from Scotland, was visiting New Zealand, and so she joined us prior to judging the hackney section of the show.

I began judging the non-hackney section at 10.30am. The classes were quite different from those I had judged in the North Island. They began with turnout, then maiden (not to have won a first at any show) and then to open classes of differing heights. Next came classes of varying heights called 'paced and mannered'. After this were classes for 'journey horses or ponies' – this was new to me. It was to be judged on the animal considered most suited to convey its passengers on a long journey. Exhibitors in the family pony class startled (even horrified) me by the things they did to prove to me the suitability of their animal for all the family. Some of the antics were just plain dangerous, in my opinion, such as crawling underneath their pony while it was put to its vehicle. One person actually passed between her pony's hind legs! However, everyone survived, so maybe I was being over-cautious.

On the day after the show, Nola Wallace and I put two of the hackney ponies, with which she had been very successful on the previous day, in tandem. We made up a set of harness with an assortment of straps we found in the harness room and a used a gig. Nola was a talented Whip and the ponies were well trained. We gave the ponies two sessions in tandem and I felt very enthusiastic about them. I would have loved to have brought them back to England.

I was then driven to Charles Cooling's hackney stud nearby, where about twenty lovely hackneys were stabled and at grass. They were superb and he had shown them very successfully the previous day and produced the only tandem at the show.

Before the third and final seminar, to be held in Christchurch, I was taken to Roger and Lucy Giles' home where all the arrangements for it had been made. It was wonderful just to relax, sitting on the bank of the river that flowed right by the garden and watch the trout swim by.

Then Lucy and I set off for Wanaka where I had a few days' holiday before conducting my final seminar. We drove for miles through more spectacular scenery, along Lindis Pass and past Mount Cook, New Zealand's highest mountain, to arrive at the 20,000-acre sheep station where we were staying with friends from the NZDS. From my bedroom were wonderful views through the huge picture window – the most beautiful part of New Zealand I had seen – a distant valley where the mountains sloped down to the edge of the Lake Hawea on one side and where some of their 9,000 sheep grazed on green hills on the other. There were magnificent, curly-horned, heavy-fleeced, Merino sheep wherever I looked.

A neighbour arrived in a small helicopter to look at and buy some rams.

'What makes a first-class Merino?' I asked.

One of the sheepmen thought for a moment then said,

'A long back, a square shape – that makes lambing easier – and strong feet.' He paused. 'They have the best wool in the world so you've got to shear as much of it as possible – no good leaving bits of it still on him – be like throwing away money!' he laughed. It was all totally new to me and quite fascinating.

Later, I watched angora goats being shorn, having their feet trimmed, their horn tips cut and deloused by a line of louse powder sprinkled along their spines before being let loose.

A couple of days later Lucy and I returned to Christchurch to prepare for the last seminar, which was to be held at the Kirwee showground. I met more members of the NZDS, including Graham Holloway whose firm had generously sponsored my holiday in Wanaka.

About seventy people arrived to see the slides on the first morning. Cordelia Hislop, who had accompanied me in the days of showing Ali, had moved to New Zealand and she had, at that time, a couple of donkeys which she drove. She booked in for the seminar at Christchurch and we had a great time catching up on the past. She was able to join up with a NZDS member who had brought a beautiful donkey to the seminar as Cordelia was not able to bring a turnout.

Chas Cooling brought a hackney horse for the single demonstrations and the Ellens brought two hackney ponies that we drove in pair and tandem. The Holloways brought their pair of ponies and I sat beside and instructed thirty Whips on the second day. The third day began at 8am with dressage and cones driving. We put the Holloways ponies in tandem and they went well as did John Glynn's 17hh Standardbreds which we drove to his lovely Ralli car. They behaved impeccably, which was a relief, for they were very big and strong and could, I imagined, really take a hold but they had beautifully light mouths.

On the final afternoon we put together as many tandems as we could muster and the New Zealand Tandem Club was born. I was honoured by being made Patron.

I later calculated that I had driven about seventy-five different animals during this trip to New Zealand and had put to five tandems.

When I left Auckland for England I came home via Singapore, where I stopped off for a couple of days' holiday paid for by the NZDS as a farewell present. Relaxing in Singapore, I recalled the different sounds that had woken me each morning during this visit.

At Roturua, it was the call of the huge magpies that frequented the Barclays' property. At the Hodders, it was the 6.28am train that woke me. At the home of Humphrey and Barbara Topham, it was the river rushing over the stones and the chirping of cicadas, cricket-like insects. At the Ellens' home, it had been a hackney mare calling to her foal that woke me. In Wanaka, it had been first the heavy rain then the bleating of the Merino sheep. But in Singapore, it was the shrill, insistent ringing of the telephone.

'Hello,' I mumbled sleepily.

'Good morning, madam, do you have a breakfast voucher?'

I thought for a moment then saw the voucher on the bedside table.

'Yes,' I replied. I glanced at the clock. It was 3am.

CHAPTER 32

California I

IT WAS A DARK, MISERABLE, DAMP WINTER MORNING when the telephone rang. I picked up the receiver.

'Mrs Sallie Walrond?' asked an American voice.

'Speaking.'

'Hi, there, ma'am!' and the caller went on to introduce himself. 'I'm calling to invite you to judge the pleasure driving classes at the Los Angeles County Fair in Pomona, California.' I was a taken aback to say the least. 'It's a very big fair, ma'am,' the caller was at pains to assure me lest my silence might mean I was not interested, 'it runs for two and a half weeks in September. We're asking you to judge four days and there are two sessions on each day: the matinée session from one till six, then the evening session, which starts at seven. It's formal so we ask our lady judges to wear an evening gown. The classes are divided into the usual sections. We'd also like you to assist with the judging of the pleasure driving mules, ma'am.' The caller finally paused for breath. I watched the rain running down the window and visions of Californian sunshine, palm trees and sandy beaches sprang to mind but I gathered my thoughts sufficiently to discuss details of judging and the show. 'You'll be met at the airport, of course, and you'll stay at the Lemon Tree Motel – they have a very good restaurant there, ma'am. The same chauffeur will drive you to the show-ground where you'll meet the other judges…' And so it went on. It was an exciting prospect and I quickly agreed that I would go. After yet more discussion regarding my judging duties, my travel arrangements, my accommodation and so on, the caller thanked me and was about to bid me goodbye.

'Oh, by the way – ' I said. 'Are all expenses paid?'

'Yes, ma'am,' he paused then said, 'there'll be about five and a quarter million spectators.'

I gulped.

'Would you confirm all this in writing, please?' I needed time to think, 'And send me a copy of the schedule.'

'Sure thing, ma'am.'

★　　★　　★

Eight months later I flew to Los Angeles; the arrangements went like clockwork. On the first day of my judging I met the other two judges with whom I was to share the judging in the driving arena. They were both American and I immediately felt comfortable with them. I knew that we were all going to get on really well, which was important. As we were going to be working closely together for four days it was essential that we should respect each other for our specialist knowledge. It was also important that we would support each other throughout, as time in the arena was tight and it was important that each judge should not overrun the time allowed for each class.

I wore a long-sleeved cotton dress for each matinée performance. The weather was warm and, at first, I tried to wear a large-brimmed hat to protect my head and the back of my neck from the sun but it was windy and several times I nearly lost the hat so, in the end, I settled on a small tight-fitting hat. Each evening, I wore a different long dress and black patent-leather shoes but they quickly became coated with dust from the arena surface.

It could scarcely have been more different from a British show. In the centre of the arena was a large, ornate gazebo erected on a platform, especially for the judges. It offered a refuge from the sun and a place to rest and relax between judging our various classes, while at the same time, refreshing ourselves with the limitless supply of cold drinks. The sides of the gazebo were open but, supported on white pillars decorated with flowers and leaves, its high conical canvas roof, scalloped around the lower edge, provided welcome shade. Pot plants and foliage provided a touch of greenery in the dusty arena and flags fluttering from tall poles added splashes of colour. There was even an electric organ at one side of the gazebo and very well played it was too – a selection of bright, cheerful tunes kept the audience entertained whenever there was a lull in the proceedings. Just before the judging was due to begin, the announcer, who was also in the gazebo, stepped out, put the microphone to his lips and announced over the public address system,

'From Suf-*foke*, England, we have – Salleeeee Wall-*rond*!'

I emerged from the gazebo in front of the crowd who clapped, whistled and cheered. I was thrilled by this wonderful reception and I waved enthusiastically back to these warm, welcoming people, grinning all over my face. When the cheering died down I stepped back into the gazebo while the announcer introduced the second judge to the crowd. There was another rapturous reception of thunderous applause and wild cheering. I felt a little deflated. The third judge then emerged to the same whistles, shouts and waves. My ego was bruised, my elation vanished and I quickly came down to earth!

I kept the schedule close by me at all times, for every class seemed to have different rules. It was impossible for me to remember which came next and so I had to check, double-check and treble-check before I walked out to judge each class. There were twelve classes to be judged in five hours so there was no time to waste or indulge in leisurely wandering up and down the line-up as often happens in Britain. All three judges had to 'kick on'!

Keith Snell, resplendent in scarlet coat and top hat, was my ring-master and hornblower. He was respected by all competitors and no one argued with his commands. Throughout the four days he was a tower of strength by keeping the classes in order. He was also extremely knowledgeable and experienced and I learnt a great deal from him.

The first class was 'Single pleasure pony obstacle course, gambler's choice'. Each driver had a set time to negotiate as many obstacles on

Judging in California, with Keith Snell at my side, keeping everyone in order. (Photo reproduced by kind permission of Duane Rieder)

the course as he could. The aim was to amass as many points as possible. Obstacles could be driven twice, and the difficult hazards gained more points than the easy ones. The driver with the most points was the winner. Great concentration was needed when judging this competition and so I enlisted the help of the mule judge on the grounds that two pairs of eyes were better than one.

The next class was the 'Unicorn (two wheelers and one leader), pleasure horse/pony, working'. In all classes designated 'working', 70 per cent is given for performance, manners and way of going; 20 per cent for the condition and fit of the vehicle and harness, and 10 per cent for neatness of attire.

I kept repeating this to myself like a mantra: 70 performance, manner and going; 20 vehicle and harness; 10 neatness – 70 performance, manner and going; 20 vehicle and harness; 10 neatness. I said it to myself again. And again, and again.

Four unicorns entered the arena: three Friesians and a hackney. The hackneys looked superb, but then the Friesians of one unicorn in particular caught my eye. It was no wonder that, in the past, these majestic black horses, with their proud head carriage and high action had been favourites for funerals.

Once the unicorns were lined up, I inspected each in turn. Knowing that I would be wearing a long dress while judging in the evening and hence unable to pick up horses' hooves for inspection, I decided to be consistent throughout all my judging and would ask the grooms to do this. I indicated to one of the grooms to pick up the off-fore foot of the leader of the hackney turnout. He looked surprised and struggled to lift the foot off the ground. By now, I had noticed that the feet on this horse left much to be desired. The horse made no attempt to co-operate and, indeed, all three animals seemed to stand as far apart from each other as their harness would permit. I asked for the rein back but they were unable to perform the movement. As a result I placed the Friesians, owned by Frank Leyendekker, in first place.

'Draught horse, singles' were next. I was not involved with them and so retreated into the gazebo to study my schedule of classes and see what came next for me. It was the class for single hackney horse or pony. There were only three entries so that this was quite straightforward. They were to be shown to a two- or four-wheeled, antique-type vehicle but, thank goodness, there were no percentages to worry about this time. Next came the pleasure driving mule reinsmanship class with marks of '75 per cent for the handling of the reins, whip, control, posture and the appearance of the driver and 25 per cent for the condition and fit of the harness and vehicle and neatness of attire'. I had to forget the previous class's percentages and learn these – but at least there were only two: 75 driver, 25 harness and vehicle.

I had to join the mule judge to give my opinion on the fitting of harness and the vehicle. Most of the mules were about 14–14.2hh, and either chestnut or brown. Their harness and vehicles were similar to those used with horses and ponies and they walked and trotted in much the same way.

The 'Combination, drive/ride, horse, pony' was next. Animals were judged 50 per cent as pleasure driving horses or ponies and 50 per cent under saddle at the walk, trot and canter. They had to be ridden and driven by the same person, as in some British ride-and-drive classes. Now I had to forget the 75/25 percentages – this was 50/50 – even easier to remember – but that didn't stop me checking the schedule again just to make absolutely sure.

I had a break while the 'Green Western Pleasure mules' were judged. 'Green' was what we would have termed 'novice', for this class was open to mules of any age in their first or second year of showing. They had to be ridden in a snaffle at 'a walk, jog and lope both ways on a reasonably loose rein without undue restraint'. They were marked on the basis of '70 per cent for performance, 20 per cent for conformation and 10 per cent for appointments'. At least I didn't have to remember these percentages and could sit back and enjoy watching the mules which, contrary to their popular image, behaved extremely well. Keith, the ringmaster, ordered them to proceed from walk into lope (canter). All were well trained, obedient, beautifully balanced and light in the hand.

The mule unicorn class was next and, again, I stepped in to join the mule judge. They were expected 'to show walk, slow trot and working trot … to stand quietly … back readily … and an ability to work as a unit with all three mules showing an evenness of tugs and the lead mule showing an alert and animated way of going conveying an image of style'. There were only two entries for this 'turnout' class.

My next class was for single pleasure ponies to be driven by a lady. Out came the schedule again to make sure I had committed these percentages to memory correctly: 40 per cent for performance, manners and way of going, 30 per cent for the condition, fit and appropriateness of the harness and vehicle, 15 per cent for the neatness, and appropriateness of attire and 15 per cent for the overall impression. I repeated the new 'mantra' to myself: 40 performance, 30 harness and vehicle; 15 neatness; 15 impression. I checked the schedule again and again as I was sure I would forget – but I didn't.

I then had a break while the single draught horses were judged. Prizes were awarded to tenth place in this class as there were so many entries among the 'heavies': Shires, Clydesdales, Percherons, Suffolks and Belgians.

In my next class, reinsmanship, there were fourteen entries. The Whips could drive either a single or a pair and the marks which had to be given were 75 per cent for the handling of the reins and whip, control, posture and overall appearance of the driver and 25 per cent for the condition and fit of the harness, vehicle and neatness of attire. Forget the 40-30-15-15 I had just learned. This class was another 75/25 percentage – at least that wasn't too difficult to remember and as there were only six in the class the result slipped into place quite easily.

The last class of the matinée performance was for 'Green trail mules' which were ridden over obstacles such as might be found on a trail ride: a wooden bridge, a gate to open, uneven ground simulated by a row of motor tyres and so on. All the mules coped extremely well and the more I saw of them, the more I admired them.

My head was spinning with percentages as I was driven back to my motel at 6pm to change into my long dress for the evening performance which was to begin at 7pm. I barely had time to redo my hair, let alone eat, so I returned to the show with an empty stomach.

The evening began with scurry driving for pairs of horses or ponies. The cones course was driven against the clock with ten seconds added for a knocked cone and 20 seconds added if a groom dismounted. There were only four turnouts and so this did not take long – and at least there were no percentages to remember!

A draught horse class for pairs to be driven by ladies or juniors was next. This was followed by single pleasure mules: 'working' – more dreaded percentages. I checked the schedule: 70 performance, manner and going; 20 vehicle and harness; 10 neatness. I must not forget…

I then had four-in-hand, pleasure horses or ponies, 'working', to be driven by a gentleman. I sighed with relief, for the percentages were the same as for the previous class. Frank Leyendekker, whose Friesians had won the unicorn class, had put a team together and again was outstanding.

Tandems of draught horses were next and they were followed by the 'Hunter under saddle mules'. These mules were asked to gallop and the riders were asked to wear 'boots, britches, stock tie, coats, hunter's cap or derby'. There were sixteen entries in this class, which I greatly enjoyed watching. Contrary to popular opinion, these mules were all so willing and obedient.

My last class of the evening was for town or formal vehicles, such as gigs or phaetons, for single pleasure horses or ponies to be judged on 'turnout' percentages. Out came the by now dog-eared schedule so that I could memorise the correct percentages … for the last time, at least for that day! There were eleven entries, all of a very high standard.

Draught horse four-in-hands followed, when drivers were given a specified test to perform. The class was judged on 'responsiveness and smoothness of the hitches in completing the course'. Prize money of $300 was given to the winner, down to $100 for tenth place. The final class of the day was for ridden mules.

To signify the end of the day's judging, fireworks were let off at 11pm at the other side of the showground but I was too tired to watch the display. I was taken back to my motel where I had a meal before falling into bed, exhausted – only to dream of percentages!

California II

A<small>FTER BREAKFAST NEXT MORNING</small> the car arrived to collect me and take me back to the showground so that I could watch the morning classes of Friesians being shown in hand. The athletic young Americans were experts at these in-hand classes. They were slim, smart and beautifully turned out. One person ran with the horse, as would be the case in Britain, but a second person 'encouraged' more action from the animal with a whip which he or she waved at, not hit, the horse. It was quite a spectacle!

Judging started again at 1pm after a snack lunch: a gambler's stakes for mules, Friesians under saddle, ride-and-drive mules, a class for 'Green English pleasure mules' then draught horses for gentlemen to drive. I only had one turnout in the working pair or tandem class but a large 'working' class for 'country vehicles to include road carts, village carts and other two-wheeled vehicles'. Seventeen turnouts entered – which took some sorting out. Then came a class for draught horse unicorns followed by mule pairs (I stepped in here in case I was needed to advise on the harness and vehicle) before my next class for pairs, after which was the draught horse pair class.

The afternoon finished with a 'combination hunter, drive and jump class for horses and ponies'. Animals were shown in harness then saddled and ridden over a hunter course of fences. They had to be ridden and driven by the same person. 50 per cent was given for the jumping performance and 50 per cent for the driven work – at least those percentages were easy to remember!

Each day the eight-horse team from the Budweiser Brewery gave an arena display. The magnificent bay Clydesdales with luxuriant white-feathered legs, came majestically into the ring drawing a dray loaded with beer barrels. Their gleaming harness was lavishly decorated with brass. The team drew up on one side of the arena, to a mock 'loading bay', then, with enormous skill the driver turned the team through 90 degrees until the rear of the dray backed up to the side of the 'loading bay'. The horses came round, crossing their legs as they went, until all eight stood facing the centre of the ring. It took a skilful driver to handle this enormous team.

One day, a different driver sat behind the team which made me realise, even more, how difficult this manoeuvre was. When the team was driven into the arena, the wheel of the dray caught the edge of the gazebo where we judges were sitting and dragged it (and us) a few inches! Then, the poor driver had trouble in bringing the team round into the final back-up position. He managed, in the end, but watching his efforts made me understand just how expert these drivers are in handling the heavy horse teams. It was a thrilling sight.

On the evening of the second day there was not a great deal for me to do. The other judges dealt with the draught horse gambler's stakes, the concours d'elegance, the $500 pleasure mule class and the six-in-hand draught horse driving competition. The Friesian specialist, Sem Groenewoud, officiated for the Friesian pair and tandem class and other judges dealt with the hunter/hack mule and the draught horse class to be driven by ladies.

My first class was the important $500, four-in-hand turnout event and my favourite Friesian team, owned by Frank Leyendekker and driven by Clay Maier, took first prize. The mule hitch teams of four concluded the second day and I returned to the motel restaurant for a meal at about midnight.

I was keen to watch the Pulling Contest on Saturday morning. These classes were divided into lightweight pairs of horses, 3,300lbs and under, and heavyweights of 3,301lbs and over. They were competing for a first prize of $1,000 down to a tenth prize of $100. The lightweight pairs had to drag a sled with a weight of 1,500lbs and the heavyweights started with the sled loaded at 2,000lbs. The pairs of horses were brought, one pair at a time, to the sled and hitched to it. They did their best to drag it for a given distance. The length of the official pull was 15 feet. The pair (which was called a team) was allowed two pulls, the longer of which was the one that counted.

The successful pairs were those that, on command from their driver simultaneously, leaned their entire weight into their collars. They lowered their heads, dug their hooves into the ground, flexed their hocks and pushed against their collars, straining with all of their might. The muscles of their shoulders and quarters rippled so that their power was almost tangible. It almost moved me to tears to see these willing horses trying their utmost to move, what appeared to me, an impossibly dead weight. Having no wheels meant that the sled stopped whenever the horses' pull lessened. Any pair that did not step forward at exactly the same time to start the pull failed to move the sled at all. However, the discipline was excellent in that no driver chastised a horse, in any way, for not moving the sled. The rules stated: 'Hitting in any way or slapping with lines not allowed.' Certainly, there was no sign of verbal or physical abuse and the drivers appeared to be good sportsmen.

My matinée judging session began with a timed obstacle course for pleasure four-in-hands. Ten seconds were added for any marker hit, any refusals and each break into canter, with three breaks incurring elimination. This brought yet another win for the already successful Leyendekker Friesian team.

My next class was for 'Country (sporting or informal) buckboards, runabouts, surreys and other four-wheeled vehicles, single horse or pony, working'. As this was a 'working' class, I checked my schedule again just to make sure I had the percentages correct. All the checking, double- and treble-checking, and reciting them to myself like a poem, meant that I had, by now, pretty well memorised them.

The next class was most entertaining: draught horses to be ridden bareback. The rules stated that the horses were to be shown at the walk, trot and canter (at the discretion of the judge) both clockwise and counter-clockwise round the ring. I did not see any of the twelve competitors fall off – but how uncomfortable and precarious they looked – and all for a first prize of just $45. I doubt I would have done it for $1,000 but, luckily, no one asked me to!

After that little light relief it was back to judging again: single turnout driven by a lady. There were sixteen entries and here my main criterion was that the horse should be an ideal 'lady's' horse: going 'politely' in a showy way to an elegant vehicle. Next came the mule hitch, a team of six. All the mules were superb and beautifully matched but one team worked together better than the others and so was proclaimed the winner.

The class for single Friesians followed and again was assessed by the specialist Friesian judge, Sem Groenewoud. My last class of the afternoon was for tandems of pleasure horses, then came the junior driven draught horses. The matinée session finished with a trail mule class.

Saturday evening began with a working hunter mule sweepstake, when mules were ridden over a course of fences about three feet high. Their jumping ability amazed me – I had no idea that mules could jump so well.

My first class of the evening was the championship for the four-in-hand and I awarded it to the beautiful Friesian team driven by Clay Maier for Frank Leyendekker. Afterwards, ringmaster Keith Snell told me that this team had won this class four times in the past five years.

The single draught horse championship was followed by the $500 western pleasure mule stake.

A class for Friesians put to Friesian Sjees was next. The rules stated that 'authentic Friesian attire and equipment to a sjees should be shown'. Friesian specialist Sem Groenewoud judged this class.

A Freisian sjees (chaise) is a two-wheeled vehicle resembling a large gig. The body is often decorated with paintings, gilding or ornate carvings. It is usually driven from the left-hand side, unlike a gig which, of course, is driven from the right-hand seat. Freisian sjees can be shown either with a single black Friesian horse between shafts or a pair driven either side of a pole. Traditionally, breast collar harness is worn and the traces are made of white rope – a striking contrast against the black coats of the horses. When a pair is put to, belly bugle harness is used to hold the pole in position. This attachment, which is rarely seen in Britain, comprises a metal fitting with two semi-circular metal bands that pass under the bellies of the horses. It is fixed to the pads, by straps, and it holds the pole in position. The draft is with traces in the normal way.

When judging was completed, I went to the horsebox area and asked the winner if I could see their belly bugle harness, for I had never seen it before. Although the competitors had packed the equipment away, they got it out for me to see and handle. They explained how it all worked and I was most grateful to them for the opportunity to learn about this unusual piece of harness.

The next class I judged, the working championship for pleasure ponies, was followed by the draught horse pair championship, then the single pleasure working championship, in which there were nineteen entries. The rosettes, known as ribbons, were normally presented by the ringmaster but I preferred, throughout the whole show, to hand them to the Whips myself, as it gives me pleasure to make personal contact and say a few words. The announcer would call out the lowest placed driver, who would come forward to take the rosette before driving round and leaving the ring. This procedure was repeated until the winning turnout came forward and drove his or her 'victory pass' to tumultuous applause from their supporters.

Throughout the judging, it was quite usual for fans and supporters of the turnout I was inspecting, to shout and applaud from the stands. As I have always maintained an impartial and unbiased attitude, I found it somewhat irritating in that they appeared to think they could influence me by the amount of noise they made.

On Saturday evening, I grew most concerned when the last class, draught horse teams of six, was still in the arena as eleven o'clock approached. Eleven o'clock was the start of the firework display. If, when the fireworks were let off, one team became frightened, it would cause chaos and injury among the forty-odd heavy horses in the arena. But, just before 11pm the gates were opened at both ends of the ring and the teams left. Even so, I did not imagine that it was much fun unhitching and unharnessing teams of six horses to a background of fireworks. However, it occurred to me afterwards that, this being California with fireworks let off at every opportunity, perhaps the horses were used to it and took no notice.

Sunday morning was set aside for the halter (in-hand) classes for the heavy horse breeds. The Suffolks and Belgians were judged together and there were separate classes for Shires, Clydesdales and Percherons. These were judged at one end of the arena, while mules and donkeys were judged at the other end.

My last session of judging was the matinée performance on Sunday. I began with the gambler's choice for single pleasure horses. Then came a commercial class open to all types of animal, for only the vehicle was to be judged. Its uniqueness and condition were paramount and the rules stated 'the harness should complement the vehicle and the animal. The performance of the equine should not be considered unless manners were bad.' All three judges joined together for this class.

The Western pleasure mules were judged next, then I had a class for hackney pairs and tandems. A reinsmanship class for draught horse pairs was next in the arena and this was followed by a pleasure driving donkey class which the mule judge and I assessed together.

My next class was a 'servant-driven' vehicle for which the coachman and groom had to be in full livery and this was judged as a 'turnout' class (horse 40 per cent, harness and vehicle 30 per cent, neatness 15 per cent and general impression 15 per cent). It was open to singles and pairs put to vehicles such as broughams, landaus and Victorias. Then there followed a competition for driving teams of four mules through a specified test.

My last class of the show was for junior reinsmanship with a single horse or pony. The first and second placings were obvious but I pondered over third and fourth. The teenage boy, who was the more competent of these two, was holding his reins incorrectly and so I went to speak to him.

'Do you realise you're holding the reins upside down?' I asked him. 'See how you have the offside rein, instead of the nearside rein, lying over your index finger? The nearside rein should be on top. Did you know that?'

'Yes, ma'am.'

'Was it a mistake that crept in just now?'

'I guess so, ma'am.'

'Oh dear. But you know I have to judge what I see at the time,

don't you?' I tried to let him down gently.

'Yes, ma'am.'

'I'm sorry but I'm going to have to put you down to fourth place because of that. Otherwise, you're a very competent Whip,' I wanted him to feel I could say something positive and indeed it was true: he was extremely competent and it was a shame he had had this slip up. I went to the other child, a girl.

'You're handling the reins very well. You're holding them correctly too,' I smiled at her and she smiled shyly back but said nothing. 'You're doing your best to drive in the approved coaching style – you've been well taught, haven't you?' She nodded. 'I'm awarding you third place,' I told her. She seemed taken aback but pleasantly so. I didn't tell her that she was not as competent as the boy but she was basically more correct.

I suspected I would receive 'an earful' from the boy's supporters and I was not wrong. They told me exactly what they thought about my judging. I explained my reasons but they were not convinced,

'I had awarded him first prize in an earlier class – his turnout is lovely. I had to judge what I saw and what I saw in the last class was wrong,' but they were still upset. The boy, however, had appeared to understand that my decision was nothing personal – even if his supporters did not – and that I was simply judging what I saw on the day.

At last, my judging was over and I could relax, feel relieved that I had coped with my huge workload, forget all about percentages and enjoy what was left of the show: the final class for draught horse teams of four. As always, I had learnt an enormous amount and although utterly exhausted, I would not have missed it for anything.

I brought back Keith Snell's excellent book on horn blowing and tapes he had made of coach horn calls. He was a master in the art of horn blowing and I was delighted to have had the opportunity of working with him.

CHAPTER 34

Guitars, Tandems and Gliders

WHEN I WAS A CHILD I never imagined that I would meet and get to know Elton Hayes, whose music I had listened to on the wireless during Uncle Mac's *Children's Hour* in the 1940s. Later, in my early teens, I greatly enjoyed Elton's rendering of 'The Owl and the Pussy-cat' and his radio programme 'Songs to a Small Guitar'.

Unbeknown to me, I had been driving past Elton's farm, about four miles from Thorne Lodge, for some time and had noticed two quality horses in a field next to the road. But it was not until 1975 that I spoke to Elton for the first time. As I was driving my tandem, Libby and Raz, past the entrance to his farm a sprightly, white-haired gentleman appeared. I pulled up and said hello.

'I heard hooves – just wanted to see whose horses were passing,' he said conversationally. 'You don't see many tandems.'

'I'm getting them fit for the Lowther driving trials,' I explained. 'I'm Sallie Walrond, by the way,' I introduced myself.

'Elton Hayes,' he replied.

'Not *the* Elton Hayes?' I asked incredulously.

'Well, yes, I suppose so.' Elton was always very modest but he did eventually admit to being the singer-guitarist of my *Children's Hour* days.

Elton's music was unique. He played classical Spanish guitar and I later learned that he had a priceless instrument made by the same maker as one played by the world-famous guitarist, Segovia. Every note that Elton played and every word he sang was crystal clear. He abhorred the pop guitarists who accompany their so-called lyrics of little more than 'Yeah, Yeah, Baby' with what he referred to as the 'three chord trick' of guitar playing. Elton's repertoire included an enormous amount of music that he had written himself. He researched lyrics, often long-forgotten ballads from manuscripts in the British Library, and wrote music to go with them. He was in great demand in the 1950s, performing at the Festival Hall in London and live on radio. His films included the role of minstrel in the Walt Disney production of *Robin Hood*, starring Richard Todd. He was given both the opening and the closing shots of the film which delighted him.

Strangely, after our first encounter, outside his farm, we bumped into each other several times: while shopping in Sainsburys and filling up with petrol at a local garage. Inevitably, we fell into conversation and he explained that he had had enough of the stresses of life in London and the theatre and he had retired from performing. He was now farming and had a large herd of breeding sows, although his first love was horses. The two horses I had seen in the field by the roadside were his: an Anglo-Arab mare and her son which Elton had bred from her. His wife, Betty, of forty years was very ill and Elton cared for her. When she died, he joined the St Edmunds Riding Club, which held regular events and shows at Thorne Court. He went hunting and he began to come out driving with me whenever I needed an extra pair of hands with the team.

★　　★　　★

Elton's guitar playing was, by now in the early 1980s, restricted to playing to friends because his fingers had become crippled with arthritis. Years of producing beautiful, clear notes from his guitar had distorted his fingers. When I was privileged to listen and watch him playing his guitar, it all looked so simple. I asked him to teach me how to play the instrument, which I felt certain that I would be able to do easily for I had been quite good at music at school. However, I found it extremely difficult, as I discovered that I have absolutely no natural ability with a stringed instrument.

But we persevered. I learned about the strings and frets and he taught me the fingering of basic chords and he even wrote music especially for me.

'A nice, easy, little piece,' he said one day. I placed the music in front of me and tried to remember all the things he had taught me. I began haltingly. I could tell there was something not quite right and tried again, and again.

Then Elton said casually, 'Stick in a B flat.'

'Where is it?'

'Right there, your fingers are lying over it.' Which fingers? My fingers were lying over lots of strings and frets.

'Elton, where is it?' I could hear the desperation in my voice.

'It's there. It should come from within you.' It didn't.

'Where is it? *Which string is it on? Which fret is it on?*' I was now almost in tears. I looked at my fingers, the strings and the frets but I could no more see a B flat than fly. It was hopeless. 'Oh, Elton, tell me where it is?' I whined sounding just like a child. Patiently, he directed my fingers to the required B flat. I played it. It sounded right.

One day, however, I got my own back! Elton was learning to drive my tandem. He wanted to earn his tandem bars and was coming almost daily to drive the ponies. He was, by now, competent with single and pair. One morning when we were about to drive out of our farm entrance, a car was parked in our way. There was a narrow gap wide enough for Elton to drive the tandem through providing that he lined up the ponies in exactly the right place. He needed to hold the wheeler off the corner so that he did not touch the car with the gig's wheel hub.

As we approached, I told Elton decisively,

'Opposition near wheeler.'

'Which rein is that?'

'Your fingers are lying over it, it comes from within you!' I said triumphantly hastily leaning across him and pulling the appropriate rein to avoid a collision.

'All right,' laughed Elton, 'point taken!'

Elton persevered until suddenly, one day, it all seemed to slip into place and he became quite proficient at handling four reins. His skill was proved when, in 1988, we took Teddy and Raz to the Tandem Club meet at the home of Peter and Polly Nichols in Wiltshire. I drove the tandem for the first half of the meet and Elton drove for the return six-mile drive. We left the Nichols' stableyard but our exit had been made very difficult by a parked car near the stone pillars of the gateway. I asked if the owner could move it, which he did, but on our return it was back again and there was another car parked behind the first one, blocking the gateway still more so the gap looked impossibly narrow.

I jumped down from the gig, to take off the leader but before I could do so, Elton had manoeuvred the ponies into a perfectly straight approach to the gateway. He held the wheeler off and drove through the gap. The gig's old-fashioned protruding hubs missed the stone pillars and the cars by no more than an inch or two. I felt so very proud of my pupil. Peter Nichols saw the manoeuvre and later commented that Elton deserved his tandem bars if he could execute a move like that.

Elton proved to be a better tandem Whip than I was a guitar player.

★   ★   ★

Bill was pursuing his gliding interests and spent most weekends flying his glider at the London Gliding Club at Dunstable Downs. I decided to follow the principle that if you can't beat them you might as well join them and so Bill arranged for me to have a flight with a club instructor in a two-seater glider. Bill was not licensed to take passengers and, in any case, his high-performance glider was a single-seater.

The day came for my flight. I sat in 'tandem' in front of the instructor as we were launched by a winch. About 3,000 feet of wire rope led from the front of the glider to a motor-driven winch at the launch point. Engine power reeled in the wire rope and the glider became airborne like a kite on a string. We were propelled upwards at such a speed and such a steep angle that my back was pinned against the seat – very exhilarating! The glider climbed and once it had reached the maximum possible height of about 1,400 feet the pilot released the cable. For a moment or two we were flying level and it was quieter. Far, far below was the airfield and the famous white lion cut into the chalk of Dunstable Downs near Whipsnade Zoo. I was just beginning to relax a little and take in the scenery when we turned and began our descent.

The glider approached the tall hedge at the edge of the airfield. It was like being carted on a courageous horse, knowing that there was not much that you can do but, providing that you sit still and follow through, you will clear the hedge with ease. The glider cleared the hedge and we bounced over the turf at sixty miles an hour. We had been airborne for about three minutes.

It had been hugely exciting and I was already visualising flying in competitions in my own high-performance machine. However, the next time I went for a flight things were very different. The instructor and I were taken up on an aero tow behind a light aircraft. It was very turbulent and after a minute or so I wished I were on terra firma.

'Can we come down? I don't feel very well,' I asked the pilot, who was sitting behind me. I was afraid lest I be sick all over the glider. Obligingly, he landed the glider but I felt terrible.

'Don't worry. Conditions are rough. Perhaps you shouldn't have gone. It's happened to one or two people today – some of them are experienced pilots,' said Bill consolingly.

Gradually my motion sickness wore off and I dismissed my experience as unfortunate. I would try again on a calmer day. A month or two later I had another flight and, once again, after a very short time I had to ask the pilot to land. Finally, I had to accept that this sport was not for me after all but at least I had given it a try.

I sometimes go with Bill to the Gliding Club to help him to rig his glider. I watch him launch and disappear into the sky.

'You know, Bill,' I once said to him, 'it takes as long to get the glider out of its trailer, fix the wings to the fuselage and heaven knows what, as it takes me to harness and put to a team of four horses!'

'It probably does but when I've finished flying, I put the glider back into its trailer and it just sits there till I want to fly next time. I don't have to feed it every day!'

CHAPTER 35

Disabled Drivers

As an instructor I had become involved with the Riding for the Disabled Association (RDA) Disabled Driving Section. Interest in driving by disabled people was increasing enough, in the 1970s, for carts to be designed especially to carry wheelchairs. These early vehicles were square, box-like, affairs but as interest grew carriage designers began to produce ingenious and better-designed vehicles so that, over thirty years, the vehicles have improved considerably. Some have four wheels and others have two. All have a ramp at the rear enabling a wheelchair to be loaded with the driver sitting in place. The chair is then clamped in position so that it cannot move. However, not all disabled drivers are in a wheelchair: some are able to mount, with help, by the steps on the vehicle. The harness is especially designed with several quick release features so that in the case of an emergency, the pony can be taken from the vehicle as quickly as possible.

All have dual-control reins so that the able-bodied Whip has one pair and the disabled driver has another pair. This second pair is sometimes fixed to the noseband of the pony, rather than the bit, if the driver has difficulty in keeping his or her hands still. It is, of course, vital that the pony is absolutely reliable. He must stand like a rock while the driver mounts and dismounts and yet must be prepared to move on when required.

A considerable number of helpers are required for every turnout and I have always thought that able-bodied people who are prepared to give up one day a week on a regular basis to act as helpers have hearts of gold. It is a big commitment. Even more to be commended are people who run a group and look after the animals throughout the year so that the disabled drivers can come for their regular drives.

Drivers' disabilities vary enormously from those with degenerative illnesses such as multiple sclerosis to others with spinal injuries sustained through accidents. Each driver has to be treated as an individual and taught with his or her particular difficulty in mind. Some are able-bodied apart from being blind.

Harry Clive, who lived locally, was running a disabled driving group and the members were keen to become involved with driving events. After much consideration, it was decided that, to start with, a theory session on dressage and cones driving would be held in a village hall rather than subject the disabled drivers in their wheelchairs to the cold outside. This was arranged and a good number of disabled drivers and their trainers attended. I used a blackboard and drew a diagram of an arena. I explained the letter markers, outlined the route to be driven and described in some detail what exactly the judges would be looking for during the test. This served to lessen the mysteries and drivers appeared to feel more confident as they, their trainers and helpers all took notes.

I had devised a cones driving course, which we used from then on. It needed twenty cones, was simple to erect, and started and finished at the same place thus making the timing and stewarding simple. Everyone went home with a copy of the dressage test and a copy of the cones course so that they could practice.

The next step was a training session with turnouts. Drivers were allotted a time to arrive at the dressage arena where I would judge their tests and were allowed twenty minutes so that, after they had driven the test, we could go through the mark sheet together and discuss ways of improving their performance. If time permitted, one or two of the movements could be driven again. Each turnout then drove round the cones course where Harry Clive and Diana Mellows, the East Region Organiser, timed and helped the drivers through the cones.

We all learned an enormous amount during this first training session. Helpers discovered how long it takes to unbox the ponies, harness up and put to before the wheelchair and driver can be loaded into the carriage. We realised that our 'time allowed' for the cones course was too generous – drivers took it very slowly which resulted in too many clear rounds, hence the overall competition rested upon their dressage scores. For able-bodied drivers, the hazards phase of combined driving competitions is usually the most exciting but I was not in favour of such a phase for disabled drivers. Negotiating hazards was just too risky and I feared that a fatal accident could result from a wheelchair strapped into a capsized vehicle.

When we next ran a dressage and cones driving day, the drivers, trainers and helpers were all much improved. These competitions became very popular among the disabled drivers; rosettes were awarded for the dressage, for the cones driving and for the overall scores, and they were greatly prized. Soon regional competitions were being held as there were several groups in the Eastern Region of England. More ambitious still were Inter-Area competitions where groups of drivers, trainers and helpers travelled long distances to compete and wore 'team colours' to distinguish their group. All participants took tremendous trouble with their turnouts. One competition was held at Wimpole Hall in Cambridgeshire and it even received radio coverage.

One day, one of the disabled drivers, Delia Dudgeon, came to me and asked if she could take the British Driving Society Test 1 which had been devised for able-bodied Whips. I did not know what to say other than that it would not be possible. For Test 1 the pony has to be harnessed and put to by the candidate. Although I thought that Delia could probably harness a quiet pony from her wheelchair it would be quite impossible for her to put to on her own. She just would not be able to pick up the shafts and put them through the tugs. What was needed was a test to be written specially for disabled drivers.

At the next meeting of the BDS Training and Test Committee I put forward my idea and offered to write a suitable test. The response was favourable and so I embarked upon writing not one but four tests and called them Preliminary, Elementary, Intermediate and Advanced. For the Preliminary test, candidates had to answer straightforward questions on stable management. They then had to direct their able-bodied (AB) helpers in the harnessing and putting to of the pony. The helpers were to do exactly as instructed by the disabled driver and any verbal assistance from the helpers would result in failing the test. Once the driver was safely in the vehicle, with the AB Whip on the seat alongside, he or she drove a simple test through cones placed wide apart solely to provide a route for the turns in both directions. After this, the driver was taken from the vehicle and he or she directed the helper in the taking the pony from the vehicle and the unharnessing.

Delia was the first candidate to take the Preliminary test and she passed with flying colours having been well trained by Trina Hall who ran a riding school and had become very involved with the RDA. Delia went on to pass the Elementary and Intermediate tests. The Advanced test, however, was very difficult. I wrote it to give a sense of purpose to the few talented people who wanted something to work towards. It involved pair harness and devising a fittening programme of feeding and stable management for a national driving trials pair. Very few people have passed this test, which was precisely my intention.

I was asked if a blind driver could take the Preliminary test. I did not think that it would be suitable and so I wrote a test especially for

Brian Moon and Mary Harris with Angie, alongside a tableful of trophies which they won in 1995. (Photo reproduced by kind permission of R.P. B. Gorringe)

blind drivers. One candidate, Brian Moon, who lived in Sussex, became a guinea pig and the first to take the test for blind drivers. I went to Sussex to test him and was quite amazed by the way in which he harnessed and put to the pony while I examined him. He then drove a dressage test and a cones course, being directed by his AB Whip. Brian then finished the test by selecting a suitable rug for the weather conditions and putting it onto the pony. He struggled manfully with the 'string vest' type of anti-sweat rug, turning it first one way then the other, so that it was first back to front, then inside out, then upside down. Eventually, he managed it and it made me realise just how difficult it is to rug up a pony when you cannot see which is the front of the rug and which is the back. His was a remarkable achievement and I was delighted to tell him that he had passed the test.

In due course, a more advanced test was needed and so I wrote one. The first requirement that the test demanded was for the candidate to assemble a set of single harness. When I wrote the test I tried this for myself. I undid all the buckles of a set of harness and laid it out on the floor. I shut my eyes and assembled it to make sure that this was possible. My worst problem had been that I could not find the browband, for I could not see where it was. This made me realise that it was not so much the assembling that caused the problems but locating the parts. So, when Brian came to Thorne Lodge to take the test, we took Brian's harness apart and laid it out carefully in a logical order so that the pieces could be found. Brian assembled it without any trouble.

His dressage and cone driving were fine as was all the harnessing and unharnessing, rugging and bandaging the pony in preparation for the journey home by horsebox. Then came the theory. We were sitting in the yard, side by side in the sunshine, while I asked him questions about stable management.

'What kind of fencing would you like to have round your field?'

'Post and rail is excellent but very expensive. Plain wire is OK so long as it's taut but I wouldn't want barbed wire – it can be very dangerous,' he began and continued to tell me about every type of fencing imaginable but he never mentioned a hedge. I wanted him to tell me that the best kind of fencing would be a thick hedge.

'There's still another kind, Brian. It's the best kind and you can see it from here.' Then I realised that, of course, he couldn't. I felt dreadfully embarrassed, 'Oh, I'm terribly sorry, Brian, I forgot you can't see…'

He turned towards me and said,

'That's the nicest thing that you could have said. It means you forgot I'm blind.'

Brian passed his test and I have since followed his driving progress with great admiration for both him and his trainer. He has achieved great success at shows in classes for disabled drivers.

The disabled driving test scheme has been very popular. Lectures, talks and discussions on the theory of driving in preparation for the tests give a sense of purpose to winter meetings when driving is not possible because the weather is too cold or wet.

I was made an inspector for the RDA Driven Section and sometimes went, with another inspector, to assess ponies and equipment for safety. Working in pairs meant that the responsibility of an inspection did not fall entirely upon the shoulders of one person. Unfortunately, in one group I had to fail one pony because I thought that it was just too sharp for the serious job required. The group organisers were not pleased with me but I later heard that I had been proved correct, for it had caused trouble with an AB Whip. I was adamant that no chances could be taken where disabled Whips were involved. They are utterly helpless when they are strapped into a wheelchair in a carriage.

Scholarships were awarded to drivers who wanted to train for the demanding role of AB Whip to accompany a disabled driver. Several came to Thorne Lodge for instruction. Some drove my ponies, some brought a pony used by the group and one person brought a pony which, once it was more experienced, would be used by the group for disabled drivers.

The disabled drivers so enjoyed their sessions and, later, the competitions. Training them and seeing their dressage improve was enormously rewarding.

CHAPTER 36

New England, USA

In 1987, two years after my trip to california, I was invited to judge in the USA once again. This was to be at an autumn show run by the chairman of the New England Region of the Carriage Association of America, Peter Morin, in conjunction with Philip and Jennifer DuBois. I had first met Peter in 1981 when I had judged in Connecticut. He made all the arrangements and I flew to Boston airport where my hosts met me and took me to their home, Otter Brook Morgan Horse Stud, at Peterborough, New Hampshire, not far from Boston.

The following day, they drove me to the venue of the show in Monadnock, about an hour and a half's drive away. At that time of the year the scenery was breathtakingly beautiful. Mile upon mile of forested hills stretched to the horizon, carpeted in reds that ranged from dark crimson to vibrant scarlet, every shade of orange from tangerine to tawny and all the yellows from deep ochre to pale lemon with, here and there, a patch of dark green where a tree hung on tenaciously to its summer colour. The rich, gorgeous patchwork covered the undulating landscape like a giant quilt. Maples, oaks, birch, hickory and beech were resplendent in their autumnal glory, which brings thousands of tourists to New England.

Otter Brook Galahad, a Morgan stallion, driven by Philip DuBois to a Meadowbrook Cart. They were winners of many types of class in the USA. (Photo reproduced by kind permission of Stan Phaneuf 05860)

The show ran for three days. On the first morning I had seven pleasure driving classes to judge in three and a half hours. These took place at the same time as the dressage tests. The complications of timing were overcome by the ingenious idea of posting everyone's dressage times well in advance. It was then left to individual competitors to change these times, among themselves, within their particular classes to suit their individual requirements. They then had to present themselves to the dressage judges on time to be judged. The system worked well as both the dressage arenas and the show rings finished on time, with everyone having driven their test and appeared in their show classes. As far as I know, this arrangement is unique.

The pleasure driving classes were all judged on 'working' percentages (70 per cent for performance, 20 per cent for harness and vehicle and 10 per cent for neatness of attire) that made judging much easier than in California. The classes were simply divided by horses and ponies, pairs and tandems, juniors and novices.

Horn blower and ringmaster was the excellent Grace Yaglou who ran proceedings in my ring with a rod of iron but she was greatly respected by all competitors. On one occasion a pony started to kick. Grace immediately brought the class to a halt 'on the rail' (at the edge of the ring) and ordered the offender to leave the arena. The class then

resumed as if nothing had happened.

The American Driving Society has a rule stated on both the schedule and the programme that 'removing the bridle whilst the horse is harnessed between the shafts incurs instant elimination and expulsion from the grounds'. I have often thought that shows and events could benefit from this eminently sensible safety ruling in Britain.

In one of the classes I judged, there were so many competitors that they were far too close to each other for safety, as well as for me to see each turnout to advantage. Grace and I discussed the situation and we decided to split the class, half being sent out of the arena to wait until the other half had been judged. No one jostled for position to escape from a possible rival and I admired their discipline and Grace's 'ringmastery'. Everyone was satisfied because two lots of awards had been given.

Not surprisingly in this area of the USA where the Morgan horse originated, they dominated the classes and I later learned that those bearing the Otter Brook prefix of my hosts' stud, had done particularly well but, of course, Philip and Jennifer DuBois were not competing on this occasion.

Most vehicles were of a low-built design with the body much nearer to the ground than, for example, gigs. Meadowbrook, East Williston and road carts were the most popular but there was one English Harewood gig and one Bennington buggy. To me, the typical, low-built, American vehicles lacked the elegance of the higher vehicles and I did so wish that these magnificent Morgan horses could have been driven to more stylish vehicles that would have complemented their beauty and presence.

Frank and Jean Kinsella's pair of Lipizzaners won the pairs and tandems class and went on to take the Paul Downing Trophy for the most consistently well-turned-out entry. This gave me great pleasure because it had been Paul Downing who had first invited me to visit the USA. I had also been impressed by Penny Rawl's delightful Shetland tandem in the multiples class. As they were the only tandem in that class I asked Grace if I could award them a special first prize. Within moments the required ribbon and prize were brought into the arena. These Shetlands were, to my mind, outstanding. They were American Shetlands, quite unlike the British Shetland with its short legs, rotund body and hairy mane and tail. These were finer boned, more lightly built, and had much longer legs, so that they really covered the ground and were forward going as well as pretty. They were liver chestnut with profuse flaxen manes and tails. (On the Monday after the show Penny brought them to the clinic, which I ran at Otter Brook Farm, and I thoroughly enjoyed driving them. They were light in my hand and obedient and gave me as much pleasure as they obviously gave to their owner.)

The short lunch break was preceded by a display of a six-horse hitch of 18-hand high Belgian horses driven to a heavy wagon. I was privileged to be taken for a short drive behind this magnificent team.

After lunch came the ride-and-drive classes. These were followed by classes for different types of vehicle: two-wheeled informal carriages and sporting vehicles; four-wheeled informal vehicles, and four-wheeled formal carriages so that there was something for everyone. The judging of all these had to be completed by 4.30pm and, somehow, it was.

Barry Dickinson, a well-known and respected Whip in the USA and whom I had first met when I visited John and Ann Friend in Wisconsin, told me that to judge in America you needed the stamina of a camel, the speed of a gazelle, the memory of an elephant and the hide of a rhinoceros! All but the last may have applied but, fortunately, I did not need to be thick-skinned because I was treated with kindness and courtesy for the entire weekend and did not hear a single grumble.

Saturday evening was devoted to the competitors' party and it lived up to the usual high standard of American hospitality. Grace Yaglou entertained us with her horn blowing, using a variety of horns. She began with a few notes from a steer's horn to which she had fitted a mouthpiece. Then she 'played' a conch shell, a washing-machine hose with a funnel attached and even extracted a few notes from the barrel of an opened gun. Finally, she blew a number of traditional coach horn calls from her own brand-named coach horn. She was a master of the art and her skills must be hard to equal by any horn blower.

Joe Zalenski, of Z brand saddlery, then entertained us with songs to his guitar. As I was learning to play this very difficult instrument, I

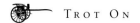

greatly admired his performance and enjoyed listening to him – and only wished that I could play like him.

Sunday dawned cold and wet – a shame because it was the day of the marathon and cones driving – and competitors were out on the course all morning in unrelenting, icy rain. It grew colder as the day progressed, with flakes of snow among the freezing raindrops. The cones driving started after lunch and competitors presented themselves at the arena whenever they were ready. There was some delay between rounds as each vehicle had to be measured and the course altered accordingly. Standard track widths of vehicles were not obligatory at that time. On completion, competitors' scores were recorded and their combined dressage, marathon and cones scores added together.

At the end of the day, we all assembled in a large marquee where we thawed out in the blast from a powerful blower heater and cupped our frozen hands around mugs of hot coffee from an enormous urn. The results were announced and ribbons given in each section as well as for the overall scores.

Monday's clinic at Otter Brook was well attended. There were four Morgan single turnouts, a pair of Morgans and the Rawls' Shetlands filling the available half-hour sessions. The DuBois' indoor school and excellent outdoor arena had good surfaces but, fortunately, the weather was dry so all was well. There was an endless supply of equipment available, ranging from a martingale crupper as used on a tandem leader to a tandem whip which enabled me to demonstrate how the thong should be folded along the stick. We set up weights and pulleys in the indoor school so that everyone could practice the traditional coaching style of rein handling.

The time flew and I had to rush to Boston to catch my flight back to England immediately after the clinic. I brought back with me a Grace Yaglou coach horn. I decided that I had better declare this item on arrival in the customs hall at Heathrow. The horn was of the type that could be split into two halves and was packed in a long, narrow box. It could have been a gun... I pushed my luggage trolley, with the horn box balanced on top, through customs and approached a customs officer,

'I've just come back from the USA where I've been judging at a show of the Carriage Association of America – that's horses and carts,' I said by way of explanation. He did not reply so I continued, 'This box contains a coach horn. It comes apart to fit in the box. I thought you might think it looked a bit suspicious. Do you want to examine it?'

He scarcely looked at me, almost yawned, shook his head in a bored sort of way and waved me through.

★   ★   ★

Back home I showed my precious new coach horn to Elton. His hands were now so stricken with arthritis that he was incapable of playing his guitar. He seized upon the horn with glee for he had already begun to play both my tandem horn and another coach horn I had had for some time. He was learning the art of horn blowing with his typically meticulous approach to music and attention to every detail. He had read Keith Snell's book and listened to the tapes that I had brought back from California. I unearthed a few horns that we had had stored away but none were good enough to satisfy Elton's acute, musically tuned ears.

He discussed the art of horn blowing with George Abbott, an expert horn blower whom we had met when I was judging at the larger shows in Britain. George would be blowing in the ring for the greater part of the day, signalling a change of pace or for the judge's chosen competitors to come into line. He was a great help to Elton in answering his queries about the technical aspects of blowing the horn.

Fortunately, the Grace Yaglou horn satisfied Elton's ears and he became very proficient in playing the traditional horn calls. He even wrote some of his own so that when he was invited to blow, on occasions such as the Tandem Club meets, he could blow a different short call to send each tandem on its way. Once, he blew thirty different calls so that he never played the same call twice. He also judged the horn blowing competition at the Suffolk County Show on two occasions.

At the Lord Mayor's Show in London in 1989, he blew the horn on the Norwich Union mail coach owned and driven by John Parker, the noted team driver and Chairman of the BDS. The coach had

stopped briefly and a group of Londoners challenged Elton,

'Play us the *Post Horn Gallop*!' Elton declined out of modesty.

'Go on, guv!'

'Bet you can't!'

Elton raised the horn to his lips and gave a rousing performance of Herman Koenig's popular novelty piece which, if nothing else, calls for lip flexibility and great technical agility. He was rewarded with a great round of applause and whistles.

CHAPTER 37

Drive and Hunt

In 1988, when tony harvey was master of the Easton Harriers, near Woodbridge, Suffolk, he invited driving enthusiasts to attend a meet of his hounds at the Bedfield Crown pub near Tannington, not far from Framlingham. But there was a condition that had to be obeyed: *all* equine participants were to arrive at the meet in harness drawing a vehicle. Those who wished to follow hounds had to saddle up at the meet and leave the vehicle and harness at the pub.

I asked Bill if he would like to come with me and ride one of the ponies. After all, he had hunted regularly as a boy and teenager. We would be out for only a couple of hours and as Bill weighs only about nine stone, Raz could carry him easily. Bill's reply was,

'Ask Elton. He'll enjoy it far more than me.' Gliders had long since replaced horses in Bill's leisure time and so I wasn't surprised he declined. But Elton was delighted to accept. Elton had hunted, throughout his theatrical career, whenever time and occasion had permitted. All horses went well for him because he was a quiet rider with very good hands. I lent him Raz to keep at his farm for about a month before the meet so that he could ride daily to prepare them both for the occasion.

On the day of the meet, we travelled by Land Rover and trailer with Raz and Teddy (my young Connemara) to Tony Harvey's home, Tannington Hall, where we unboxed and put to: Raz in the lead of tandem wearing a driving bridle and a riding saddle on top of which I fitted the leader harness; behind her Teddy wore a driving bridle, a full collar and, like Raz, a driving saddle over the riding saddle. I fitted a false breeching which saved having to use a crupper. We took the Harewood gig because we could store the harness in its huge boot while we were hunting. We put to and, dressed in our hunting (rat-catcher) tweeds, we set off in convoy with others from the unboxing area.

Eight and a half couple of hounds were loaded into an open top dray with a net over them to prevent their jumping out. The vehicle was drawn by Blossom, a sturdy piebald cob, owned and driven by Mary Garton.

On arrival at the meet we took the ponies from the gig, removed their harness and stowed it in the boot of the vehicle. We exchanged the driving bridles for riding bridles and were soon ready to move off. Several well-known East Anglian Whips were present, including John Parker who followed with his grey team drawing a cross-country vehicle. Mary Garton unharnessed and rode Blossom. Others whom I knew from driving events included Sue Scott with her horse, Bertie Wooster; Jean Carlisle's Shetlands were ridden by children; Mike and Gill Daniells hunted their Friesians; the artist Anne Grahame Johnstone rode her Welsh Cob, Scole Cam, and several more enjoyed the fun.

Hounds found a hare quite quickly and we had an exciting hunt. When we moved on along a lane, I was particularly impressed by Tony's hound control. He spoke to them quietly and they came as one alongside his horse, forming a neat pack under his hunting whip, which he held out sideways. It was a very impressive demonstration of complete control of hounds on a public road. Hounds drew again and after the second hunt, we called it a day knowing that we still had to harness up, put to and drive back to Tannington Hall.

Raz, as tandem leader, was still game to carry on having done no pulling as such, but Teddy was very tired. It was he who would pull the gig back to our trailer and Land Rover and so for the journey home I put Raz into draught so that she could help Teddy pull the load.

Raz had, by now, replaced Libby as my tandem leader and she had become an excellent leader in her own right – as good a leader as she had been wheeler. So good, in fact, that because she never kicked or bucked I frequently put her in front of visiting animals belonging to pupils who were keen to learn about tandem driving. Also, I always made sure that any animal I put behind her was very experienced as a single. I usually fitted overreach boots onto Raz's hind legs to protect her from possible treads from the wheeler's front feet but it did not happen and there were never any problems.

CHAPTER 38

1991

THE YEAR 1991 WAS MEMORABLE IN MANY WAYS. It had been four years since I had judged in New England and Peter Morin, chairman of the New England Region of the Carriage Association of America, once again invited me to that beautiful part of the world, this time to speak at the CAA New England Region weekend get-together. I was to entertain the members after dinner on the Saturday with an illustrated talk on carriages. I accepted and packed more than my usual number of slides, just in case I was asked to perform again on the Sunday.

When working abroad I always carried my lecturing material in my hand-baggage so that if any luggage was lost or delayed I would at least have my slides and could go ahead, even if my dress left much to be desired. If time permitted I could always buy more clothes but I could not replace my slides at a moment's notice. Because of increased airport security, this time when checking in at Heathrow I was told that my slide boxes had to go through the x-ray machine. I was very much afraid that this would damage the pictures.

'Let me open the boxes and take out all the slides, then you can see for yourselves,' I offered.

'Sorry, that's not allowed,' came the adamant reply. (I could hardly believe there was a rulebook somewhere that specifically stated that boxes of slides must not be opened for inspection.)

'If I open them you can inspect them even better than the x-ray,' I pointed out.

'I'm sorry, madam, we can't do that.'

I dug in my toes and demanded,

'Would you please let me speak to your manager?' The supervisor and a manager arrived. They were sympathetic but would not budge but tried to reassure me,

'I can promise you that the x-ray machine will not damage your slides, madam.' I was not convinced and could feel hot tears of frustration – even despair – welling behind my eyes. 'I'm afraid we cannot let you onto the aircraft unless all your hand-luggage is x-rayed,' said the manager.

I knew I had no choice but to give in. I would miss my flight if I dwelled much longer and Philip and Jennifer DuBois, my hosts in 1987, and Peter Morin would be waiting for me at Boston. Reluctantly, I watched the boxes of slides roll away on the conveyor belt and disappear into the wretched x-ray machine. I was absolutely certain that its rays were wiping off every vestige of every picture on every slide. I had no idea how I would entertain the audience without my slides.

They emerged, I grabbed them and hurried to the departure lounge where I opened the boxes with fumbling fingers, my heart in my mouth, dreading seeing totally blank slides. But they were quite undamaged behind their glass mounts. I wanted to cry again – this time with relief. Even so, it had not been a good start.

As before, my hosts met me at Boston and drove me to their home at Otter Brook Farm to spend the night. The next day we went by car to the Sheraton hotel at Sturbridge, not far from Boston, where the 'get-together' was being held. The conference centre here was vast with a huge indoor swimming pool surrounded by palm trees, a conference room seating well over 250 people and an exhibition hall so large that sleighs and carriages for the evening auction were easily accommodated.

My talk was to follow dinner on the Saturday evening. Although I enjoy giving talks, the 'butterflies' in my stomach beforehand make it impossible for me to really enjoy a meal and I prefer to eat after my talk but that is not always possible. This was one of those occasions when I had to eat first and I managed a little of the excellent dinner. The slide-show was so well received by the full house that I was requested to show another set of slides the following morning. I was glad I had packed the extra slides.

After I had finished speaking, the auction was held. There were all kinds of interesting items offered for sale. I was longing to look around, browse through them and even bid, but I was constantly surrounded by people asking me questions. Of course, that was the reason I was there – I was not on holiday – but I spotted the auctioneer holding up a beautiful, light, swept-back collar, about 20 to 21 inches. I felt sure the collar would be perfect for my latest dun Connemara pony, Piper. I was sorely tempted to bid and watched with interest. Somebody called out a bid. Then someone else joined in. It was such a lovely collar... I took a deep breath ready to put in an offer.

'Ah, Sallie, there you are! I did enjoy your talk so much this evening...' A woman came up to me, oblivious that I was about to bid. I smiled at her in a distracted sort of way then looked back at the auctioneer still holding up the collar. Yes, it would set off Piper's head and neck beautifully... I took a deep breath again. 'I've just bought a new horse and I want to drive him but he's never been in harness before. Now, what do you think is the best way...' My companion rattled on. Above her somewhat strident tones I heard the crack of the auctioneer's gavel and the collar was sold. Well, perhaps it wouldn't have fitted Piper anyway.

Eventually, I extricated myself from the lady with the new horse and wandered around the stalls. I saw a set of brass sleigh bells on a black leather band that encircled the horse's body. They were just like those that Ann Friend had given to me when I had visited Wisconsin. I had used these bells at Lowther and often thought that it would be nice to have a second set so that both the leader and the wheeler could wear them. They looked expensive and I glanced at the price ticket: $249.50 cents. I pondered about being very extravagant but decided that this was too good an opportunity to miss. The bells were lovely and I would probably never get another chance to buy such a set again. I produced my $250 to pay for them. The stallholder looked somewhat taken aback on being presented with so much money and promptly gave $225 and 5 cents back to me.

'What's all this? I gave you $250 dollars,' I said puzzled.

'No, no! See, the price is here. It's $24.95 cents, ma'am.' I looked more closely – and indeed it was. I was thrilled – it made up for missing the collar!

I then returned to where Peter Morin was sitting and saw *the* collar on the table in front of him. He too had fallen for it and it had been he who had been the successful bidder. I told him how much I had admired and wanted it but had not had a chance to bid because of the interruption. I felt almost glad that I didn't have the collar because if I had known he was bidding, I would not have bid against him. I knew it would look superb on either one of his hackneys or a DuBois Morgan horse.

Next day, just as I was leaving Otter Brook Farm to go to the airport for my flight home, Peter said, 'Just a little something to remember your trip to New England,' and he presented me with the collar! 'Seems like you wanted it so much – we'd all like you to have it!' he beamed. I scarcely knew what to say for I was overwhelmed by the generosity of my hosts.

In view of the hiatus with the boxes of slides at customs at Heathrow, I anticipated huge problems with a horse collar and so, before I flew out of Boston, I made the officials examine it minutely to check that it was not filled with drugs. I impressed upon them that this was an old horse collar and made them take note that the stitching had not been cut or renewed. I made such a point of all this that I think they were glad to be rid of me and the collar when at last I boarded the aircraft! I simply wanted them to remember me – after all there couldn't be many middle-aged women bringing horse collars through customs – and, if there were to be a problem when I arrived at Heathrow they could confirm my story over the telephone.

When I disembarked and eventually walked through the 'Nothing to declare' channel at Heathrow, I wore the collar slung across my shoulders. No one queried it – perhaps they thought it a new fashion accessory!

★   ★   ★

That winter there was a heavy fall of snow in Suffolk and the countryside looked beautiful. It was a wonderful opportunity to get out the sleigh and try the new bells. The *East Anglian Daily Times* was full of photographs of cars stuck in snowdrifts or marooned in ditches and children tobogganing and snowballing in public parks. I rang them and asked if they would like something different: a picture of a horse-drawn sleigh.

They sent a photographer round immediately.

He was accompanied by a 'Father Christmas'. The newspaper's editor had plans that the picture, complete with 'Father Christmas', might be suitable for the *EADT* Christmas card. My young, dark brown, Connemara mare, Tina, wore a good set of harness and the sleigh bells, I was bundled up against the cold in a fur-trimmed bonnet and Father Christmas looked just perfect sitting in the sleigh. The photograph was indeed good enough to be used later as *EADT*'s official Christmas card.

Piper, my dun Connemara, was coming on nicely and he got on well enough with Raz for me to drive them in pair and tandem. Tina, however, hated Piper and so I decided to find a suitable home for her. Raz, although getting on in years, was still well and sound and I found two ponies were quite enough work. At least, Piper and Raz were both dun, even though they were a hand apart in height.

★   ★   ★

I had been the BDS Area Commissioner for East Anglia for over twenty-five years and decided to retire from the post in 1992. The area was very active; I had a good Assistant Area Commissioner in Jo Jenkins and a hard working and very supportive committee of people such as Angela Sixsmith, June Hales, Anne Grahame Johnstone and Miriam Rawlinson. It seemed sensible to prepare to hand over to others while the area was flourishing.

What I did not know, but apparently 300 or so other people did know, was that a surprise party and presentation were being organised. Minta Winn, one of my first pupils, had had plenty to do with the arrangements. Elton had been delegated to think of some cunning way of getting me to the local village hall on the appointed day at the appointed time. He had been specifically ordered not to tell Bill because they knew Bill would be bound to let it slip. So, when Elton told me that some friends of his, who lived locally, wanted to meet me because they were interested in carriage driving and we had been invited to go for Sunday morning drinks, I believed him. Actually, I loathe Sunday morning drinks: they end up lasting hours and I dislike having to dress up in the middle of the day then having to change into scruffy clothes to put ponies to bed in the evening afterwards. So it was with great reluctance that I agreed to accompany Elton, but I was delighted when snow fell and I was told that the drinks party had been cancelled.

Nothing more was said for about three weeks and then Elton announced one day that the drinks party had now become a lunch party and I was to be ready for him to pick me up at midday on 17 March.

Elton suggested I wear my 'little black dress' because, he said, 'it does so much for you' and so, to please him, I did. He even checked which jewellery I planned to wear and how I was going to do my hair. I thought that he was being somewhat fussy but, I imagined, he wanted me to look my best to meet his friends at this wretched lunch party. Elton was his usual dapper self, in his beautifully cut sports jacket and his white hair neatly trimmed, a gentleman and a gentle man through and through. And so, for Elton's sake, I tried to go with good grace.

Our route took us towards the village hall. Its car park is to the rear but is visible from the main road.

'There are a lot of cars parked there,' I commented.

'Oh, probably a car boot sale,' replied Elton casually. Then he turned down the lane that leads to the hall.

'Where are we going, Elton?' I queried.

'The lunch is being held here,' he said. Strange that there should be a car boot sale *and* Elton's friends' lunch on the same day, I thought, but said nothing for I was thinking how over-dressed I was for a village hall lunch party. Elton parked his car and we got out. It was not until I walked towards the door of the hall that I saw the large yellow BDS banner. I now realised that this was no ordinary lunch party. The hall was packed with BDS members, past and present

The weather vane, before it was mounted on the coach house roof. (Photo by Elton Hayes)

The weather vane, before it was mounted on the coach house roof. (Photo by Elton Hayes)

chairmen, Jenny Dillon, the present secretary, Pam Stewart-Smith from Surrey and countless friends from all over the country.

'What's going on? What is all this? What's it all about?' I asked.

'If you'll just keep quiet for a minute, we'll tell you,' replied Tony Russell, a harness-maker friend 'It's for you! A surprise party to say thank you from us all!'

I was terribly moved and scarcely knew what to say. I glanced across to Elton. He was grinning,

'You knew about this all along, didn't you?' I whispered.

'Of course.'

I was presented with a wrought iron weather vane: a silhouette depicting my tandem and gig designed by Anne Grahame Johnstone and made at Brandeston Forge by blacksmith Hector Moore, assisted by his wife, Mary. In place on the coach house roof it provides a constant reminder of that incredible day.

The only thing that marred the day for me was that Bill had not been there to share it with me. When I told him about it, as soon as he returned from his gliding club, he was, of course, delighted but said, 'I'm actually glad they didn't tell me because I could never have kept that a secret from you!'

★   ★   ★

Later that year, the chairman of the BDS, Peter Nichols, told me that I must attend the BDS Annual General Meeting at the Royal Mews in London in April. I had intended to go, for I always went. Peter seemed most concerned, almost insistent, that I be there. I went and, as the meeting progressed, I realised why Peter had wanted to be certain that I would be there.

I was presented with the BDS Medal of Honour which was very exciting. I was so thrilled when the *BDS Journal* was published in 1992 to read what Tom Coombs, a past chairman of the BDS, had written about me:

Presentation of BDS Medal of Honour to Mrs Sallie Walrond

At the 1991 Annual General Meeting, John Richards presented a BDS Medal of Honour to Mrs Sallie Walrond. The society awards its Medal of Honour purely as a token of its esteem to a member who has given long, honourable and distinguished service to the BDS and the general interests of driving. It is not related to the holding of any office and does not require its recipients to undertake any duties or responsibilities. It is awarded only rarely, the last awards being made in 1988 to Mr Richard James, Mr George Mossman and Miss Anne Norris. The medal committee recommended to council that a medal should be presented in 1991 to Mrs Sallie Walrond.

Twenty-five years spans most of the history of the BDS and, when Sallie was presented with the society's rare and much coveted Medal of Honour at the AGM on April 29th, 1991, for 25 years of most distinguished service as Area Commissioner for East Anglia. This was one of the best deserved awards ever made on behalf of all the members, or ever likely to be. It was universally acclaimed and it was complemented by an earlier presentation of a wrought-iron weather vane, depicting Sallie driving her famous tandem, which she received from all the members of her own area at a special party given in her honour in Suffolk on March 17th.

Sallie Walrond has been a continuously elected member of the BDS Council for almost as long as she has been an Area Commissioner, and her modestly brief contributions to its deliberations are a source of inspiration and fundamental good sense for all our activities. A bastion of orthodoxy and a dedicated custodian of tradition, she is founder president of the Tandem Club, whose members must all demonstrate to her their competence at this difficult driving art, but she has always moved with the times and was one of the first and most successful competitors in driving trials when these were considered to be indecorous by some of her contemporaries. She judges these competitions with the same scrupulous discernment that has gained her the respect of all exhibitors in the show ring.

Sallie has always been a gifted and inspiring teacher, both of horses and of the humans who aspire to ride and drive them. Many of her innumerable human pupils have made their mark on the equestrian scene but only a few of her fellow BDS members may know that some of Britain's top racehorse trainers have queued up each year to persuade her to undertake the breaking of their young horses. They are confident that the elementary education which they get from her will give them the best chance to realise their full potential.

Sallie has travelled all over the world to judge, lecture, instruct and generally to advise people on how to get the best, and the most fun, out of their driving horses. Her books on driving and carriages and their accoutrements and turnout are read world-wide and widely quoted by tyros and experts alike, who recognise the undeniable authority born of practical experience with which her lucid explanations are invested. Her *Encyclopaedia of Driving*, which has been reprinted several times, will be a boon to countless generations to come as a record of the traditions, conventions and esoteric harness accessories of a bygone age which, but for it, would by now have been mostly forgotten.

Sallie is evergreen; perpetually youthful in temperament as well as appearance, she is popularly, and probably quite correctly, assumed to have become an expert on horses in harness and taken office in the BDS just after she left school. The BDS council must now tackle the pleasurable problem of devising an appropriate award to celebrate her 50th jubilee.   T.C.

Tom had been very influential throughout my life. He had taught me about judging coaching classes and had helped enormously with the text of the revised edition of *The Encyclopaedia of Carriage Driving*. I had judged private driving classes alongside him in championships at such prestigious shows as Royal Windsor. I had worked with him as a member of the BDS Council when he was chairman. He had visited Thorne Lodge on many occasions, had driven my tandem, attended the Suffolk Hunt Ball with Bill and myself and became a great friend.

★   ★   ★

The need for carriage driving instruction was increasing to such an extent that the Light Harness Horse Training Board was formed to establish examinations for carriage-driving instructors. This was a chicken-and-egg situation: of the few established carriage-driving instructors, who could examine whom? To solve the problem, a few people, including myself, were appointed 'verifiers' and eight of us were given the right to use the letters LHHI (Light Harness Horse Instructor) after our names. The BDS Training and Test Committee, chaired by Linda Tate, took on the writing and running of the BDS test scheme. These qualifications are now recognised worldwide and are much sought after.

★　　★　　★

Once again I was invited, this time by the Kinsellas, to judge at the Kent Show in Connecticut. A judges' clinic was also scheduled in conjunction with this show and I was asked to give a two-hour talk on the day before I was to judge. I agreed to do this but emphasised that I was certainly not about to tell these very experienced American judges how to judge classes in their own country. I was quite sure that they knew far more than I was ever likely to know. I decided that I would tell them about my judging experiences in Britain and sprinkle my talk liberally with anecdotes – it went down extremely well – and there followed an open discussion on judging in general in which we learnt much from each other. The two hours passed very quickly.

Soon after I began judging on the Saturday morning, the sun broke through the cloud and it promised to be very bright and hot with temperatures in the 80s. I wore a wide-brimmed hat and sunglasses to counteract the heat and glare, for I knew I would be standing in the shadeless arena all day with only a ten-minute break for lunch, while competitors in the ride-and-drive class changed from harness to saddle.

The first six pleasure classes were all judged on 'turnout' percentages (40 per cent for the horse, 30 per cent for vehicle and harness, 15 per cent for neatness of attire and 15 per cent overall impression) and the later classes were judged on 'working' percentages (70 per cent horse, 20 per cent vehicle and harness, and 10 per cent neatness of attire). At least having only two lots of percentages made my job quite easy. It had been agreed that the American judges who had attended the conference on the previous evening would watch my judging, in a group by the rail, throughout the day – a somewhat daunting prospect. The plan was that after each class had left the arena, I would go to the rail for a brief discussion before the next class came into the ring. Fortunately, as each class, except for one, came into the arena, there was, as far as I was concerned, a clear winner, unless it suddenly behaved very badly. It was, therefore, a matter of sorting out the remainder. On each occasion, when I went to the rail, the American judges agreed with my winner.

The exception was the class for pairs and tandems. I had to think very hard before coming up with my result and the American judges could not understand the reasons for my decision.

'Why didn't the pair of coach-type horses win? They sure looked fine to me,' asked one judge.

'They were pulling away from the pole at times,' I explained, 'Couldn't you see?'

'No, ma'am. From the rails here they were going OK.'

'What the judge sees and what the spectator sees are two different things! You get a totally different view from the middle of the ring,' I said.

'What about that lovely pair of chesnuts? What was wrong with them?'

'Again, from in the ring I could see one them was not always level behind, just on the corners.' I hoped I didn't sound too much of a know-all.

'I never saw that,' said one of the judges, surprised.

'You can't from here,' I replied.

'And how about those other chesnuts? The young ones?'

'Yes, they are going to be superb in a year's time but I have to judge what I see on the day, not what the turnout might be in the future.'

'And the tandem?'

'I thought that the vehicle was a little small for the horses.' One of the other judges nodded in agreement and I felt relieved that someone shared my opinion. 'Besides, did you notice there was a bit of a "hiccup" in the far corner of the arena when the groom had had to get down?' They nodded. 'Well, the leader's trace became detached from the wheeler – it happened twice – and the groom had to sort it out. It could have been disastrous.'

'Hmmm, I see now why you placed the Morgan pair first,' put in one judge, 'they weren't spectacular but they had worked well as a pair.'

'Yes,' and I added, 'they were safely and correctly turned out and were an ideal drive for their lady Whip.'

This quizzing by the American Driving Society judges had really put me to the test. However, they concluded that, providing judges have good reasons for their placings and stand by their decisions, all is well. After all, judging is purely the opinion of one person on one day. In the end, there are usually only two satisfied people: the winner and the judge!

I finally walked out of the arena at 6pm. I was glad of a bath and change of clothes before sitting down to dinner that evening with 200 people. It had been a long, hot, tiring day and I staggered off to bed exhausted.

On Sunday morning, a journalist, who wanted to write an article about my visit, interviewed me at breakfast as this was the only time that I was going to be available. I had to judge the junior Whips in the morning and the gambler's stakes in the afternoon. I always found judging of the cloverleaf difficult. It involved driving three circles in two different directions to make a cloverleaf pattern. Drivers take different routes to negotiate the obstacle according to the American Driving Society rules and so I appointed a knowledgeable steward to watch this particular hazard for me.

In spite of this precaution, a problem arose. Both the steward and I declared that one competitor had not driven it correctly. The competitor disagreed and made herself felt in no uncertain terms.

'I have that recorded on tape!' she stormed. 'I can prove I was correct.'

'Please go and get your recording,' said my steward, 'then that will settle the matter.'

We waited for her to bring along her video recording so we could see for ourselves but we heard not another word and she disappeared.

The flight from London had been a miserable and uncomfortable experience. I had been squashed between two very large and unpleasant men who spilled over into my central space without so much as a brief apology. I had mentioned this to Frank and Jean Kinsella and thought no more about it. However, it transpired that they knew someone who knew someone who knew someone who worked for the airline and so, when I checked in for my return flight, I was upgraded into Club class. This was luxury I had never before experienced. I was fed on caviar, smoked salmon and champagne and, more importantly, was allocated an enormous seat. It made all the difference to my flight back to England.

Within a few days of returning home, I received three invitations to lecture and judge in the USA for later in 1991 and the following year, 1992, but I refused. I really had had enough of travelling abroad and preferred to stop while I was still wanted. Elton's philosophy when performing in the theatre was that 'you should always leave them wanting more'.

My mother had returned to England after living in Florida for many years and so, to have more time with her, I began to cut down on my teaching. She was living in a flat in Bury St Edmunds and relied on me to contact her daily. She spent time at Thorne Lodge with Bill and myself every week but, as her health began to deteriorate, became more demanding. I worried about her and it became increasingly difficult to be away for long periods.

★   ★   ★

One evening shortly before Christmas, a fox appeared in the straw shed near the stables. She had an injured shoulder and, unable to bear weight on one front leg, was doing her best to walk on her other three pads. I telephoned a friend, a vet who was particularly interested in foxes, and asked his advice. He told me that if given shelter and food she might recover if the injury was not too serious. I decided to give her a helping hand and, when a large rabbit hopped into our garden, I rushed upstairs and took the rifle out of the gun cabinet. I opened the bedroom window quietly, took careful aim, said a little prayer and fired. The rabbit fell dead instantly, thank goodness. I fed it to the fox,

Foxy. (Photo by Anne Grimshaw)

which seemed grateful for the meal.

The next day was Christmas Eve. I had already done all my shopping but I braved the crowded supermarket to buy a large supply of dog food, everything from luxury brands to economy tins, to tempt the fox. I wanted to be sure to give her a choice. The vet had told me to get dog biscuits too but I soon discovered that she did not like these. Foxy, as I called her, used to come out of her hiding place in the straw when I called her each day with her breakfast in a soup bowl. She ate well and appeared to be getting better. We even saw her kill a rabbit in the garden. Then she began to deteriorate.

One evening when Bill and I went out to see if she was there, she came towards us from the back of the barn and lay down in the straw right in front of us as if asking for help. We were terribly upset, realising that the time had come to help her to die. Bill went into the house and got the 12-bore shotgun. I kept talking to her and she lay quite still with her eyes shut. Bill put her out of her misery. I dug a hole among the trees, carried her to it and buried her. Through my tears I was able to see that her shoulder was completely rotten. The smell was awful. We did, however, get some comfort from the fact that we had done our best for her and that, for about five weeks, she had been well fed and warm in our straw shed.

CHAPTER 39

Judges

Judging appointments have taken me the length and breadth of Great Britain. I have kept all my judge's badges and they hang in the hall at Thorne Lodge. Every single badge tells a story and brings back many memories. Some show committees treat their judges much better than others. My favourite shows to judge were always the Suffolk County and the New Forest.

It was fortunate that the Suffolk County Show was fairly local as it was vital to arrive by 7am to beat the crowds pouring in through the gates later. Judges and stewards would meet in the restaurant where a first-class, freshly cooked breakfast was served in comfortable conditions. The loos were superb and near to hand. Judges were welcomed by their stewards and the chief light horse steward, Colin Willcox, took immense trouble to go through all the timings, numbers entered, specials to be presented and would make arrangements about the meeting place where a particular steward would be ready to escort the judge to the ring in good time for the class.

The New Forest Show provided a similar reception, where stewards such as Robin Ford and Lionel Hunt were second to none. Another steward, Mary Ford, took charge of the road drive through the New Forest. She was always in complete command of any situa-

tion, be it locking and unlocking gates on forest tracks or organising the removal of parked cars causing an obstruction.

At the other end of the scale would be the shows where judges had the distinct impression that they were tolerated but not welcomed. One of my pet hates was having to queue up for the loo, with the general public, just before I was to start my long session of judging.

There was one occasion when I had a steward who assured me that he had stewarded at this big show for years. He wandered to the side of the ring and lit up a cigarette just as the class came in. He then sat down on a chair and left me to get on with the stewarding by myself! I wondered why the show committee tolerated him. Sometimes the steward and I had to consult on matters such as the timing for the final judging in the main ring. I would then ask him to stand behind me and talk to me over my shoulder because this way any conversation between us would not be noticed from the ringside and possibly misinterpreted by spectators as his telling me how to place the turnouts. When I was chair of the BDS Judges' Committee, such a complaint was brought to my notice. There had been concern from the ringside that a steward had been influencing a newly appointed judge on how to place the competitors. I looked into the matter and,

Judging the private driving championship with Major Tom Coombs at the Royal Windsor Horse Show in 1993. (Photo by Elton Hayes)

295

as I suspected, this had not been the case. The steward had been explaining, at length, that the judging was to be completed in another ring and the judge was merely querying the timings. But it had not appeared so to spectators who could not, of course, hear what was being said.

The BDS runs a probationer judges' scheme for people who hope to become fully fledged judges on the official BDS panel of judges. They have to attend a number of shows and work alongside several judges who assess their suitability and competence. I used to like to meet candidates before the class to get to know them before we went into the ring. Then, once we were in the arena I would ask them to tell me, as the turnouts passed a certain point, what their immediate reaction was on this first appearance. During the line-up, after we had inspected each turnout, I would ask them for their comments. After the individual show, I would then ask them for the order of their placings before I told them mine.

On one occasion, I was to judge a class in the ring before it took part in a road drive. The probationer judge who was to have met me, was not at the ringside at the appointed time and so I began judging the class alone. She arrived a few minutes later and came into the ring.

'Sorry I'm late,' she breezed. 'The road drive's next, isn't it? I hope there are some bushes along the route – I shouldn't have had that second gin!'

'There are some loos over there,' I replied coolly and pointed her in the direction of the nearest 'ladies'. Off she trotted and I carried on without her.

Needless to say, I did not write in my report that she was likely to make a suitable judge. When, at the end of the summer, her name came up for discussion by the Judges' Committee, there were murmurs that she had 'a problem' and so, of course, her name was not added to the panel. It was a shame and I felt sorry because she certainly had the necessary knowledge and exhibiting experience.

Occasionally, after judging a private driving class, a competitor would telephone me and aggressively demand to know, 'Why did you put me fourth last Saturday?' My usual reply was: 'Because I so much preferred your turnout to the one that I placed fifth.'

If these people who telephone, because they are cross and feel aggrieved, realised that they are never forgotten for their bad manners perhaps they would refrain. They are, fortunately, so rare that their names will be imprinted on my memory forever. It is quite different when a newcomer to exhibiting genuinely asks for help and honestly does want to know why they were not placed higher up in the line. I then get great pleasure from doing my utmost to help. Usually, such instances are dealt with on the day of judging when it is possible to help the competitor to rectify mistakes so that when I next see their turnout it will be greatly improved.

I had been on the combined driving judges' panel since the competitions began in 1971 and, by 1994, I decided that the time had come to take myself off the list of judges. Judging at most events entailed being away from home for about three nights. The distances I travelled were frequently very long and I increasingly felt that I just could not spare the time involved. I had also reported some driving events for *Horse and Hound* but this was a very demanding task which, after the initial novelty wore off, I no longer enjoyed.

After forty years on the BDS judges' panel I decided that I would relinquish that too. I wanted to leave before I became a 'doddery old fool'. I had seen, first of all as a member of the judges' committee and later as chairman, how sad it was when judges, who in their younger days, had been excellent and well respected, became unpopular as they could no longer cope with the demands of judging. A few of these elderly people would insist that they were still capable of handling large classes at high-level shows when it was patently clear they were not.

Show committees would refer to the BDS panel of judges when choosing a judge for the following year's show and would, quite correctly, assume that if a name was on the list then that person was presumably fit and able to cope with the job. If there had been problems with the judge, the show secretary would inform the BDS judges' chair.

After I became chairman I realised even more, how tricky the situation was when, after a show, the secretary would telephone to tell me about problems with the judge. I did not intend to let this happen to me in my capacity of a judge. I asked to be taken off the list but agreed to be on a list known as 'consultant judges'. This would enable

me to fill a gap if a judge had been unable to go to a show at the last minute and, at the same time, fulfil BDS rules.

This happened in May 2003 when the judge who had been booked for the coaching class and the horn blowing competition at the Suffolk County Show had to withdraw at the last moment due to ill health. I was invited to take his place and greatly enjoyed the events.

I also feel that when I reach the stage of being unable to judge, no one will ask me to step in and I will be blissfully unaware that I am no longer wanted!

CHAPTER 40

Dun Ponies

For some time I had been concerned about the feet of my newest Connemara pony, Piper. His shoes came off very easily and I never knew from one moment to the next if all four shoes were still on his feet. I tried everything I knew and had long discussions with the vet and farrier but Piper's feet did not improve in spite of all the care and attention they received. The hoof horn was brittle and hardly seemed to grow at all.

For example, I had turned him out to graze in my 20-metre training ring. I had checked that all four shoes were safely on but when I looked barely an hour later, one hind shoe was missing. I searched the ring but could not find the shoe. A little later, I happened to look out of the bedroom window that overlooks the garden. The ring is separated from the garden by a five-foot hedge and there, on the lawn, I could see the shoe. Piper had obviously been playing around, bucked and kicked and the shoe had flown off over the hedge.

I am fortunate to have two superb farriers in Barry and Fred Lambert who struggled for years with Piper's feet. But, in spite of all the problems, thanks to Barry and Fred, Piper won consistently. He took first prize in one of the classes at the BDS show. He won both ridden and driven dressage as well as ridden and in-hand mountain and

Piper at the BDS Show in 1995, where he won a class. Elton Hayes is acting as groom. (Photo reproduced by kind permission of Peter Higby)

moorland classes. But, in the end, I realised that his feet were never going to improve and I gave him away to Raymond and Brenda Waters.

Brenda had driven him in pair and tandem with Raz with whom she had initially learnt to drive. She knew all about Piper's feet but she desperately wanted to have him and give him another chance. He remained with the Waters in cosseted luxury, receiving all the love and care that Raymond and Brenda could give him until the end of his days, when his feet finally gave out and he lay down in his stable for the last time. It was a terribly sad day for he was a wonderful pony in every other way.

I wanted to replace Piper and I saw a dun Welsh Cob foal advertised for sale and bought him. He was a great mover and I had visions of him becoming a huge success both in harness and under saddle. I imagined him at Olympia, in the ridden mountain and moorland class and perhaps at the Horse of the Year Show in the working hunter pony class. He had enormous natural ability but he and I just did not hit it off. It was just one of those things and was most disappointing. He was more of a man's horse and I preferred the polite temperament of the Connemaras. He went on loan to a very knowledgeable and experienced teenager whom I had seen showing her pony at Olympia, but she too did not get on with him any better than I had. He then found his niche with a couple who ride, drive, jump and do dressage with him with great success. He is much loved and I am delighted that he has found such a good home.

I was still searching for another pony to complete my dun tandem. Raz was, by now, in her twenties so I did not expect her to go on 'in active service' for much longer. I looked at the English Connemara Pony sales list and to my delight, saw that there was a dun two-year old 13.2 hand gelding for sale at the Scottsway Connemara stud near Cambridge. I telephoned the owner, Carole Prentice, and arranged to go and see Scottsway Sunrise. After the dreadful experiences with Piper, the first thing I looked at was his feet. They appeared to be an excellent shape. Later, I went to see his mother, Scottsway Sahara, who was in foal again to Wisbridge Erinmore. I had seen him on a previous occasion being galloped over rough ground and knew that he had good feet. Sahara's feet also looked excellent. She was by Carole's stallion, Kirtling Tam O'Shanter. I saw him and his feet looked good too.

I was impressed by this two-year-old's polite attitude towards me when I later led him out to the field at the stud, for he was light in my hand even in his headcollar. Carole had, quite clearly, given him a very good start. While leading, I inadvertently let go of him. Carole was leading another youngster and I had taken Sunrise. We went through one gate and then across a field to a second gate. As I conscientiously stopped to latch this second gate, Sunrise swung his head and I dropped his rope. I was extremely embarrassed as he set off at an extravagant trot across the field with the rope swinging between his legs. I was sure that Carole must be furious with me but we watched him trot round. He looked splendid and certainly, there were no foot problems here. He returned to Carole of his own free will within a minute or two and all was well.

The deal was settled and Carole agreed to deliver him for me. Sunrise's dam, Sahara, was due to foal in April the following year and, so impressed was I with Sunrise, that I asked Carole if she would give me first refusal if the foal was a dun colt.

And so, Scottsway Sunrise arrived at Thorne Lodge in October

1996. I called him Sandy as he was out of Sahara and I wanted a name of two syllables. Six months later, I telephoned Carole to tell her that Sandy, now aged three, had won a strong mountain and moorland in-hand class that morning at the Riding Club show at Thorne Court.

'That's splendid!' replied Carole delighted. 'And I've got some news for you. Sahara had a dun colt foal last night!'

'Wonderful!' I was tempted to say I'd go and see it the following day but, on the principle that you should see youngsters when they are at their best, that is, at three weeks, three months and three years, I waited for three weeks before I went to see the new arrival, Scottsway Sunset, and agreed to buy him.

Carole kindly agreed to keep him until he was two years old so that he could have the same excellent start that his brother had had. This included being led and boxed to nearby grazing. One field was at a pig farm where the sounds and sights of hungry pigs, not to mention tractors and various other farm machinery, would stand him in good stead. His feet would be trimmed, he would have the requisite vaccinations and injections and he would be castrated. A wait of two years gave me time to get Sandy going before starting all over again with another youngster.

Raz went on permanent loan to Dr Terence Wheeler and his wife, Liz, where, at the time of writing, she is living in the lap of luxury. She wants for nothing and, at rising thirty-two, is still sound and looking

Raz, aged thirty-two, teaching the Wheelers' grandchildren, Jack and Tabitha, how to handle ponies. (Photo reproduced by kind permission of Dr and Mrs Terence Wheeler)

wonderful. She is teaching the Wheelers' grandchildren about looking after ponies and helping them begin their riding careers. They all love her. She is a very lucky old pony.

Sandy was driven at shows as a four-year-old and won a number of classes. The following year, as a five-year-old, he qualified for the BDS end of season championships at Burghley. About three weeks before we were due to go to Burghley I was exercising him in my Offord speed cart on the set-asides near Thorne Lodge. As I drove him over a 'walk through' between two wide, deep ditches, he suddenly spotted an old railway sleeper that had been newly placed there to prevent the side of the 'walk through' from falling into the ditch. He spun right-handed and faced the yawning chasm. Then down the bank he went, tipping me into the ditch, my head just an inch or two from his hind legs as the wheels passed either side of me. He leapt up the opposite bank, hauling the vehicle up the steep bank.

A myriad of thoughts flashed through my mind: the first was that, we would no longer be going to Burghley. I just *knew* that this was the end of Sandy's career. We were about a mile and a half from Thorne Lodge and I imagined Sandy would set off for home on his own. The route eventually led onto a village road, past parked cars and houses, before returning to the farm track which, after half a mile, emerged onto a road. Sandy would have to cross this road to get to the Thorne Lodge driveway. The chances of his negotiating all that without hitting something seemed slim.

I watched as he hauled the cart up the bank and began to walk, quite purposefully, towards home. From the bottom of the ditch, I said as gently as I was able, under the circumstances, 'Sandy, whoa!' and, to my amazement, he stopped. I clambered out of the ditch talking to him all the time, 'Sandy, whoa, good boy! Whoa, good boy. Sandy, Whoa!'

He stood absolutely still. I could not believe my luck and I reached him before he changed his mind. I gave him a big hug and a peppermint and told him what a good boy he was. Never mind that my ribs, back and left knee were hurting terribly and that he had crossed a ditch with a cart behind him, he had not galloped off. I walked round the cart expecting to see terrible damage but nothing was broken or even scratched. My nylon exercise whip was nowhere to be seen and

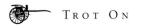

so I led Sandy back to the ditch where I saw it lying in the bottom. I pulled one of the reins out of the terrets and held on to it while I scrambled down to retrieve the whip. After all this I mounted and drove home.

We continued towards home and on the way we met Edward who works for Tim.

'Sorry I look a bit of a mess,' I apologised to him, 'but I've just spent part of the morning in the ditch over there. Somebody's put a sleeper by the "walk through". Sandy thought it was a monster out to get him and he went across the ditch.' Edward looked embarrassed.

'It was me. I did it to stop the bank collapsing. You know, when I put it there I wondered if it might cause a problem. Heavens, Sallie, I'm really sorry. I'll go and move it.' Edward tried to make amends but I assured him that it was not his fault.

'Leave it, Edward. I'll go round again tomorrow. Sandy knows it's there now and I can't have him getting "a thing" about that ditch.'

'Well, if you're sure,' said Edward doubtfully.

'Yes, I am, honestly.'

I drove the same route on the following day and made certain that we did not have a repeat performance.

We went to Burghley after all and Sandy was placed a good third being beaten by Minta Winn for second place.

★   ★   ★

My new two-year-old, Scottsway Sunset, arrived at Thorne Lodge in the spring of 1999. After much deliberation and consulting friends, I chose to call him Desert, later shortened Dez, to connect him with Sahara. The names Sandy and Dez are good for pair and tandem as they sound quite different and each pony knows that he is being spoken to. The names Libby and Raz had worked so well in the past that I wanted similar sounding names for my next tandem.

I schooled Dez in the same way I had Sandy and, when he was four, I took him to a few public outings as a single as well as in pair beside Sandy, harnessed to a spider phaeton that I had had custom-built by Mark Broadbent.

I am fortunate to have the support of three loyal helpers when I take Sandy and Dez to shows. Pat Zilli, whom I grew to know through the Riding Club, lives less than a mile away. She has the right slim figure for the black livery coat that I had made for her with a dun-coloured collar. This blends with my dun-coloured coat which has a black collar. She wears livery if the occasion is dressy, otherwise she wears smart, fawn, well-cut tweeds.

I also have the help of Peter and Denise Durrant. I got to know Denise when, as a physiotherapist, she visited Elton on a weekly basis after he suffered a severe stroke in 1995. When he eventually came out of hospital he tried to continue to live at his farm but found it impossible. His left side had been affected although, thank goodness, his brain, speech and hearing remained sharp until he died. He moved into Thorne Lodge and an extension, which he helped to design, was built so that he could be as comfortable as possible. Denise continued to visit him weekly and worked on his muscles to try to keep him as mobile as possible and ease some of his constant pain. Bill and I cared for him until he finally died of cancer in 2001.

Naturally, Denise had become a good friend to us all and she and her husband, Peter, came to dinner. Peter is, like Pat, the right size and shape to be a passenger in the gig. I discovered that he liked horses and had ridden and so I struck a bargain with him. I asked him if he would consider coming to some shows if I taught him to drive. He agreed and so I consider myself to be very fortunate in that the four of us go off to shows together and work as a team. We all get on extremely well and this adds enormously to our enjoyment.

★　　★　　★

The year 2001 saw the dreadful epidemic of foot-and-mouth disease. Many events were cancelled as livestock movement of all kinds was severely restricted. Consequently, we were able to get to only one or two shows. As a pair, Sandy and Dez had a walkover at the BDS Area Show run by Linda Swain at Stockwood Park, Luton, Bedfordshire. A professional photographer there took some pictures of them that were good enough to use in the new edition of *Driving a Harness Horse* which was to be reproduced in colour as a companion to the new edition of *Breaking a Horse to Harness*.

In that same year, I had the honour of being given an award for services to carriage driving by the Worshipful Company of Coachmakers and Coach Harness Makers of London. The cup is usually presented at the BDS show at Windsor but, because of the foot-and-mouth epidemic, this was cancelled. Instead, Bill and I were invited to The Worshipful Company of Coachmakers and Coach Harness Makers of London, Court and Aerospace Industry Livery Dinner. We queried, in our minds, the aerospace connection and then decided that it was all about travel – whether to outer space or by coach and horses!

The dinner was to be held at Ironmongers' Hall in the City of London on 21 November and we accepted with enthusiasm, as neither of us had ever attended a Livery Company dinner before. This was to be a very grand affair and we neither wanted to drive to London by car ourselves nor travel by public transport with Bill in black tie and me in a long gown. Pam Greene's son-in-law, Rob, is a professional chauffeur and he agreed to take us, as he knows London well.

We arrived early at Ironmongers' Hall and waited in reception until we were ushered up the sweeping staircase to the first floor. Here we were presented by the toastmaster to the Master, David Almond, past masters and other dignitaries wearing their ceremonial purple-trimmed gowns over their dinner jackets. There were drinks before dinner and then all were called into the dining room, apart from those who were to be sitting at the top table and myself. After a photo call, we processed into the dining room, led by the toastmaster carrying a mace. We were welcomed by a slow united hand-clap as we walked to our seats. I was escorted by the Immediate Past Master, The Hon. Roy Constantine, and sat with Bill on one side and on the other, the young Alastair Colebourn, who had won the bursary award for 2001, which had been presented for his interest in space travel about which he had written a paper. He was most interesting to talk to and it was amusing that we should be attending the dinner in such different capacities connected with travel. Richard James, BDS Vice President, was sitting opposite which was a comfort, as was the Chairman of the Awards committee, David Shalit, who was very kind in guiding us through the procedure of the handling the loving cup that was passed round after dinner.

The three-course meal was delicious and was followed by the loving cup, toasts and speeches. Alastair received his bursary and then the Master began to say all sorts of very flattering things about me. I was escorted to the top table to receive the large, lidded, solid silver cup on a plinth. I expected to receive it and then hand it back immediately but everyone insisted that I should take it home, which worried me in case it became damaged or stolen. I was also given a superb certificate to keep. I had strict instructions not to engrave the silver band on the plinth as this has no names of previous winners on it. However, I made enquiries and discovered that previous winners have been HRH Prince Philip, Mark Broadbent, John Parker and Joseph Allen of J.A. Allen books. I also discovered that I was only the third woman to receive the award during the twenty years which it has been presented.

★   ★   ★

I had decided by now, to retire from all of my honorary appointments with the BDS and so I wrote to the President of the Society, Colonel Sir John Miller; the BDS Chairman, John Parker; the Vice Chairman, Linda Tate, and the secretary, Jenny Dillon, outlining my plans for retirement and that I would not be standing for election to the BDS council again. There were plenty of young enthusiasts who were willing and keen to act on the council. I had arranged for Minta Winn to take over the running of the Tandem Club, whose financial position was so sound that I handed over about £3,500-worth stock of silver tandem bars to the BDS for safe-keeping. Carriage builder Mark Broadbent and Claudia Bunn, a highly respected carriage driver and judge who had been on the judges' committee for many years, agreed to take over the chair of the judges' committee. Sarah Wildy, a Light Harness Horse Instructor who is very involved with driving for the disabled, said that she would administer the Disabled Drivers' test scheme which had become very popular. I would no longer be an examiner and would retire from the training and test committee that Linda Tate had run so efficiently for a great many years. I agreed though, that if asked, I was willing to help with material for any new tests and I am happy to say that I have, in fact, been asked and it gives

me great pleasure to do this.

Bill came with me to the BDS Annual General Meeting in 2001. I was honoured to be made a Life Vice President of the BDS by Col Sir John Miller. This was splendid because I am entitled, if I wish, to attend council meetings. I also receive the minutes from all the meetings and thus I can keep up to date with BDS activities. I was presented with a beautiful tandem whip, mounted on a board, made especially for me by Kevin Stillwell, the BDS Honorary Solicitor who makes driving whips as a hobby. It was a very moving occasion and, of course, I had to say a few words of thanks,

'I've been so touched by everyone's kindness. It's quite overwhelming. Even though I am no longer on the various committees and panels, I do hope that people will still telephone to ask my advice. However, when everyone stops telephoning me, I shan't mind because I shall be too ga-ga to notice, so don't worry about hurting my feelings!'

★   ★   ★

In 2001 Bill asked me what I wanted for my sixty-seventh birthday. I did not want shawl and slippers or a bus pass or a flat in sheltered accommodation. What I wanted, more than anything, was to put the ponies into tandem – but I needed help. So, on my birthday, I put Dez between the shafts of my Bennington buggy and Sandy in the lead with Bill holding him. I mounted the buggy and Bill threaded the leader's reins through all the terrets then hooked on the leader's traces. He stood on the back step of the buggy so that he could dismount quickly and grab a pony if necessary.

I asked the ponies to walk on, which they did, and we drove out of our gateway and down the farm track which leads to the set-asides. We drove for forty minutes and the ponies behaved as though they had been driven in tandem all their lives. They went just as well the next time and on every occasion since. I decided that while my nerve was still strong and I had such super ponies, I would drive them in tandem the following season of 2002.

They competed, in tandem, at five shows and won eight first prizes as well as a championship and a supreme championship. They took

the first and second prizes for driving in the East Anglian Native Pony Society Performance Award Scheme in 2002.

At last, I have my tandem of dun ponies. It is almost sixty years since I saw the dun horse driven to a phaeton at the Seven Sisters Riding School in Hayes, Middlesex, that sparked my ambition to drive a turnout with ponies of the glorious, golden dun.

Sandy and Dez winning their class at the BDS East Anglia Area Show in 2002. Peter Durrant is the passenger. (Photo reproduced by kind permission of Richard Weller-Poley)

CHAPTER 41

2003

I HAD MADE PROVISIONAL PLANS for the 2003 show season and was feeling optimistic; Sandy and Dez were going well, the gig was smart and it would be fun to show the two dun Connemaras, my dream ponies, in tandem.

But one Sunday afternoon in February I suddenly felt ill with a bad cold and a raging headache. Bill would be back later from his gliding club but in the meantime I could have an hour or two's rest in bed. It might help. I lay on the bed, pulled a blanket over me and closed my eyes. The comfort and the warmth made me feel a little better and I dozed fitfully for I would have to get up to feed the ponies before it grew dark.

Eventually, I opened my eyes to look at the bedside clock. I couldn't see it. There was some dim grey light where the window was but everything else was dark. I felt my heart miss a beat. I was now wide awake. I covered my right eye. All I could see with my left eye was a black circle. I closed my left eye, I could see through my right eye. I tried the left one again. Only blackness.

My heart was racing. Panic flooded over me. I was blind in my left eye. How long until Bill came home? What about the ponies? What if my right eye did the same? I'd be blind. I wouldn't be able to do anything – ever again. How would I be able to look after Bill and Thorne Lodge? There would be no ponies, no tandem, no showing. It was too terrifying to think about.

I told myself to keep calm. I still had some vision in my right eye. It was growing dusk. The ponies had to be fed come what may. I staggered to the stables, fed them and settled them for the night. They lived out, had grazing, shelter and water and could look after themselves to a certain extent. Then I returned to bed and lay with my eyes closed. Sometimes I opened them but everything was dark. I panicked again, then told myself that Sunday evenings in February were dark. I tried to sleep but it was impossible and I longed to hear Bill's key in the door. It was late evening when he returned and we decided to see how I was in the morning. I spent a miserable night lying on the bathroom floor near the loo, feeling terribly sick with a stabbing pain behind my left eye.

The next morning I felt a little better and crawled out to feed the ponies with Bill's help, before telephoning the doctor's surgery at opening time. I told the receptionist my story.

'Come round to the surgery now and the doctor will see you immediately.' I could hear the concern in her voice.

Within minutes of my arriving at the surgery, the doctor had examined my eyes and had telephoned the eye clinic at the West Suffolk Hospital.

'I've told them your condition and they will be waiting for you. Get there as soon as you can,' he said.

Bill drove me to the eye clinic, where I was taken into a room for my eye to be examined. The doctor carried out various tests and took endless care in examining both eyes. He then called consultant ophthalmologist, Mr Andrew Ramsay, who diagnosed acute glaucoma. Within an hour he had skilfully lasered both eyes.

I could see again! If I had not felt so utterly weak, I'd have jumped for joy. There is no doubt that my sight was saved through the wonderful efforts of all those professional people. Amazingly, by midday I was home again with vision in both eyes. However, Andrew told me that as well as glaucoma, I also had cataracts in both eyes. He made arrangements for these to be removed in two separate operations at the Nuffield Hospital in Bury St Edmunds. It was reassuring to know

that Andrew would be performing the operations as, by now, I had complete faith in his skills.

My life seemed to grind to a halt. I was given eye drops and drugs that prevented me from driving a car, let alone my 7.5-ton, 30-foot long horsebox. Bill and friends rallied round to do chores … and life went on. I did, however, manage to drive the ponies quietly each day but kept off public roads walking round the park and the set-asides on the farm. My reactions were too slow to venture into a trot. Luckily, Sandy and Dez were well behaved so I had no problems. I cancelled all commitments with other peoples' animals because I could not risk an accident.

Bill and I were also, at this time, trying to learn how to use a computer. I had been telling my friend Anne Grimshaw, about my idea for this book and asked if she would edit it. Anne agreed but said that I must learn how to use a computer if I was going to produce another book as it would be so much easier in the editing process. My trusty 'steam' typewriter was apparently hopelessly outdated and my work now had to be produced on a 'floppy disk'. I had no idea what this was and decided that I had better find out.

David Jones, the husband of a past pupil, Canny, is a great expert with computers and he guided us through the purchasing of the computer and all that went with it. He set it up and initially taught me how to use the word processing software – or at least enough of it so that I could start on the book. Bill, Canny and I then enrolled on a ten-week computer course at the West Suffolk College. We somehow managed to complete this to the satisfaction of the tutor and even received certificates to prove our competence. I have no illusions about my skills – or lack of them – with a computer but it was fun to complete the course.

Whilst undertaking the computer course, practising with the computer at home, doing the homework set by the tutor and writing the book, I had to make numerous visits to the eye clinic as my left eye developed complications. Andrew Ramsay assured me that these were quite common and went to great lengths to explain what was happening behind my eye. His constant care, skill and attention was reassuring and he was proved right in the end. I was taking various prescribed drugs and applying copious quantities of eye drops to persuade the left eye to work properly. Life was pretty miserable at times. By April, the sight had stabilised and Andrew decided to operate again in July to remove a cataract from the right eye.

'Have a breather for a couple of months,' he said, 'and enjoy your ponies.' I did and in May the tandem won their class at a small show. Then I had a surprise telephone call from Colin Willcox, the chief light horse steward of the Suffolk County Show.

'Do you have any plans for the Suffolk County Show?' he asked.

'I'm showing my tandem,' I told him.

'Oh, I see,' he sounded disappointed. 'I was hoping you'd be able to judge the coaching class. The judge who was booked has been taken ill.'

'I'll do it,' I replied immediately making a snap decision. Colin brightened,

'Really?'

'Yes. Be happy to,' I agreed. It would be fun to judge again even though I had taken myself off the panel of judges many years ago. It was flattering to be invited and to know that I was still wanted. 'I'll cancel showing the tandem.'

'Are you sure?'

'Yes, Colin.'

When I had showed the tandem I had been surprised at just how exhausted I had been afterwards. Perhaps I had tried to do too much after my eye operation. In my present state I didn't think I could do the ponies justice.

And so I judged the coaching class at the Suffolk County Show with John Parker, Chairman of the BDS. It was hugely enjoyable. I was also invited to judge the horn blowing competition the following day with Richard James, a Vice President of the BDS. The schedule stated that, as each coach was driven separately around the ring, each contestant was to blow two traditional calls on the horn as well as music to entertain the passengers on the coach.

I took the music manuscript of the most commonly played calls and we asked each competitor to name the calls he intended to blow. We marked five calls for each contestant on the lines of dressage marks with ten for excellent down to five for sufficient and the result slipped easily into place. The whole experience was great fun for us all.

ABOVE: *Scottsway Sunrise (Sandy) at Burghley, 2003. (Photo reproduced by kind permission of Chris Rushforth)*

RIGHT: *Perfect conditions, in January 2004, for sleighing along the lane by Thorne Lodge with Sandy. Patricia Zilli is on the rear seat. (Photo reproduced by kind permission of the East Anglian Daily Times, Terry Hunt, Michael Hall and Sharon Boswell)*

With the second eye operation pending, it was impossible to make definite plans for the ponies, as I did not know whether similar complications would occur with the right eye and prevent me from feeling well enough to drive the lorry and do all the work which showing entailed. Andrew performed the second operation in July and there were no complications so that, in August, I was able to take Sandy to one of the remaining shows that had a qualifier for the Mountain and Moorland Class at the BDS championships at Burghley and he qualified. So it was off to Burghley in early September. I was thrilled when he was placed second, for this gave him the title of Reserve Champion Mountain and Moorland pony for 2003.

A couple of weeks later at Keysoe he qualified for the Mountain and Moorland class at the BDS championships in 2004.

I cannot thank the staff and doctors at the Long Melford surgery and the West Suffolk Hospital enough for their help and support during a horrendous few months. Most of all, I shall be forever grateful to Andrew Ramsay, for saving my sight. Without him, I would no longer be able to drive ponies and say 'Trot on!'

About the Co-Author

ANNE GRIMSHAW

I FIRST KNEW SALLIE WALROND through a black-and-white photograph in a book I had been given for Christmas in the 1960s. She was driving Ali to a skeleton gig at a show. I had always wanted to drive and looked at the picture enviously. As a less-than-natural rider, I felt I might do better driving – but there it rested for many years, for there was simply no opportunity for me to pursue learning to drive.

BACKGROUND

I was born in Lancashire and grew up in Yorkshire, not in the Broad Acres of 'God's own county' but on the fringe of the industrial area of the old West Riding which, in the 1950s and 1960s, was an equine desert. I begged my parents for a pony but the answer was always no: we had neither the facilities nor the money; my mother had no experience of horses and was a little scared of them and my father's health would not have allowed him to help me with the hard physical work involved, although he had ridden in the past and liked horses. To try to make up he would take me to horse shows and sometimes, after his day's work, for a riding lesson at a riding school thirty miles away. Of course, now I see that he did what he could to satisfy my desire to learn to ride. His reasons for not buying me a pony were perfectly

Anne Grimshaw with Cottenham
Loretto. (Photo by Sallie Walrond)

valid but at the time, of course, I did not see it that way.

So I copied what the children in the book, *The Twins and Their Ponies* by Ursula Moray Williams, did: I made hobby horses. The head was one of my father's old socks stuffed with my mother's laddered nylon stockings nailed onto a broomstick. A strip or a small circle of white material sewn on the front made a blaze or a star. Black buttons were eyes, triangular pieces of cardboard covered with an off-cut from the cuff of the sock made the ears and a piece of washing line made a bridle and reins. Fortunately, men's socks were the same colour as horses and so I had four: Smokey, a grey and named after cowboy Will James' horse in the story of that title; Lucky Star, a brown or rather khaki – a left-over sock from my father's army days (I can't remember where that name came from); Corrymeela, another grey (named after a horse in, if I remember rightly, *Janet Must Ride* by Diana Pullein-Thompson) and Rosina, a cream (don't know where that sock came from as my father did not wear cream socks) named after the mare in the book *Rosina Copper* by Kitty Barne. They served me well long after the age I should have given up such toys.

The only experience I had of real horses up to the age of ten was the greengrocer's horse that pulled a cart around suburban roads near my home and a week-long family holiday in Filey where there was a riding school and I was able to have a riding lesson (on the leading rein) every day.

By twelve I was deemed old enough to go alone on the bus to the only riding stables for miles around, whose ponies knew two speeds: slow and stop. There was simply nowhere within reasonable reach of home where I could learn to ride properly and progress. I had, therefore, to be content with drawing horses and reading about them. I covered every scrap of paper and margins of school exercise books with drawings of horses: mustangs with flying manes and tails, show hacks with beautiful heads and plaited manes, whiskery cart horses, dressage horses, jumping horses, rearing horses, trotting horses, galloping horses ... I read almost nothing except books about horses: pony stories, veterinary tomes, old army books on horse management, how-to-ride guides, show jumpers' biographies, equestrian art – anything, so long as it was about horses. All this, did not, of course, go down well at school – a girls' grammar school geared to academic excellence and, ultimately, sending its girls off to university or teacher training college.

Later, as an adult with my own transport and money, I would make a four-hour round trip to an excellent equestrian establishment on the edge of the Yorkshire Dales but I had neither the time nor money to go frequently enough for my riding lessons to be of any real benefit.

So, I reckoned that the only way to gain experience was to have my own horse. It was a long, long wait and I was twenty-four before I realised my dream and bought a horse. But it was not so much a dream as a nightmare and I sold him quickly, my confidence and my bank balance shattered. I did not ride again for several years.

Then a good riding school opened not far from home and, at last, I took regular lessons and hacks for four or five years. One day, my instructor made a casual remark about my riding, 'But you enjoy it, don't you?' Did I? Did I really enjoy riding? I had, finally, to be honest with myself: no, I didn't. I hadn't done for years. I almost dreaded going for my ride. Would I miss it if I didn't go? So I stopped riding. It was a strange sense of relief and yet I still wanted to ride.

But now, perhaps with age and maturity, I have come to terms

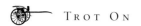

with my ambivalence towards riding. I enjoy being around horses and I do enjoy driving – and I'm much better at it, thanks to Sallie.

CAREER AS A PROFESSIONAL LIBRARIAN

In the mid 1970s, shortly after I had begun my career as a professional librarian, I decided to undertake a Fellowship of the Library Association by producing a thesis, a bibliography of British equestrian literature (except racing). As far as I knew, there was no such a book (except a very old one published in the 1880s) but before embarking on the project, I put a letter in various equestrian magazines asking if anyone knew of the existence of any such a bibliography.

No one did and so I proceeded with the thesis. Among the replies to my letters was one from Sandy and Biddy Watney who told me they had a large collection of books on equestrian topics and I was welcome to visit them and see the books. I jumped at the chance for I knew they were experts in the world of driving. Whilst staying with them, they took me out in their gig drawn by their chesnut Welsh Cob, Shandy. I loved it and Sandy gave me a brief driving lesson. They recommended Sallie Walrond as a driving instructor.

Sallie Walrond! The black-and-white photograph in the book! I booked a week's course of lessons. I immediately felt that my driving 'career' was going to be considerably more rewarding and successful than my attempts at riding. And so, in 1978, I became one of Sallie's pupils – not one of her most talented, nor a protégé likely to win her kudos in the show ring – but she and her ponies helped me back into the horse world after my disastrous attempt at horse owning.

Since then I have been a regular visitor to Sallie and Bill's home at Thorne Lodge in Suffolk, more so since moving from Yorkshire to Hertfordshire in 1983. It has always been a breath of fresh air (literally) to drive through the rolling Suffolk countryside around her cottage where I could see for miles and miles, my eye muscles stretching to focus on a distant horizon under glorious 'Constable skies'. In 1998 when my mother died and my last link with Yorkshire was broken, I was immensely grateful to Sallie for her kindness and support and I like to think of Suffolk as my second home.

★   ★   ★

BOOKS AND WRITING

The Horse: an Annotated Bibliography of British Equestrian Literature 1851–1976 had formed the basis of my Fellowship of the Library Association. That, in turn, stood me in good stead to undertake a Master's degree in librarianship in 1981 while I was working as a librarian in a college of higher education in Yorkshire. Now, however, I no longer work as a librarian but am editor of a business technology journal based in Hertfordshire.

But it is writing for my own pleasure in which I take greatest the pride and interest. As well as the horse bibliography, Sallie knew of my other published books: *An Annotated Black Beauty* (published by J. A. Allen like several of Sallie's books); *A Day That Made History: D-Day – the Normandy Landings*; *The Last Flight of Lancaster LL919*; and *Wings on the Whirlwind*. In late 2002 Sallie told me of her plan to write her autobiography and asked me if I would 'look through it' when it was finished. I made a few suggestions and what I hoped were constructive comments, whereupon she invited me to join her as co-author.

It has been a delight to edit Sallie's autobiography. Over the years she has told me of the people, places, horses and events but it was difficult to visualise 'the big picture'. Now, all those stories fall into place. I could 'identify' with so much of what she wrote about, particularly her childhood. Although a few years older than me, Sallie and I share the same memories of yearning for a pony, being willing to do *anything* to acquire a horse, saving every penny towards buying a pony, putting up with discouragement of our horsey pursuits by teachers at school, cajoling pet dogs into the role of horses, drawing horses with tack or harness correct to the minutest detail. We made friends with tradesmen's ponies; we wore itchy, cavalry twill jodhpurs and lace-up shoes; we were taught to ride on a leading rein while out hacking and we read every horse book we could lay our hands on. We both grew up at the very end of the horse-drawn era.

Apart from teaching me to drive, Sallie has helped and supported me in my writing: listening while I read out stories I'd written, reading my four (as yet) unpublished novels – and commiserating with me over yet another publisher's rejection slip – and, more recently, in public speaking by giving constructive criticism on my slide-talk presen-

tations on various subjects from working horses to photographing gardens and tracing wartime RAF aircrew to the American Civil War.

EVENTS

I shared in some of the events that Sallie writes about. For instance, I sat up beside her one time when she drove the team. It was March and snowing. The ponies turned their heads against it as they trotted into the wind, so did the passengers – but everything and everybody was covered in the freezing white stuff. As a result, I never buy Christmas cards with pictures of coaches in the snow…

I saw Foxy several times in the barn. The only foxes I had seen before had been in the distance or in a wildlife park. But here was a fox, a wild animal that trusted me enough, even though she was badly hurt, to sit a yard or two away from her while I took photographs. It was a sad episode but, for me, a wonderful, and humbling, experience to be so close to a truly wild fox.

But there are events that stick in my mind that Sallie has probably forgotten so, I'll add one or two that I particularly remember.

The first time I visited Thorne Lodge as a pupil, I sat in the kitchen while Sallie prepared supper. On the Aga was a large pan with a lid. It had been there a long time and she stirred it occasionally. It smelled less than delicious – and there was an awful lot of whatever it was. I wondered if this was to be our supper for the rest of the week… In due course, supper was served: paté and French toast, roast chicken and a selection of vegetables, lemon soufflé, cheese and biscuits and coffee. Perhaps the stuff in the big pan was for tomorrow. The next day Sallie lifted it off the Aga and said,

'Help me carry that pan of boiled linseed and barley out to the ponies, will you?'

I didn't dare tell her I thought it had been intended for us!

I was at Sallie's on the day in 1981 when HRH Prince Charles married Lady Diana Spencer. We wanted to watch the proceedings on television but I was also there to learn to drive and so, just after dawn, we took out the pair and the dog cart. The occasional car passed us on the main road and we got some decidedly odd looks from drivers and passengers – they probably thought we were on our way to London to take part in the wedding! Sallie does not have a television and so I had taken my portable TV. The reception was poor and the only way we could see a picture was by perching the TV on a small table in the spare bedroom with its aerial poking out of the window! Nevertheless, we settled ourselves on the bed for the next few hours to watch – taking a coffee break only when we were sure there weren't any horses about to appear!

When Elton Hayes came to live at Thorne Lodge I was delighted to meet him. He was a gentleman in every sense of the word, incredibly wise and with a kind but quick sense of humour and bright as a button right up until his death. I remembered, as a child, listening to him on the radio singing *The Owl and the Pussy Cat* and seeing him at the cinema as the minstrel Alan-a-Dale in a favourite film *Robin Hood*, starring Richard Todd. However, it was one Christmas before Elton went to live at Thorne Lodge that Sallie, Bill and I had a musical evening: Sallie on the accordion, me playing the flute – and Bill on castanets! Great fun but perhaps it was as well that Elton's sensitive, musical ear was not present.

I have particularly fond memories of one of Sallie's ponies, Raz. I had wondered, after many years out of the saddle, how I would feel if I rode again. Sallie understood my yearning and my hesitation and offered Raz if I wanted to try again. If my nerve gave out at the last minute, so be it. On the morning of my ride I woke feeling huge excitement, I couldn't wait to put on my jodhpurs and hat and actually get on horse again. I hadn't felt that way since I was a child. I sat on Raz while Sallie walked alongside then I walked and trotted round the dressage arena in the park at Thorne Court and back to the stables. I was thrilled! I hadn't even cantered, let alone jumped, but I didn't care. Raz and Sallie had given me back a little of my lost confidence and I'm grateful to both of them for that.

OTHER INTERESTS

Apart from my life-long interest in horses, driving and writing, I have been a keen genealogist for thirty years with a particular interest in researching military ancestors. I love history (except the boring stuff we had to do at school to get through exams!) and began my interest in military history when I was a teenager with the American Civil War – I've no idea why but perhaps I read *Gone with the Wind* at an impressionable age! From there it expanded to encompass wars in which my family had been involved, most recently the Second World War (my father) and the First World War (my grandfather) and, further back, the Napoleonic Wars (a second cousin five times removed!) These spawned a request from a friend to trace an RAF airman who had been killed in 1944 when his Lancaster bomber was shot down over France. From that blossomed an interest in aeroplanes and aviation – so much so that I had a flying lesson – just one…

My interests have taken me abroad: the RAF and aeroplanes to eastern France where the crew of the Lancaster bomber are buried; to the Arras area of northern France where my grandfather drove his horse-drawn ammunition wagon in the attack on Vimy Ridge in April 1917; to Tunisia and Italy to follow in my father's wartime footsteps of 1942–5, and to Belgium where my distant ancestor fought with the Duke of Wellington against Napoleon at Waterloo in 1815.

But most of my travelling has been to the USA. First it was to the Black Hills of South Dakota where, as a student librarian, I worked in the public library of Rapid City as part of the work experience while at library school. It was in South Dakota that I had my first taste of riding western style which I found so much more secure and relaxing than English style but, of course, back home in Yorkshire in the early 1970s there was no opportunity to ride à la cowboy.

It was on an American Civil War battlefields tours to the eastern USA in 1981 that, totally unexpectedly, I drove a Morgan stallion called Richard to a hooded buggy along the main street of Gettysburg at midnight… I didn't use the classical style of rein handling advocated by Sallie as Richard didn't know about that. It was a rein in each hand, the whip in the socket (not that I was likely to need it at the speed Richard went), the battery-powered, hazard-warning lights flashing on the back of the buggy and rear-view mirrors that showed a police car… I tried to make too tight a turn and the wheels of the quarter-lock buggy made a horrible screeching noise, Richard's iron-shod hooves pounded the tarmac, dogs barked and the harness rattled and jingled as we bumped over the railway tracks. No, it was not what Sallie had been teaching me.

I enjoy playing the piano and flute (not at the same time) but whether anyone hearing me enjoys them as much, I couldn't say.

More successful than my musical (and horse-owning) forays has been photography. Several of my photographs appear in this book and I have spent many happy hours wandering around Thorne Lodge and Thorne Court photographing plants and the garden as well as the villages and cottages of the Suffolk landscape.

And now I have come full circle: my first knowledge of Sallie Walrond was a black-and-white photograph in a book I looked at when I was a teenager. Now, forty years on, here I am helping put together another book containing photographs of Sallie…

Books by Sallie Walrond

1969   *Fundamentals of Private Driving*, The British Driving Society

1971   *A Guide to Driving Horses*, Thomas Nelson & Sons Ltd

1973   *A Guide to Driving Horses*, Wilshire Book Co. USA

1974   *Encyclopaedia of Driving*, Horse Drawn Carriages Ltd

1974   *Encyclopaedia of Driving* (leather bound), Horse Drawn Carriages Ltd

1977   *A Guide to Driving Horses*, Pelham Books Ltd

1978   *Fahren Lernen*, German edition

1979   *The Encyclopaedia of Driving*, Country Life

1980   *Looking at Carriages*, Pelham Books Ltd

1981   *Breaking a Horse to Harness*, Pelham Books Ltd

1982   *Your Problem Horse*, Pelham Books Ltd

1983   *Les Voitures à Chevaux*, French edition

1984   *Chevaux a Problèmes*, French edition

1984   *Probleempaarden & Paardeproblemen*, Dutch edition

1985   *Probleme mit dem pferd was tun*, German edition

1985	*Breaking a Horse to Harness*, J A Allen & Co Ltd
1988	*The Encyclopaedia of Carriage Driving*, J A Allen & Co Ltd
1991	*I Problemi del tuo Cavallo*, Italian edition
1992	*Driving a Harness Horse*, J A Allen & Co Ltd
1992	*Looking at Carriages*, J A Allen & Co Ltd
1993	*Your Problem Horse*, Swan Hill Press
1994	*Judging Carriage Driving*, J A Allen & Co Ltd
1994	*Starting to Drive*, Kenilworth Press
1995	*Driving Questions Answered*, Kenilworth Press
1996	*Driving Do's and Don'ts*, Kenilworth Press
1998	*Fahren Lernen 1*, German edition
1998	*Fahren Lernen 2*, German edition
1998	*Mennen Problemen en Oplossingen*, Dutch edition
1998	*Handling your Problem Horse*, Swan Hill Press
2000	*Breaking a Horse to Harness* (colour edition), J A Allen & Co Ltd
2001	*Pferde Richtig Einfahren*, German edition
2001	*L'attelage*, French edition
2002	*Driving a Harness Horse* (colour edition), J A Allen & Co Ltd
2002	*Driving a Harness Horse* (colour edition), Trafalgar Square USA